MICHILLANEOUS

More than 450 fascinating, amusing, informative, surprising and entertaining lists about Michigan people, places, phenomena, oddities and events. The ultimate book for every Michigan reader who has everything and wants more.

by
Gary W. Barfknecht

Friede Publications

ISBN 0-9608588-0-6

To Amy
Who keeps me thinking

To Heidi
Who keeps me laughing

To Ann
Who keeps me

CONTENTS

INTRODUCTION   viii

INVITATION TO PARTICIPATE   ix

1. DEATH SENTENCES   1

3 Dogs Who Shot Their Masters...2 Odd Accidents...5 Conspicuous Nuclear Accidents and Near Misses...5 Deadly Accidents...3 Disastrous Forest Fires...4 Violent Explosions...3 Spectacular Plane Crashes...2 Highway Landings...3 Fatal Parachute Jumps...2 Who Survived Terrible Falls...2 Conspicuous Suicide Sites...6 Ways To Commit Suicide...3 Mass Poisonings...2 Pronounced Victims of Toxic Shock Syndrome...5 Strange Coincidences...2 Who Were Buried Alive...5 Miraculous Survivals...10 Odds Against Your Death...5 Life Expectancies...6 Most Common Fatal Accidents...2 Tragic Drownings...6 Elements of a Boating Fatality...2 Most Dangerous Hunting Seasons...5 Deadliest Years to Drive...6 Driving Casualties...4 Dangerous Highways...4 Lethal Years...10 Biggest Killers...8 Counties With No Hospitals...5 States Where We Die...3 Unusual Autopsies...2 Ancient Autopsies...7 Counties With Only One Mortuary...5 Unusual Funerals...5 Memorable Cemeteries...2 Peculiar Tombstones

2. LET US ENTERTAIN YOU   21

32 Entertainment Personalities Born In Michigan...6 Entertainers Who Died While Performing in Michigan...6 Great Gate Crashings...2 Alleged Song Thefts...2 Notable Rock Music Markets...5 Rock Stars Represented by T. Patrick Freydl...4 Loudest Radio Stations...2 Top-Ranking TV Markets...4 Ranking Magazine Markets...7 Well-Known Novels With a Michigan Setting...3 Movies Filmed in Michigan...2 Movies Filmed on Mackinac Island...2 Movie Theatres With Bars...Michigan's Ten Favorite Beers...Michigan's Favorite Whiskeys...2 Remarkable UFO Sightings...3 Haunted Houses...4 Michigan Monsters...5 Sightings of Bigfoot...2 Monster Hunters...Legal Bag Limits of 3 Unusual Game Animals...3 Fish Tales...8 Record Fish...3 Popular Snowmobile Races...3 Large Snowmen...6 Largest Ski Areas...6 Most Economical Ski Areas...4 Most Popular State Parks...4 Largest Roadside Parks...11 Occupational Vanity Plates...3 Couples' Vanity Plates...14 Rejected Vanity Plate Requests...8 Interesting Vanity Plates...2 Dullest Highways...9 Fantastic Voyages...5 Unique Mackinac Bridge Crossings...6 Ways Not To Cross the Mackinac Bridge...7 Outstanding Bridges...9 Man-Made Wonders...Detroit's 5 Tallest Buildings...6 Major Fine Arts Centers...6 Embarrassing Errors at the Ford Museum Dedication...15 Well-Known Summer Theatres...7 Music Festivals...17 Prominent Food Festivals...11 Historic Festivals...27 Prominent Ethnic Festivals

3. HONORABLE MENTIONS   48

12 World's Largests...6 World's Longests...3 World's Highests...3 World's Greatests...10 Guinness World Record Holders...5 Miss America Winners...2 Prohibited Pageants...5 Male Pinups...4 Beauty Pageant Winners...2 Disabled Winners...3 Sound Winners...2 Domestic Winners...7 Big Money Winners...3 Special Appearances...3 Notable Smokers...2 Special Scholars...2 Awarded Prisoners...5 Who Have Recently Written to Ann Landers...4 Featured Families...2 Recently Awarded Heroes...2 Who Received the Congressional Medal of Honor Twice...12 Silver Buffalo Award Winners...7 Pulitzer Prize Winners...4 Great Scientists Born in Michigan...10 Famous People Born in Michigan...4 Michigan Astronauts...6 Notable Centenarians...3 Longest-Serving Governors...2 Supreme Court Justices...14 Cabinet Members...10 Presidential Candidates Who Won in Michigan But Lost The Election...5 Memorable Map Omissions...2 Conspicuous Map Additions...11 All American Cities...12 Areas in Which Michigan Ranks First in the Nation...8 Second Bests...5 Thirds...10 Fourths

4. JUSTICE FOR ALL   70

5 Most Criminous Cities...5 Safest Cities...4 Nude Crimes and Misdemeanors...2 Cases of Wood Rustling...6 Unique Thefts...4 Body Snatchers...2 Recent Grave Robbings...4 Rare Offenses...6 Most Common Non-Criminal Offenses...7 Most Common Crimes...6 Convicted Public Officials...4 Memorable Cases of Prostitution...3 Rights...4 Penalties...6 Creative Excuses for Speeding...2 Poisonings...3 Skyjackings...4 Iranian Hostages From Michigan...2 Famous Missing Persons...5 Infamous Murders...2 Teachers Murdered in Front of Their Classes...3 Abused Wives Found Innocent of Murdering Their Husbands...6 Notable Executions...2 Notorious Gangs...2 Major Interracial Riots...2 Worst Prison Riots...13 Michigan Prisons...4 Museums That Were Once Jails...8 Oldest County Jails Still in Use...5 Smallest County Jails...11 Interesting Attorney General's Opinions...9 Attorney General's Opinions That Were Probably Important To Someone...8 Unusual Lawsuits...5 Fantastically Large Awards Levied Against Michigan Automakers...7 Awards For Unusual Reasons...11 Fantastically Large Awards...First 2 Crime Victims Who Were Compensated.

5. THE WAY WE WERE   96

First 4 White Men to Visit Michigan...First 3 Books in the World to Mention Michigan...3 Countries That Have Claimed or Held Michigan...5 Earliest Permanent Settlements...10 Oldest Counties...7 Oldest Incorporated Cities and Villages...14 Old Buildings...2 Castles...2 Michigan Kings...9 Michigan Historical Field Museums...8 Items in the Capitol Cornerstone...First 6 Newspapers...6 Oldest Radio Stations...6 Oldest Colleges...Original Names of 6 Colleges...Former Names of 8 Cities...7 Cities Named After Women...4 Townships Named After Women...6 Ships Named "Michigan"...8 Places Named in an Unusual Manner...2 Townships Named After Stoves...3 Unique Ghost Towns...2 Abandoned Gold Mines...4 Working Mills...7 National Transportation Firsts That Took Place in Michigan...First 3 Railroads...First 3 Major Roads...6 National Auto Firsts...3 National Auto Firsts That Didn't Happen in Michigan...3 Memorable First Automobile Trips...11 National Sports and Entertainment Firsts That Happened in Michigan...2 International Entertainment Firsts That Took Place in Michigan...9 National Business Firsts That Occurred in Michigan...8 National Education Firsts That Happened in Michigan...4 National Law and Order Firsts That Took Place in Michigan...33 State Firsts...15 Women—First in the State...6 Michigan Women—First in the Nation...Michigan in 6 Wars...Number of Michigan Men and Women Killed in 6 Wars

6. NATURE'S WAY   126

5 Earthquakes...7 Cities Hit by Meteorites...8 Michigan Weather Extremes...4 Most Deadly Tornadoes...4 Memorable Winter Storms...5 Destructive Floods...4 Counties in the Great Lakes State With No Water...4 Counties With the Most Water...3 Counties With the Most Lakes...11 Largest Lakes...3 Longest Rivers...3 Notable Rivers...8 Picturesque Waterfalls...6 Natural Wonders...3 Mountain Ranges...4 Interesting Geographic Points...3 Towns That Lie on the 45th Parallel...4 Smallest Counties...4 Largest Counties...10 Natural Landmarks...6 State Symbols...5 Champion Trees...4 Special Christmas Trees...5 Unique Trees...5 Most Common Trees...6 Poisonous Plants...9 Monster Vegetable Records...6 Fruit Tree Populations...4 Livestock Populations...3 Counties With the Most Cattle and Calves...3 Counties With the Most Chickens...3 Counties With the Most Sheep and Lambs...5 Counties With the Most Pigs...13 Animal Jaywalkers...6 Counties With No Veterinarians...8 Endangered Species...3 Whales...3 Albino Animals...4 Unique Pets...2 Extraordinary Dog Lovers...4 Special Dogs...1,688 Items Caught by "Mr. Butler"

7. THE FACTS OF LIFE   147

10 Creative "I Do's"...3 Loving Years...7 States Michigan Brides Most Often Come From...8 States Michigan Grooms Most Often Come From...3 Reasons For Getting Married in Hell...2 Most Wedded Cities...3 "I Don't's"...9 Grounds For Divorce...5 Most Pregnant Years...4 Childless Years...5 Unique Births...2 Significant Surrogate Births...5 Remarkable Multiple Births...5 Most Pubescent Birth Years...4 Years in Which "Mature" Mothers Had the Most Children...4 Years in Which "Mature" Mothers Had the Fewest Children...160 Years of Growth...5 Most Populous Counties...6 Least Populous Counties...7 Largest Cities...5 Most Elderly Counties...7 Most Youthful Counties...5 Most Densely Populated Counties...5 Least Densely Populated Counties...3 Most Rapidly Shrinking Counties...5 Counties With the Smallest Families...5 Most Rapidly Shrinking Cities and Villages...6 States We Most Often Move To...260 Who Were Asked to Leave...5 Countries With the Most Aliens Permanently Residing in Michigan...5 Leading Sources of Newcomers...5 Fastest Growing Cities and Villages...3 Fastest Growing Counties...8 Counties With the Largest Families...8 Numbers of Rooms in Michigan Houses...3 Unique Dwellings...4 Counties With the Most Mobile Homes...5 Common Appliances...6 Phoney Years...4 Counties With the Most Septic Tanks or Cesspools...16 Worst Toxic Waste Dumps...4 Conspicuous Instances of Chemical Pollution...6 Air Pollutors...7 Water Pollutors...7 Polluted Rivers...2 Cases of Trash...Michigan's 4 Best Cities...11 Ranking Cities...4 Most Scholarly Counties...4 Most Uninstructed Counties...3 Most Learned Years...5 School Districts With the Most Students...5 School Districts With the Fewest Students...3 Counties With the Most Minority Students...3 Counties With the Fewest Minority Students...3 Counties With the Highest Private School Attendance...8 Counties Where No One Attends Private Schools...3 Most Instructive Years...6 Largest Colleges...7 Notable Churches...3 Conspicuous Crosses...2 Religious Groups With National Headquarters in Michigan...8 Most Popular Religions...3 Unusual Rituals...2 Unique Examples of Medical Research...5 Notable Weight Watchers...8 Momentous Organ Transplants...7 Successful Limb Re-Attachments...

8. MAKING CENTS   177

5 Unique Budget Problems...2 Cities That Were Bought and Sold...General Motors' 4 Largest Quarterly Losses...4 Incredibly Large Losses...2 Recent Bank Failures...3 Major Cities That Have Defaulted...4 Most Needy Counties...4 Most Financially Independent Counties...3 Most Socially Secure Counties...3 Most Socially Insecure Counties...7 Poorest Counties...5 Richest Counties...5 Largest Banks...6 Smallest Banks...6 Richest Cities...8 Poorest Cities...8 Most Distressed Places...6 Counties With the Smallest Paychecks...2 Anchormen's Salaries...5 Detroit Tiger Arbitration Cases...5 Record Profits...Michigan's 8 Richest Men...4 State Officials' Salaries...5 Large State Government Expenses...5 Counties That Get the Most Defense Dollars...4 Largest Federal Government Dispersals...5 Taxing Years...7 Least Taxing Cities...6 Most Taxing Cities...5 Most Generous School Districts...5 Most Frugal School Districts...5 School Districts That Pay Their Teachers the Most...4 School Districts That Pay Their Teachers the Least...5 Most Inexpensive Colleges...5 Most Expensive Colleges...3 Largest Foundations...12 Top Political Campaign Contributors...7 Lobbyists' Unusual Gifts...3 House Winners...5 Large Lottery Payouts...First 3 Lottery Millionaires...3 Record Lottery Sales...5 Unique Lottery Numbers

9. GETTING DOWN TO BUSINESS   193

7 Memorable Promotional Campaigns...5 Top Advertisers...6 Unique Products...11 Michigan Inventors...4 Michigan Production Firsts...4 Wartime Auto Industry Products...22 Products of the Year...3 Most Extravagant Counties...4 Most Frugal Counties...7 Rare Businesses...Foreign Investments in 32 Michigan Communities...3 Michigan Businesses Owned by Ted Nugent...22 Fortune-500 Companies...4 National Franchises Headquartered in Michigan...5 Largest Motel Chains...5 Largest Department Store Employers...6 Interesting Occupations Licensed by the State...3 Relative Professions...11 Licensed Professions...3 Most Dangerous Jobs...4 Most Working Years...6 Most Jobless Years...8 Most Unemployed Cities...2 Conspicuous Resignations...3 Most Striking Years...3 Least Striking Years...4 Notable Strikes...3 Years With the Most Strikers...4 Years With the Fewest Strikers...5 Significant Auto Strikes...2 Largest Automobile Recalls...23 Models Made in

vi

Michigan...6 Counties With the Most New Cars...5 Counties With the Fewest New Cars...2 Shortest Highways...3 Unusual Highway Materials...7 Incomplete Highways...6 Brick Highways...5 Mackinac Crossings...4 Least Trucking Counties...5 Most Trucking Counties...6 Oil Refineries...4 Largest Oil Producing Counties...3 Nuclear Power Plants...3 Largest Ports...3 Mineful Counties...5 Years of Iron Mines...5 Least Mineful Counties...5 Most Agrarian Counties...5 Years of Farms...5 Largest Cash Crops...4 Breweries...14 Wineries...5 Largest Wineries...5 Most Common Ethnic Periodicals...4 Smallest Newspapers

10. ATHLETE FEATS   222

6 Remarkable Feats...9 Olympic Gold Medalists...44 National Champions...5 1980 World Champions...2 National Halls of Fame Located in Michigan...2 National Sports Organizations Based in Michigan...3 Athletes of the Year...3 Retired Numbers...23 Sports Illustrated Cover Athletes...3 Record Home Attendances...19 Tigers in the National Baseball Hall of Fame...2 Hall of Famers Who Spent Their Entire Career in Detroit...Detroit Tigers' First 3 Years...7 Pennant-Winning Years...2 Longest Tiger Games...3 Tiger Rookies of the Year...6 Detroit Tiger Most Valuable Players...4 American League Home Run Champions...8 American League Batting Champions...3 Tigers Who Hold All-Time Major League Records...7 Tigers Who Have Hit For the Cycle...2 Tigers Signed Out of Prison...2 Who Missed a Chance to Manage the Tigers Because They Were on Vacation...10 Animal Nicknames...3 Weighty Tiger Nicknames...An All-Time, All-Michigan-Born Professional Baseball Team...3 Major League Umps From Michigan...3 National Amateur Softball Champions...5 National College Football Champion Years...9 College Football Hall of Famers...3 Heisman Trophy Winners Drafted by the Detroit Lions...5 Hall of Fame Lions...6 NFL Rookies of the Year...4 Lion All-Time Pro Records...2 Who Died While Playing for the Lions...3 NFL Championships...9 College Hockey Championships...2 Former Names of the Red Wings...11 NHL League Championship Years...7 Stanley Cup Championships...3 Red Wing Winners of the Hart Trophy...6 Red Wing Lady Byng Winners...3 NBA Records Held by Detroit Piston Kevin Porter...2 NBA Records Set by the Detroit Pistons...6 Professional Boxing Champions...8 A.B.C. Hall of Famers...4 Bowlers With Six or More Sanctioned 300 Games...2 Highest Sanctioned Series...6 Bowlers of the Year...5 National Coaches of the Year.

INDEX   245

MAP OF COUNTIES   259

INTRODUCTION

This book is a rather extended answer to my wife who offhandedly asked one bitter cold evening, "What's the coldest it's ever been in Michigan?" I said, "I don't know," then wondered out loud what the hottest temperature was.

The "I wonders" continued for the next several weeks — I wonder what the record snowfall is. I wonder if Michigan or Michigan people hold any world or national records. Are there any Olympic gold medalists from Michigan? I wonder how many famous entertainers were born in Michigan. Have any movies been filmed in Michigan? I wonder if anyone in Michigan has reported seeing Bigfoot, UFO's or haunted houses. Has anyone from Michigan ever hijacked an airplane? Who are Michigan's most infamous murderers? What cities have the highest crime rates? I wonder what cities levy the highest taxes.

After a few trips to the library I concluded four things:

(1) Anyone who wanted answers to these and other "I wonders" would have to plod through dozens of research sources just to answer one question;

(2) Most research sources present only facts and in a rather tedious, boring, cumbersome and uninteresting fashion;

(3) Michigan readers should have *one* book that featured a wealth of information on a variety of subjects presented in a condensed, readable and entertaining manner;

(4) I would do this book.

So, for the next two years, I researched and collected thousands of fascinating, amusing, informative, vital and trivial Michigan facts, stories, phenomena, oddities, opinions and observations. I then assembled these items into more than 450 easy-to-read lists and put them between the covers of *Michillaneous.*

Presented in this list form I think you will discover that *Michillaneous* is a serious reference book that entertains but also a fun book that painlessly answers all of your "I wonders."

INVITATION TO PARTICIPATE

We want the next edition of *Michillaneous* to be even more comprehensive and entertaining than this, the first. To achieve that goal we need your help. Tell us what you liked about this book, but also tell us what we could do to improve it.

Most of all, tell us what we may have left out of this book that we could include in the next. Send us your ideas or actual lists for *Michillaneous II*. We will credit you if we use your list. Be sure to include a self-addressed, stamped envelope for return of your idea if it is not acceptable.

Send to: Gary W. Barfknecht, Friede Publications, 510 North Lapeer Street, Davison, Michigan 48423.

Michigan's worst airline crash (see page 6).

Zilwaukee elevator explosion (see page 5).

1

DEATH SENTENCES

Shooting The Hand That Feeds Them
3 DOGS WHO SHOT THEIR MASTERS

1. MONROE - 1981

A German shepherd, who was being trained to attack and disarm intruders, shot his owner. While the owner chatted with relatives, the dog used its teeth to pick up a .22 magnum pistol from a table and dropped it on the floor causing the gun to discharge and strike the man in the fleshy part of his left arm.

2. DANSVILLE - November 8, 1981

A 34-year-old factory worker leaned on the muzzle of his twelve-gauge shotgun as he excited his two beagles by dangling a freshly shot rabbit over their heads.

One of the dogs, as they jumped up and down, pawed the trigger of the gun sending a blast into the man's liver, lower stomach and lung. Doctors spent five hours removing the No. 6 shot.

3. YPSILANTI - January 4, 1982

A German shepherd knocked a double-barrel, twelve-gauge shotgun to the floor causing it to discharge and spray shot into an adjacent room where a woman was sitting. The 31-year-old victim suffered a leg wound.

Why Me?
2 ODD ACCIDENTS

1. WILLIAMSBURG CRATERS - April 19, 1973

Residents of Williamsburg, a small town of three hundred residents northeast of Traverse City, awoke to find hundreds of craters that had mysteriously appeared throughout their town. The craters, many of which spewed water, mud and volatile gas in three-foot geysers, forced virtually all residents to evacuate for nearly a month and turned the town into a moonscape.

State geologists theorized that natural gas from an oil company's well being drilled four miles south of town escaped through a hole in the casing, traveled through porous rock and subterranean water and burst through the earth's crust.

2. BUG OFF - Spring, 1981

An invasion of fish flies caused several traffic accidents and near misses in Ira Township (St. Clair County). The short-lived insect collected and died on several roads and intersections creating conditions similar to driving on ice. Fire department personnel hosed the flies out of many intersections when motorists and motorcyclists slid through stop signs and collided.

6 CONSPICUOUS NUCLEAR ACCIDENTS AND NEAR MISSES

1. 1966

When coolant flow was blocked, the uranium fuel core at the Enrico Fermi (Monroe) experimental fast-breeder reactor partly melted and flooded the plant with high-level radiation. A University of Michigan study calculated that, had the core completely melted and "run away," 133,000 people in the Detroit-Monroe area could have been killed.

2. MARCH, 1980

Seventeen employees at the Donald C. Cook Power Plant (Bridgman) drank coffee made with radioactive water which resulted from wastewater backing up into the pure water system.

3. JANUARY 7, 1971

An unarmed Air Force B-52 bomber crashed into Lake Michigan ten miles from Big Rock Point Nuclear Plant (Charlevoix) killing nine crew members. Had the plane crashed eleven seconds later, it could have hit the nuclear facility.

4. APRIL, 1978

When the Palisades Nuclear Plant (South Haven) reopened after a routine refueling operation, two safety valves were inadvertently left open and remained so for eighteen months. Though no radiation escaped, a loss-of-coolant accident would have resulted in radiation escaping into the air. Nuclear Regulatory Commission (NRC) officials, stressing the "very serious safety significance" of the incident, fined Consumers Power

$450,000, the largest in NRC history.

5. SUMMER, 1978
A Big Rock Point employee allowed a local golf course to borrow demineralized water for use in their golf cart batteries. The water was later discovered to be radioactive.

6. AUGUST, 1973
More than twice the allowable limit of radioactive iodine was released into the air from the Palisades Nuclear Plant during a routine purging operation. The Atomic Energy Commission fined Consumers Power $19,000 for that and sixteen other violations.

5 DEADLY ACCIDENTS

1. ISHPEMING - November 3, 1926
Fifty-one miners, working eight hundred feet below the surface of the *Barnes-Hecter Mine,* died when a swamp bottom sank suddenly into the shaft and washed away the workers in a wall of mud and quicksand.

The collapse left an indentation sixty feet deep over a 60,000-square-foot area of the swampland and filled the shaft with six hundred feet of water.

2. SALEM - July 20, 1907
An eleven-coach excursion train, carrying eight hundred employees of the *Pere Marquette Railway* from Ionia to Detroit for an annual holiday, collided head-on with an oncoming freight train near Salem, killing thirty-three and injuring one hundred.

A special hospital train from Detroit sped to the accident scene to treat and remove the injured victims, mostly men who were sitting in a smoking car in one of the front coaches.

The engineer and fireman of the freight—which was supposed to have waited at Plymouth for the excursion train to pass—jumped from their engine and escaped injury, but the excursion crew died.

3. CALUMET - December 24, 1913
Five hundred youngsters, mostly children of impoverished striking miners, packed into a second-story ballroom at Calumet's *Italian Hall* to hear music, see Santa Claus, open small gifts and temporarily forget about the bitter strike that divided their town.

Suddenly, an unidentified man—said to be wearing the badge of a group bitterly opposed to the strikers—burst into the crowded hall and yelled, "Fire!" Panic-stricken adults and children rushed toward the single fire escape, pressed through the narrow exit and tumbled over each other down a steep staircase.

Firemen, who rushed to the hall, found no fire but a gruesome pile of seventy-two dead bodies, mostly children.

4. DURAND - August 6, 1903

The first sixteen cars of a circus train, traveling in two sections from Charlotte to Lapeer, stopped at Durand at 4 a.m. When the air brakes of the closely following, 22-car second section failed, it plowed into the rear of the first train, telescoping a caboose into a sleeper car and burying dying and injured victims in a mass of twisted wreckage. Twenty-three members of the Wallace Brothers Circus died and forty were injured.

5. MONROE - July 1, 1975

A 24-foot recreational vehicle, carrying a family en route to a two-week Florida vacation, nicked a guard rail, slammed into a bridge support, burst into flames and burned to the axles faster than bystanders could reach the trapped victims. Ten people, including five children, died.

3 DISASTROUS FOREST FIRES

1. SEPTEMBER 5-8, 1881

The summer of 1881 had been unusually dry and the lumber industry was in its prime. Loggers had left a wilderness of slashings and stumps throughout the Thumb area.

Farmers, taking advantage of the dry spell, set fires to clear their lands but, on September 5, the wind took the smaller fires and pushed them until they became one.

By the time the fire had reached eastern Tuscola County, northern Sanilac County and eastern Huron County, the winds had reached hurricane proportions, tearing roofs from buildings, knocking down large trees and rolling boulders as if they were pebbles.

People and animals frantically fled the rapidly moving, 100-foot-high sheets of flame to survive. Some lowered themselves into wells; others huddled in streams under wet blankets while fish floated to the surface, cooked by the intense heat. Many survived by rushing to green cornfields and burying themselves in the soil.

Many perished. The wall of flame overtook galloping horses and running people and left them roasting on the ground. Entire families suffocated when the oxygen-starved fire sucked the air out of their homes. Others suffocated from smoke.

A heavy rain finally doused the blaze but not until it had killed an estimated 280 people, burned over a million acres of land and left 15,000 people homeless. These victims became the first in the nation to be helped by the Red Cross's disaster relief program and resulted in official federal government recognition for the new organization.

2. JULY - AUGUST, 1975

Because of bureaucratic confusion and indecision, a small fire spread to become the second most expensive forest fire in U.S. history.

The fire started innocently in late July when lightning struck in the Seney Wildlife Refuge. The Refuge manager, thinking he could fight the fire alone, tried to walk to the blaze but couldn't reach it. Ten days later, the Refuge staff took heavy equipment to fight the rapidly spreading fire but the manager halted their efforts. Since federal regulations prohibit fighting fires in wilderness regions, he was undecided whether his people should fight the fire or who would pay for the costs involved.

Several more days of indecision and phone calls to his superior in Minnesota followed. Finally, on August 19, when more than a thousand acres were burning, federal fire fighters moved in to begin the first active suppression of the blaze.

By the time the blaze—which, according to a U.S. Department of the Interior report, could have been confined to one acre—was controlled, it had consumed 72,000 acres and cost over $8 million to put out.

3. MAY 4-7, 1980

On May 4, though short-staffed that day, eleven Forest Service employees ignored or misread the very high fire danger forecast and intentionally set a fire near Mio to improve the habitat of the endangered Kirtland Warbler.

The fire, scheduled to burn only two hundred acres of pine trees, jumped barriers and ultimately burned over 25,000 acres, killed one fire fighter, destroyed thirty-three homes, forced thousands to evacuate, caused $2 million in damage and cost $50,000 to put out.

4 VIOLENT EXPLOSIONS

1. PORT HURON - December 11, 1971

Unaware that deadly methane gas was filling their confined work space, construction workers poured a concrete liner inside a six-mile-long tunnel being constructed under Lake Huron. Suddenly the gas ignited, exploded like a bomb and sent concrete, steel and bodies flying. When rescuers cleared the debris, they found the bodies, some virtually unrecognizable, of twenty-one dead workmen.

2. ZILWAUKEE - January 22, 1976

A spark from a welding torch ignited dust in a grain elevator which exploded, killing five, injuring ten and leveling ten grain silos and a weighing office. Rescuers on the bitter cold day had to use hot-water bottles to warm victims and thaw frozen intravenous fluids. (Photo page *x*)

3. TAYLOR - December 14, 1979
When an automatic gauging system failed to indicate that a 1.2-million-gallon storage tank was full, gasoline overflowed into a surrounding moat and the fumes drifted over a vacant field to a nearby mobile-home park. When the fumes reached a heater pilot light in one of the units, they ignited, shot back to the 500-foot-wide, five-story-high tank and engulfed it in a massive blast that shot up flames that could be seen twenty miles away. Eight thousand people evacuated the area while fire fighters from eighteen southeastern Michigan communities fought the blaze.

4. ANN ARBOR - June 16, 1979
Five thousand residents, living a half mile from the University of Michigan campus, evacuated their homes and apartments when a large propane tanker exploded with a blast that rattled windows ten miles away and sent an orange fireball hundreds of feet into the air.

3 SPECTACULAR PLANE CRASHES

1. FREELAND - April 6, 1958
When ice accumulations jammed its horizontal stabilizers during a snowstorm, a Capitol Airlines, four-engine, turbo jet slammed into a mucky cornfield and exploded while approaching Tri-City Airport. Forty-four passengers, including twenty from Michigan, and three crew members died in the fiery crash, Michigan's worst. (Photo page *x*)

2. ALPENA - September 26, 1976
An Air Force KC135 tanker jet, carrying twenty men on a training mission, ripped a fifty-yard-wide, half-mile-long swath through a wooded area before crashing into a swamp. Fifteen of the servicemen died.

3. MACKINAW CITY - September 11, 1978
During a pea-soup fog, a small plane, carrying three U.S. Marine Corps Reserve officers, crashed into the Mackinac Bridge and plunged two hundred feet into the water. As a result of the impact, a piece of wing found on the roadway bore a perfect imprint of one of the bridge's steel suspension cables. Scuba divers removed the three bodies from the fuselage which was left in the eighty-foot-deep water as a bed for fish.

2 HIGHWAY LANDINGS

1. PLYMOUTH TOWNSHIP - January 1, 1982

Moments after taking off from Detroit City Airport, a Cessna 172 began to lose power and altitude so the pilot, eighteen-year-old Brian Brunt (Farmington Hills), landed the plane on I-75 and calmly taxied off an exit ramp.

2. HOUGHTON LAKE - March 29, 1972

Ralph Bower (Midland) headed through snow squalls from Flint to Midland in his single-engine Cessna but, because of bad landing conditions at Midland, air traffic controllers directed him to Roscommon. Finding similar unfavorable landing conditions there, Bowers calmly landed on northbound U.S. 27.

3 FATAL PARACHUTE JUMPS

1. WHITEHALL - March, 1966

During his first-ever jump, a seventeen-year-old skydiver fell 2,650 feet and landed headfirst on a blacktop road when his two parachutes failed to open.

2. ARGENTINE TOWNSHIP - July, 1980

When his chute failed to open, a 33-year-old Ypsilanti parachutist fell 5,500 feet into the backyard of a suburban home.

3. IONIA - April, 1968

A 36-year-old veteran skydiver, using main and reserve parachutes he had packed himself, jumped 10,500 feet to his death. Witnesses saw the Grand Ledge man struggle to tear the chutes' cover off before he hit the ground half a mile south of Ionia Airport.

2 WHO SURVIVED TERRIBLE FALLS

1. CHRISTINE CANDELLA (Visiting from New Jersey) - June, 1977

As her parents were waiting to be seated at a cocktail bar on the seventy-third floor of the Detroit Plaza Hotel, the 2½-year-old squeezed between some decorative mirrors and fell through a twelve-inch gap between the floor and revolving bar. She fell two stories before landing in the service area of the seventy-first-floor restaurant but suffered only a hairline fracture and several bruises.

2. BRUCE SHANNON (Vienna Township) - July, 1980
    The 43-year-old father of five swung in a "bosun's chair" sixty-seven feet above the concrete floor of a Pontiac foundry where he was cleaning machinery. The chair failed to hold him and, though he suffered a broken neck, arm and jaw, a collapsed lung, a torn diaphragm and a crushed kidney as a result of the seven-story fall, he recovered after several operations.

2 CONSPICUOUS SUICIDE SITES

1. HYATT REGENCY HOTEL (Dearborn)
    Only eighteen months after opening in February, 1976, three people had successfully committed suicide by jumping from upper-floor interior balconies to the main-lobby floor.

2. MACKINAC BRIDGE - April 22, 1974
    A young Royal Oak man left his Chevrolet van, lights on and motor running, and leaped to his death from the middle of the Mackinac Bridge. His was the first known suicide leap from the bridge.

6 WAYS TO COMMIT SUICIDE

1,280 people committed suicide in Michigan in 1977. The six most common methods of reaching that dubious goal were:

1. SHOOTING OR BLOWING UP	53.4%
2. HANGING	14.8%
3. CAR EXHAUST OR GAS	13.2%
4. POISONING	12.7%
5. JUMPING	2.0%
6. DROWNING	1.5%

Guess What's Coming To Dinner?
3 MASS POISONINGS

1. PONTIAC - March 28-31, 1977
    The worst outbreak of botulism in the nation's history occurred when fifty-nine people contracted the dread disease after eating food containing improperly home-canned peppers at a Mexican restaurant. Though all but two of the victims were hospitalized—some in critical condition—quick identification of the toxin, one of the deadliest poisons known, prevented

fatalities. The restaurant's owners were fined $420 after pleading no contest to two misdemeanors.

2. JACKSON - November, 1981
Seven of 325 persons who attended a United Way luncheon contracted typhoid fever and twelve more were suspected of having the rare disease. State health officials traced the source to ice served in beverages at the luncheon.

3. FLINT - May 16-18, 1978
Eighty-five people who ate at a popular smorgasbord-type restaurant during Mother's Day weekend contracted confirmed cases of salmonella, a type of food poisoning that causes diarrhea, stomach cramps and convulsions. Laboratory reports confirmed salmonella bacteria in two employees but authorities were unable to determine whether the employees were the source of the outbreak or whether they had contracted it like the customers.

2 PRONOUNCED VICTIMS OF TOXIC SHOCK SYNDROME

During late 1980, a wave of the disease called "toxic shock syndrome" swept the country. Particularly vulnerable appeared to be women who wore tampons. Doctors at the U.S. Center for Disease Control in Atlanta, Georgia, who confirmed four hundred cases and forty deaths from toxic shock from 1975-80, speculated that tampons may favor the growth of bacteria which produce the poison or toxin that brings on the sudden symptoms. Victims suffer vomiting, diarrhea, fever and a sunburn-like rash on the hands and feet that later peels. Blood pressure usually drops rapidly followed by shock and sometimes death.

The exact number of cases in Michigan is unknown because doctors here are not required to report them to state health officials. Two of the nearly fifty reported cases include:

1. MARCY BINDER (Royal Oak) - September, 1980
The twenty-year-old newlywed, who was struck by the disease while on her honeymoon, became the state's first known fatality from toxic shock syndrome.

2. PEGGY CRUSAN (Detroit) - November, 1980
This victim, who at one point doctors had given only two hours to live, survived to file the first Michigan lawsuit against the manufacturers of the tampons she had been using.

5 STRANGE COINCIDENCES

1. DETROIT - Spring, 1975
A baby fell fourteen stories and landed on Joseph Figlock who was walking below. One year later, it happened again. Figlock and both babies survived. (From *The Book Of Lists II*, William Morrow and Company, Incorporated, copyright 1980)

2. WILLIAMSTON - 1979
As a mischievous kid of seventeen, Melvin Beach used his jackknife to carve his initials and the date (1919) on the bottom plate of a snapping turtle, then returned it to Doan Creek. Sixty years later, a neighbor found the brownish-colored turtle and took it to Beach who, like the turtle, had not moved far. Beach again released the turtle, which had only grown to ten inches, this time into a neighbor's private pond.

3. WYOMING (Michigan)
The 1977 Kelloggsville High School graduating class included three sets of twins and a set of triplets. Kelloggsville's 1975 graduating class included six sets of twins.

4. GRAND RAPIDS - December 27, 1981
A lonely British soldier stationed in Ireland, who wanted to talk to someone in America, dialed a telephone number by matching the digits on his military identification tag. The number belonged to the Tom Troyer family who talked to the soldier for ninety minutes.

5. MENOMINEE - December, 1981
Twin brothers Ken and Keith Mattson were involved in separate, minor traffic accidents a half hour and five miles apart. Three days later, the brothers, this time riding in the same car, were involved in another minor accident.

2 WHO WERE BURIED ALIVE

1. DANNY CULP (Traverse City) - February 19, 1980
The eleven-year-old was sledding with twelve friends and two adults at Sleeping Bear Dunes National Lakeshore (Glen Haven) when a huge wall of snow collapsed and buried him under six feet of snow. Paramedics, U.S. Coastguardsmen, and Park Rangers frantically shoveled a thirty-by-sixty-foot area before finding the boy, semi-concious but miraculously alive, one-and-a-half hours later.

2. LAWRENCE SHANNON (Grand Rapids) - February, 1978

Late in October, 1977, the 82-year-old man and his eighty-year-old wife left Grand Rapids in their motor home for a leisurely cross-country trip to their daughter's California home.

But, on February 6, 1978, they took a wrong turn in Sequoia National Park during a heavy rainstorm and headed up a road that dead-ended at a Boy Scout camp closed for the winter.

Rockslides forced them to stop, the van's engine broke down and it began to snow heavily. Two days later, Mrs. Shannon, who had Parkinson's disease and a history of high blood pressure and strokes, died.

Shannon wrapped her body in a blanket, turned off the heat in the motor home and began a daily routine of drinking melted snow, rationing his small supply of food and walking on an exercise path he shoveled around the buried van. He kept the motor home's roof free of snow and, a month later, was finally spotted by the Boy Scout Camp Director who had chartered a helicopter to survey snow damage to the camp.

A New Lease On Life
5 MIRACULOUS SURVIVALS

1. JEFF LUCZAK (Bay City) - February, 1979

The thirteen-year-old and his brothers playfully fought with snowballs when an errant throw smashed a large side-door window. As Jeff stepped inside to clean up the mess, a strong wind caught the door and plunged a large, dangling dagger of glass into his chest and heart. Jeff jerked the glass out and his brothers packed the wound with snow.

An ambulance arrived only to get stuck in the driveway and the medics had to wait and switch the unconscious boy to another before taking him to Bay City Medical Center. There, heart surgeon Dr. David Reyes opened Jeff's chest, scooped out handfuls of blood, plugged holes with his fingers and, without a needed heart-lung machine, repaired the heart wall during four hours of surgery.

Jeff had stopped breathing in the ambulance, in the emergency room and during surgery but, in spite of the freakish ordeal, fully recovered and now plays on his school's golf and basketball teams.

2. PATRICIA GRIFFIN (Plymouth) - September 26, 1966

While playing with a friend in her family's driveway, the five-year-old leaped from a partially opened garage door onto the trunk of the family car. Suddenly, terrified screams brought her mother and a neighbor who found the car's radio antenna driven into the girl's right eye. The adults could not free her easily so they removed the antenna from the car and, with it protruding from the frightened girl's eye, drove her to Annapolis Hospital.

Doctors there rushed her to nearby University of Michigan Hospital where neurosurgeons were amazed to discover that the antenna had slipped through a tiny aperture above the tear duct, passed through the eye socket without damaging the eyeball and lodged one inch into a non-vital area of the brain without hitting any major blood vessels. After careful surgery to remove the antenna, Patricia left the hospital with no damage other than a very evident black eye.

3. ALEXIS ST. MARTIN (Mackinac Island) - June, 1822

The young trapper recovered from a severe gunshot wound in his abdomen but the outside of the wound never healed. Dr. William Beaumont, the island's physician, was able to peer inside St. Martin's body and, for years, studied the process of human digestion firsthand.

St. Martin, later known as the "man with a window in his stomach," lived to be eighty.

4. BOEING 727 (Flint) - April 4, 1979

A TWA Boeing 727, carrying eighty passengers at 39,000 feet, suddenly swerved to the right, completed a 360-degree barrel roll and nosedived five miles at a speed the plane's instruments could not record. Harvey "Hoot" Gibson, the pilot, tried to slow the descent by extending wing flaps, spoilers and leading edge slats, but they were torn from the plane. He finally regained control by putting the landing gear down and made an emergency landing at Detroit Metro Airport.

5. KEVIN WILLIAMSON (Mason) - August 23, 1979

The six-year-old squeezed under a fence around a Detroit Edison booster station, climbed to the top of a transformer, avoided a 40,000-volt line but grabbed a live, 4,800-volt wire. His mother found the boy, frightened but suffering only third-degree burns on his right hand. Authorities speculated that he lived only because he was not well-grounded.

10 ODDS AGAINST YOUR DEATH

If you were born in Michigan, the odds against your eventual death from ten specific causes are:

	MEN	WOMEN
1. HEART DISEASE	3 to 2	4 to 3
2. CANCER	4 to 1	5 to 1
3. STROKE	11 to 1	6 to 1
4. ACCIDENT	20 to 1	35 to 1
5. FLU OR PNEUMONIA	35 to 1	35 to 1
6. CIRRHOSIS	49 to 1	90 to 1
7. DIABETES	54 to 1	31 to 1
8. ARTERIOSCLEROSIS	61 to 1	166 to 1
9. SUICIDE	61 to 1	166 to 1
10. MURDER	70 to 1	249 to 1

5 LIFE EXPECTANCIES

Life expectancies for Michigan men and women for five selected years.

	MEN	WOMEN
1. 1900	53.4	55.1
2. 1920	55.1	56.0
3. 1940	63.4	67.4
4. 1960	67.1	73.3
5. 1977	69.3	76.3

6 MOST COMMON FATAL ACCIDENTS

Based on the number of people killed in Michigan in 1977.

1. AUTOMOBILE	1,993
2. FALLS	564
3. FIRE OR EXPLOSION	311
4. DROWNING	238
5. POISONING	156
6. CHOKING	105

2 TRAGIC DROWNINGS

1. MUNISING - September 22, 1959

Twelve members of a Skandia family—Mrs. Dora Larson, ten of her eleven children, and her brother-in-law—all drowned when their overloaded, twelve-foot motorboat swamped in Lake McKeever. The family, none of whom could swim, were en route to pick cranberries when the boat capsized forty feet from shore and resulted in Michigan's worst small-boat tragedy.

2. EAST TAWAS - July 16, 1943

Nine young people attending a church camp drowned in Lake Huron. The victims, ages twelve to twenty-two, leaped from an excursion boat which they mistakenly thought was sinking.

6 ELEMENTS OF A BOATING FATALITY

In 1973 the Michigan Department of Natural Resources, using statistics from hundreds of Michigan boating accidents, drew a composite picture of a boating fatality.

A boating fatality will happen:

1. In an aluminum boat with an outboard motor.
2. While pleasure cruising.
3. On an inland lake.
4. On a calm Saturday afternoon in July.
5. When the boat capsizes because of driver neglect.
6. To a passenger not wearing a life vest.

2 MOST DANGEROUS HUNTING SEASONS

The two firearm deer-hunting seasons since 1950 when the most hunters were shot and killed.

1. 1952	15
2. 1975	13

5 DEADLIEST YEARS TO DRIVE

The five years during which the most people died on Michigan's highways.

1. 1969	2,487
2. 1968	2,392
3. 1966	2,298
4. 1972	2,258
5. 1973	2,213

6 DRIVING CASUALTIES

During 1977 in Michigan:

1. One out of every 4,551 persons living in Michigan was killed in a traffic accident.

2. One person was killed every 4 hours, 29 minutes.

3. One out of every 53 people living in Michigan was injured in a traffic accident.

4. One person was injured every 3 minutes, 10 seconds.

5. One out of every 16.4 licensed drivers was involved in an accident.

6. A traffic accident was reported every 1 minute, 24 seconds.

14

4 DANGEROUS HIGHWAYS

1. WOODWARD AVENUE (M-1), from 11-Mile Road to 14-Mile Road.
Family Weekly Magazine (December, 1973) listed as one of the most
dangerous highways in America this stretch in Detroit which, in 1972, had
637 accidents including two fatalities.

2. U.S. 131, between Howard City and Cadillac.
During the first nine months of 1977, this 41.5-mile stretch of road,
which is scheduled to be converted to four lanes, had 305 accidents, killing
four and injuring 173.

3. M-37, just north of Manistee River Bridge in Wexford County.
This ½-mile "S" curve is notorious for accidents, especially when
snowy. Guard rails are mowed down as quickly as they are installed and oil
tankers and trucks carrying cherry juice spill their loads on the sharp curves
making conditions even worse.

4. M-21, between Lapeer and Port Huron.
As many as twenty people a year have died on this thirty-mile stretch.

4 LETHAL YEARS

Four years with the most Michigan deaths.

1. 1972	79,210
2. 1973	78,522
3. 1971	77,395
4. 1968	76,855

10 BIGGEST KILLERS

The ten leading causes of death in Michigan in 1978.

1. HEART DISEASE	29,406
2. CANCER	15,249
3. STROKE	6,520
4. ACCIDENTS	3,970
5. FLU AND PNEUMONIA	2,003
6. DIABETES	1,551
7. CIRRHOSIS	1,351
8. ARTERIOSCLEROSIS	1,146
9. SUICIDE	1,132
10. MURDER	932

8 COUNTIES WITH NO HOSPITALS

1. ALMA
2. ANTRIM
3. KEEWEENAW
4. LAKE
5. MISSAUKEE
6. MONTMORENCY
7. OSCODA
8. ROSCOMMON

5 STATES WHERE WE DIE

2,104 Michigan residents died outside the state in 1977. The five states our residents most often died in were:

1. FLORIDA	497
2. OHIO	297
3. INDIANA	252
4. WISCONSIN	183
5. ILLINOIS	101

3 UNUSUAL AUTOPSIES

1. WAYNE COUNTY MORGUE

For six years two morgue employees charged and counter-charged each other with body snatching, decapitating and mutilating corpses, illegally selling glands and other ghoulish acts.

The bizarre feud began in 1975 when pathologist Millard Bass told reporters that his boss, Wayne County Medical Examiner Werner Spitz, had performed unauthorized gunshot experiments on corpses and had sold glands, brains and bodily fluids from bodies at the morgue to support his research foundation. Prosecutors substantiated most of the claims but did not file charges against Spitz because they found no criminal intent.

Spitz, in turn, fired Bass in 1976 claiming that the pathologist had decapitated bodies and stripped flesh from more than a dozen others. Spitz led police to a cache of bones in a Greektown storeroom Bass rented, and investigators also found a vat of nine human heads and other miscellaneous body parts in a Wayne State University workroom used by Bass. Spitz also claimed he had found vertebrae in Bass' office that fit like a puzzle with those of a decapitated body in the morgue.

County prosecutors criminally charged Bass, but after a flurry of publicity the charges were dismissed at a preliminary hearing.

In 1978 Bass sued Wayne County for malicious prosecution and won $1.8 million in damages which a judge later reduced to $564,000.

2. POWERS - 1977

After completing an autopsy on a young Menominee County murder victim, the County's Deputy Medical Examiner, without notifying the girl's parents, shaved her head and cut off her hands before funeral-home personnel closed the casket for the funeral

The shocked parents did not discover what had been done until the body parts were grimly displayed as evidence months later at a preliminary court hearing held for the man eventually convicted of beating their daughter to death.

3. KALAMAZOO - 1970

Argonne National Laboratory (Chicago) researchers exhumed the of a woman who had been buried for forty-two years so they could study the long-term effects of radioactive substances on the human body. The woman, who died at age seventy-two in 1928, had received radium shots to combat Hodgkins disease.

What's Wrong With Mummy?
2 ANCIENT AUTOPSIES

1. DETROIT - 1971

Dr. Adrian Cockburn, the director of several clinics in the Detroit area, performed an autopsy on a 2000-year-old Egyptian mummy to research and investigate the history and evolution of infectious diseases. The body of the 35-year-old minor government official still held waste products, bodies of parasites and bacteria intact.

2. DETROIT - 1973

Twenty microbiologists, anthropologists, surgeons and pathologists from the United States, Canada, Egypt and Czechoslovakia performed a seven-hour autopsy on a 2,700-year-old mummy at Wayne State University. Under the direction of Wayne State University pathologist Robin Barraco, the researchers determined, through x-rays, that the 26-year-old man had died of a skull fracture. When they opened the previously untouched remains they were able to locate an incision through which organs had been removed to be mummified separately.

7 COUNTIES WITH ONLY ONE MORTUARY

1. ALGER

2. CRAWFORD
3. KALKASKA
4. LEELANAU
5. LUCE
6. MACKINAC
7. OSCODA

Keeweenaw County has no mortuary.

5 UNUSUAL FUNERALS

1. BRIGHTON - October 19, 1979

As the widow, friends and relatives accompanied the casket of a Brighton man to its grave, the bottom of the casket suddenly came loose and, according to a subsequent lawsuit, the body, "surrounded by rags, newspaper, shredded paper and what appeared to be panty hose, rolled onto the ground."

2. FLINT - June 7, 1978

The dozen mourners who lined their cars behind the hearse of Mr. Stewart M. Fine, head of a company that fenced guns and other stolen goods, received two shocks. First, Mr. Fine didn't exist and never had and, second, they were arrested.

Agents of the U.S. Bureau of Alcohol, Tobacco and Firearms and Flint Police created the fictitious Stewart Fine and his company in an elaborate, eight-month-long sting operation. At the rate of twelve to fourteen a day, customers brought stolen televisions, weapons, cars and credit cards to a grubby, concrete-block warehouse. "Mr. Fine's" clerks, actually armed undercover agents, paid customers but also secretly photographed and identified them.

The sting operation closed when "Mr. Fine" died and his clients were told that the funeral procession could be used to secretly drive stolen cars to Detroit to sell. As the cars lined up behind the hearse and the suspects stepped out to put funeral flags on them, they were arrested.

3. DETROIT - August, 1970

Designed as the ultimate in social convenience for friends who want to let a grieving family know they sympathize but don't have the time to walk into the funeral home or go to the funeral, a Detroit mortuary installed a drive-in window.

Visitors drive into a canopied horseshoe driveway and, after viewing the deceased in a display window, drop a signed card into a box mounted across the window.

18

4. DETROIT - February, 1971

To aid the families of deceased persons who don't have enough strong friends to carry them out, the Wayne State University placement service added a "rent-a-pallbearer" to its list of odd jobs for students who want to earn extra spending money.

5. EAST LANSING

For the past ten years Michigan State University has conducted an annual mass cremation, funeral and burial for the families of people who donated their bodies to the school's anatomy department.

5 MEMORABLE CEMETERIES

1. LIVONIA - 1965

Many of the three hundred Memorial Day visitors to the Brookdale Park Cemetery could not find the graves of their loved ones and were shocked by the woefully unattended grounds. Their complaints launched an investigation that revealed shocking, improper burial practices including stacking as many as two hundred bodies like cordwood in a shed, mass burials, missing or misplaced bodies and empty graves.

A series of court-ordered exhumations uncovered graves marked with the names of bodies contained there but found empty, graves containing bodies other than those thought to be buried there, and bodies supposed to be buried in the cemetery but not found anywhere.

The former superintendent of the cemetery testified that caskets containing bodies of more than two hundred persons, including thirty-five babies, were stacked to the ceiling in a shed for as long as five months before being buried in unmarked graves. The superintendent added that he had buried the thirty-five babies in three communal graves and that some graves in the cemetery held the caskets of as many as eighteen children stacked one on top of the other.

2. DETROIT - October, 1976

Taking the pet-rock craze to its ultimate end, two southwest Detroit bar owners opened a pet-rock cemetery in their parking lot. Each of the twenty-three plots was covered with synthetic grass, bordered by white concrete block, marked with tombstones and decorated with plastic flowers and candles.

3. FLINT - September, 1976

A Flint businesswoman opened the Golden Gate Pet Rock Mortuary and Crematorium which crushed "dead" pet rocks, burned them, put them in glass containers and returned the ashes, a death certificate and a "newborn" rock to customers who paid $19.95 for the last rites.

4. MUSKEGON - 1972

The city of Muskegon removed one hundred tombstones from its municipal cemetery when families had fallen behind in the payment of annual care fees. They stopped after loud public protest but, under their city's 1943 law, they could have also exhumed the bodies and resold the plots.

5. DETROIT

One hundred-thirty-five-year-old Elmwood Cemetery is Michigan's oldest active graveyard.

Grave Images
2 PECULIAR TOMBSTONES

1. NORTH BRANCH TOWNSHIP

A nineteen-year-old woman, killed by a hit-and-run driver in 1974, continued to look for her killer through the eyes of her picture, encased in plastic and attached to her tombstone by her parents. According to local legend and several witnesses, the eyes in the picture glowed.

Two years to the day of her death, a driver, said to be the man who killed her, drove by the cemetery and, blinded from a sudden intense shining light from her eyes, lost control of his car and was killed.

3. JACKSON - 1973

A young inventor created a tombstone that does more than just stand there. The "talking tombstone," as he called it, chats, sings, plays stereo music, shows movies and slides and is bullet-proof.

Friends or relatives can store solar-battery-operated slides, films, tapes and stereo equipment inside the polycarbonate structure so they might play back voices and view photos of the departed loved ones at each visit.

Elmwood Cemetery

LET US ENTERTAIN YOU

32 ENTERTAINMENT PERSONALITIES BORN IN MICHIGAN

1. JUDY GARLAND (Grand Rapids, 1922) - Actress

2. LILY TOMLIN (Detroit, 1939) - Television and movie comedienne

3. ED McMAHON (Detroit, March 6, 1923) - Johnny Carson's long-time announcer

4. DANNY THOMAS (Deerfield, January 6, 1914) - Comedian

5. ROBERT WAGNER (Detroit, February 10, 1930) - Actor

6. GLEN FREY (Royal Oak) - Member of *The Eagles* rock group

7. LEE MAJORS (Wyandotte, April 23, 1940) - Actor

8. SONNY BONO (Detroit, February 16, 1940) - Songwriter and actor

9. DIANA ROSS (Detroit, March 26, 1944) - Recording star

10. JAMES McGINNIS (Detroit) - Joined the circus at age fourteen, adopted the name "Bailey" and joined Phineas T. Barnum

11. KIM HUNTER (Detroit, November 12, 1922) - Actress

12. MARLO THOMAS (Detroit, November 21, 1943) - Actress

13. DELLA REESE (Detroit, July 6, 1932) - Recording artist

14. HARRY MORGAN (Detroit, April 10, 1915) - Actor, most recently as Col. Potter on *Mash*

15. DICK ENBERG (Armada) - Sportscaster and play by play announcer

16. STEVIE WONDER (Saginaw, May 13, 1950) - Recording artist

17. ARTE JOHNSON (Benton Harbor, January 20, 1934) - Comedian

Harry Morgan

Robert Wagner

Lee Majors

Tom Selleck

Pam Dawbar

Gravestone of Debora de Costello, one of six entertainers who have died while performing in Michigan. When the young orphan's body finally washed ashore, she was buried in Empire's St. Philips Cemetery.

18. DICK MARTIN (Detroit, 1922) - Comedian

19. MARTIN MILNER (Detroit, December 28, 1931) - Actor

20. FRANCIS FORD COPPOLA (Detroit, April 17, 1939) - Film director

21. GEORGE PEPPARD (Detroit, October 1, 1928) - Film and theatre actor

22. TOM SELLECK (Detroit) - Television actor and model

23. BETTY HUTTON (Battle Creek, February 26, 1921) - Actress

24. PAM DAWBAR (Detroit) - Actress and model

25. JOHNNY DESMOND (Detroit, November 14, 1921) - Composer

26. JULIE HARRIS (Grosse Pointe Park, December 2, 1925) - Actress

27. ALICE COOPER (Detroit, February 4, 1948) - Rock star

28. ELLEN BURSTYN (Detroit, December 7, 1932) - Actress

29. MICHAEL MORIARITY (Detroit, April 5, 1941) - Actor

30. PIPER LAURIE (Detroit, January 22, 1932) - Actress

31. WILLIE TYLER and LESTER (Detroit) - Ventriloquist and his streetwise sidekick

32. DAVID WAYNE (Traverse City, January 30, 1914) - Actor

6 ENTERTAINERS WHO DIED WHILE PERFORMING IN MICHIGAN

1. HARRY HOUDINI - October 31, 1926
After an October 23rd performance in Montreal, a college student, thinking that Houdini had flexed his muscles, hit the great escape artist full force in the stomach. Though his appendix had ruptured, Houdini traveled to Detroit, performed, then collapsed offstage. He died of an infection seven days later in room #401, Grace Hospital (Detroit).

2. DEBORA de COSTELLO - Autumn, 1920
The Empire Fair Committee had hired the parachutist and her Japanese pilot to perform in their cloth-winged, wooden-propellered plane. To open the performance, the young girl jumped over Lake Michigan, opened her chute and the prevailing winds were supposed to blow her back to shore where she could land at the fairgrounds. But the wind suddenly shifted, blew her out over the lake, collapsed her chute and she fell into

Lake Michigan and disappeared.

3. "CAPTAIN EDDIE" KNIPSCHILD - August 2, 1964
As 22,000 watched at floodlighted Tiger Stadium, the performer placed his foot into a strap eighty-five feet up a swaying pole and began his act. Suddenly the strap broke and the 55-year-old fell to his death.

4. DIETER SCHEPP - January 30, 1962
Making his first appearance with the famed Wallenda Family high-wire act, the 23-year-old East German died when a seven-member "human pyramid" collapsed and he fell thirty-six feet to the concrete floor of the Detroit State Fairgrounds Coliseum.

5. RICHARD FAUGHNAN - January 30, 1962
The only American member of the German Wallenda troupe fell to his death as seven thousand children and adults watched the "human pyramid" collapse during a Shrine Circus performance.

6. PATRICIA COWAN - April 10, 1978
While the young actress auditioned in Highland Park for a part in a play called *Hammer*, the playwright suddenly attacked her with a sledgehammer and bludgeoned her to death.

The Great Pretender
6 GREAT GATE CRASHINGS

Barry Bremen (Southfield), a 34-year-old insurance salesman, has made a hobby of popping up unexpectedly at major sporting events, usually in full view of a national television audience. Because of his exploits, he has also appeared as a guest on the *Tonight Show* and *Today Show*.

1. During the 1979 NBA All Star basketball game played at the Pontiac Silverdome, Bremen wore a number-thirteen jersey, participated in warm-ups and sat on the bench for the entire first half before being discovered.

2. Bremen played in two U.S. Open practice rounds at Toledo in 1979 and Baltrusol, New Jersey, in 1980. On the first two holes at Toledo he outdrove the two "real" pros he was with.

3. He donned falsies and wig and, wearing a matching outfit, joined the Dallas Cowboy cheerleaders on the field during a December, 1980 playoff game.

4. He posed as former Detroit Lion Lem Barney and sat on the bench during football's 1980 Pro Bowl.

5. While wired with sound by a national television network, he imper-

sonated a New York Yankee during the 1980 All Star game.

6. Disguised as an umpire, he stood at home plate for the playing of the national anthem during a 1980 World Series baseball game in Philadelphia.

2 ALLEGED SONG THEFTS

1. Carol Hinton (Rockford) claimed that Stevie Nicks of the rock group *Fleetwood Mac* stole lyrics from a poem she wrote in 1978. Though the lyrics to the top-ten song *Sara* were remarkably similar to and sometimes identical to Hinton's poem *Sarah*, Nicks attributed the similarities to "karma," a Hindu word meaning "fate."

2. Catherine Hoste (Detroit) claimed that Elvis Presley plagiarized the melody of a song she wrote in 1946 and used it in his tune, *I'm Yours.*

2 NOTABLE ROCK MUSIC MARKETS

1. LANSING
   Based on *American Radio*'s 1977 figures, Lansing is the tenth best rock music market in the nation with a 57.5 share of the total Lansing listening audience.

2. FLINT
   Based on *American Radio*'s 1977 figures, Flint is the sixth worst rock music market in the country commanding only a 24.9 share of Flint's radio audience.

5 ROCK STARS REPRESENTED BY T. PATRICK FREYDL

T. Patrick Freydl (Detroit), Michigan's foremost rock lawyer, negotiates contracts and handles the business affairs of several musical and entertainment artists including:
   1. BOB SEGER
   2. BILLY JOEL
   3. TED NUGENT
   4. STYX
   5. THE ROCKETS

4 LOUDEST RADIO STATIONS

Based on broadcasting power in watts.
1. WJFM (Grand Rapids) - FM 93.7 - 500,000 watts
2. WOOD (Grand Rapids) - FM 105.7 - 265,000 watts
3. WUOM (Ann Arbor) - FM 91.7 - 230,000 watts
4. WOMC (Detroit) - FM 104.3 - 190,000 watts

2 TOP-RANKING TV MARKETS

1. MARQUETTE
According to 1977 figures, Marquette is the second best market in the entire country for television's *60 Minutes* and third best for *The Lawrence Welk Show.*.

2. ALPENA
Alpena is the second highest area in the country for percent of cable television penetration. As of 1977, sixty-five percent of Alpena-area homes were connected to cable television.

4 RANKING MAGAZINE MARKETS

1. BARAGA
Fifth in the nation for readers of *Grit*.

2. WASHTENAW
Sixth in the nation for readers of *Psychology Today*.

3. KEEWEENAW
Seventh in the nation for readers of *Grit*.

4. ARENAC
Eighth in the nation for readers of *Brides Magazine*.

Ninth in the nation for readers of *Cosmopolitan*.

7 WELL-KNOWN NOVELS WITH A MICHIGAN SETTING

1. *ANATOMY OF A MURDER* (Robert Traver)

Somewhere In Time, one of two movies filmed on Mackinac Island. (Photo courtesy of Universal Studios).

Four novels with a Michigan setting.

A fictionalized version of an actual murder in the town of Big Bay, written under a pseudonym by Michigan Supreme Court Judge John D. Voelker.

2. *WHEELS* (Arthur Hailey)
Details the lives of people running the automobile industry.

3. *HIAWATHA* (Henry Wadsworth Longfellow)
Expands upon legends of the lake country in this epic poem.

4. *NORTHWEST PASSAGE* (Kenneth Roberts)
Describes a quest for a route to Asia.

5. *MOTOR CITY BLUES* (Loren D. Estleman)
The Whitmore Lake author introduced his Detroit private eye, Amos Walker, in this novel.

6. *DOLL MAKER* (Harriette Arnow)
Observes the people who live and work in automobile manufacturing areas.

7. *CROOKED TREE* (Robert C. Wilson)
Story of possessed black bears stalking humans in the Upper Peninsula.

3 MOVIES FILMED IN MICHIGAN

1. *ANATOMY OF A MURDER*
Otto Preminger filmed the movie at the Thunder Bay Inn, Big Bay (near Marquette), in 1969. The movie, starring James Stewart and Ben Gazzarra, was based on an actual slaying that took place in Marquette County in 1952.

2. *WORD OF HONOR*
The television movie, starring Karl Malden, was filmed in and around West Bloomfield, Bloomfield Hills, Plymouth, Royal Oak and Pontiac.

3. *JIMMY B. AND ANDRE*
The television movie, about a Detroit bar owner who befriends a black ghetto youth, was filmed largely in Detroit's Lindell AC nightclub.

2 MOVIES FILMED ON MACKINAC ISLAND

1. *THIS TIME FOR KEEPS* (1946)
   Starred Esther Williams.

2. *SOMEWHERE IN TIME* (1979)
   Starred Christopher Reeve, Jane Seymour and Christopher Plummer.

2 MOVIE THEATRES WITH BARS

The only two movie theatres in the country where, as of 1978, patrons could buy drinks at lobby bars and carry them to their seats.

1. DEARBORN ENTERTAINMENT CENTER (Dearborn)
2. QUO VADIS (Westland)

MICHIGAN'S TEN FAVORITE BEERS

Based on the number of barrels sold from January to July, 1980.

1.	MILLER	881,116
2.	PABST	671,231
3.	BUDWEISER	423,129
4.	MILLER LITE	409,897
5.	STROH'S	383,694
6.	MICHELOB	205,861
7.	OLD MILWAUKEE	138,045
8.	MICHELOB LIGHT	103,756
9.	COLT 45	88,046
10.	BUSCH	83,661

MICHIGAN'S 5 FAVORITE WHISKEYS

1.	AMERICAN BLEND	75%
2.	STRAIGHT BOURBON	23%
3.	BONDED BOURBON	1%
4.	STRAIGHT RYE	.2%
5.	STRAIGHT CORN	.1%

2 REMARKABLE UFO SIGHTINGS

1. HOUGHTON - August, 1965

U.S. Air Force personnel reported solid radar contact with seven to ten unidentified flying objects (UFO's) moving at about nine thousand miles per hour in a "V" formation over Lake Superior. Two other radar stations in North Dakota and Minnesota also spotted the objects and a third station in Canada reported electronic jamming of its radar. Jet interceptors gave chase over Duluth, Minnesota, but could not maintain the speed of the UFO's and were outdistanced.

2. WASHTENAW COUNTY - Spring, 1966

A rash of elliptical UFO's with pulsating red and green haloed lights flew in formation, dipped, hovered and landed over a three-day period in the Ann Arbor-Dexter area. At least a dozen law enforcement officers and more than fifty other reliable citizens witnessed and pursued the objects, and Selfridge Air Force Base personnel confirmed radar contact. Two congressmen, including then Rep. Gerald Ford, requested a Congressional investigation but were denied. An Air Force consultant was practically laughed out of the area when he hurriedly attributed the entire phenomenon to "swamp gas," but to this day no other explanation has been postulated.

3 HAUNTED HOUSES

1. JACKSON

A one-story frame house, built in 1837 in the shadow of the Michigan State prison, plagued the Victor and Beatrice Lincoln family with flying dishes and knives, pounding sounds and other inexplicable happenings from 1961 to 1964.

Although the family had lived in the house for years, nothing out of the ordinary happened until September, 1961, when Beatrice heard footsteps in the basement, which is located over abandoned tunnels where prisoners mined coal years earlier. Pounding followed, like someone trying to break a door down. Startled awake by the racket, Victor grabbed a shotgun and went into the basement but no one was there and the sounds stopped.

Other events followed. Locked doors unlocked and opened. A string of electric Christmas lights suddenly flew from the tree to the floor. Beatrice, alone in the house, made a bed, left the room and returned minutes later to find the blankets pulled down. In February, 1962, a paring knife flew from the table and struck her in the leg.

A curious probation officer stopped by to investigate, and while he was there, water taps in the bathroom and burners on the gas stove mysteriously turned on.

The Lincoln family moved out in 1964. Another family bought the house and has resided there uneventfully.

Residents of an Alma College fraternity house (above) say that the ghost of a former member eerily floats through the house. And several owners of an older Fenton home (below) claim that a minister's ghost is more a nuisance than frightening.

31

2. FENTON

One of Fenton's oldest homes, often featured on historic house tours, is occupied by an unthreatening but irritating ghost named "Norman," according to several owners of the friendly and cheery dwelling.

The spirit, named after Reverend Norman Hough, a Baptist minister who died in the house in 1926, opens doors, knocks things off walls, unrolls toilet paper, causes loud inexplicable crashes and footsteps, breaks mirrors and ashtrays, plays music and creaks around after midnight.

3. ALMA

Members of the Tau Kappa Epsilon fraternity at Alma College say a former member of the house, who died in a canoeing accident fourteen years ago, may be haunting the aging building.

Members of the fraternity, all of whom won't stay in the house alone, claim that a ghost wearing a white T-shirt has been roaming the corridors, making noise and playing practical jokes since 1975. Many have reported catching glimpses of a headless limbless torso covered with a white T-shirt floating just off the floor from room to room.

Others have turned off mysteriously running showers only to have them go back on as soon as they step out of the room.

4 MICHIGAN MONSTERS

1. BARRYTON - September, 1977

Footprints measuring 16½ inches long and 9½ inches wide with 58-inch strides marked the soil in the backyard of Bob and Becky Kurtz. The day after the footprints appeared, their normally ferocious watchdogs scurried into the house where they remained for two days and numerous deer, that normally gathered in a nearby swamp, also disappeared for several days. Bear hunters and other authorities who investigated said the tracks, which disappeared in a grassy orchard, were not made by a bear or faked by pranksters but had to be made by an unidentified creature weighing close to eight hundred pounds.

2. GROSSE POINTE - 1884

In Legends of Le Detroit, published in 1884, author Marie Caroline Watson Hamlin vividly described the attacks of a predatory werewolf. According to her writings, "the monster resembled a baboon with a horned head, a skin of bristling black hair, brilliant restless eyes and a devilish leer on its face."

3. PETOSKEY - 1895

National newspapers ran stories about several sightings of a huge sea serpent swimming in Little Traverse Bay and one resident even produced a photograph. The origin of the creature remained a mystery for thirty-five years when the then aging photographer finally confessed that his picture was a phony.

4. GULL ISLAND - 1900
The island's Indians spotted a huge, thirty-foot, green serpent sunning itself offshore and refused to fish for weeks. One young brave finally ventured out to fight the beast only to discover two huge logs covered with seaweed.

5 SIGHTINGS OF BIGFOOT

Bigfoot is a legendary, eight-foot-tall, 600-pound, hairy creature that walks on two legs and leaves giant footprints and a foul odor. Himalayan mountain climbers first reported seeing the beast in the 1950's and, since then, the beast has been reported to roam wooded areas from Maine to California. Reported sightings in Michigan include:

1. SISTER LAKES - 1964
A migrant berry picker reported seeing a hairy, nine-foot-tall, 400-pound monster threading its way quickly through the area's tangled vines and dense forests. From all around the state, thousands of monster hunters with clubs, rifles, camouflage apparel and dogs poured into the town but no one saw the beast again.

2. MONROE - March, 1979
A man was bitten by his own dog as he tried to keep it from attacking a hairy creature that towered above the 8½-foot eaves of his garage.

3. MONROE - 1965
A mother and daughter reported being attacked by a Bigfoot after accidentally hitting the creature with their car.

4. GRAYLING - 1976
Three military men reported being chased into their truck by a Bigfoot that then climbed on top of the vehicle trying to get at them.

5. LANSING - December, 1978
A General Motors welder and his wife reported that they had seen a Bigfoot in their driveway and followed the creature's ten-by-thirteen-inch tracks through the snow into an apple orchard.

2 MONSTER HUNTERS

1. WAYNE KING (Caro)

In 1977 the 45-year-old autoworker established the "Michigan-Canadian Bigfoot Information Center" by installing four business telephones in his home. Since then he has received over two hundred accounts of sightings of the legendary creature, also called "Sasquatch" and the "Abominable Snowman."

King is serious in his goal to prove that Bigfoot exists in Michigan and claims that there are probably twelve of the creatures in Benzie County alone.

2. MARK McPHERSON (Ypsilanti)

The 29-year-old Wayne County Community College administrator spent $3,000 on a 1976 expedition in search of Scotland's Loch Ness monster. McPherson navigated the 24-mile-long Loch Ness in a small boat and unsuccessfully searched the 975-foot-deep waters for "Nessie" with a sonar device, binoculars and cameras.

2 OLD-FASHIONED HUNTERS

1. ROBERT MANLEY (Fulton)

Using only a hand spear topped with an eleven-inch blade fashioned from a 1950 Ford truck spring, Manley has hunted and killed three black bears. He has also hunted with throwing spears, knives, throwing knives and boomerangs.

2. BILLY D. KILLIAN (Flint Township) - November, 1978

The National Flintlock Rifle champion shot a fifteen-point, 230-pound buck at fifty yards with his muzzle-loading flintlock rifle.

LEGAL BAG LIMITS OF 3 UNUSUAL GAME ANIMALS

The 1980 legal hunting limit on three animals not considered "normal" hunting game but legal to hunt in Michigan.

1. SNIPE   8 per day, 16 in possession
2. CROW   No limit
3. SKUNK   No limit

3 FISH TALES

1. In 1978 Ted Goodwin (Benzonia) caught a ten-pound, three-ounce burbot, otherwise known as ling, lawyer or lush. Because the fish is so ugly,

most fishermen throw them back and Goodwin's catch was listed as the first state record for a burbot. In January, 1979, Tom Courtemanche (Pinconning) topped the record with an eighteen-pound, four-ounce catch. Both fish were caught in Munuscong Bay (Chippewa County).

2. The largest fish ever caught in Michigan waters, a 193-pound, 87-inch lake sturgeon, was *speared* by Joe Maka (Grand Haven) in Mullett Lake (Cheboygan County) on February 16, 1974.

3. Bill Pivar (Eagle River, Wisconsin) caught a record 45-pound northern muskie in Thousand Island Lake (Gogebic County) in 1980. Because the lake lies right on the Michigan-Wisconsin border, the fish is listed as a record catch for both states.

8 RECORD FISH

Record weight in Michigan for eight game fish as of 1981.

1. NORTHERN PIKE - Thirty-nine pounds
   Caught in 1961 by Larry Clough (Ludington) in Dodge Lake (Schoolcraft County).

2. WALLEYE - Seventeen pounds, three ounces
   Caught in 1951 by Ray Fadely (Yorktown, Indiana) in Pine River (Manistee County).

3. SMALLMOUTH BASS - Nine pounds, four ounces
   Caught in 1906 by W. F. Shoemaker in Long Lake (Cheboygan County).

4. BLUEGILL - Two pounds, ten ounces
   Caught in 1945 by F. M. Broock (Bloomfield Hills) in Silver Lake (Cheboygan County).

5. WHITE CRAPPIE - Two pounds, ten ounces
   Caught in 1977 by Bob Cox (Westland) in Kent Lake (Livingston County).

6. SUNFISH - One pound, nine ounces
   Caught by Randy Czubko (Jackson) in Crooked Lake (Washtenaw County).

7. BULLHEAD - Three pounds, seven ounces
   Caught in 1977 by Arthur Kemp (Kent City) in Lime Lake (Kent County).

8. CARP - Sixty-one pounds, eight ounces
   Caught in 1974 by Dale France (Michigan Center) in Big Wolf Lake
   (Jackson County).

3 POPULAR SNOWMOBILE RACES

1. TC 250 (Traverse City) - January

2. INTERNATIONAL 500 (Houghton - Hancock) - February

3. INVITATIONAL (Mackinaw City) - March

3 LARGE SNOWMEN

Taking advantage of the heaviest Upper Peninsula snowfall in ninety years and responding to a challenge issued by the Osmond family on television, three fifty-foot-high snowmen were built throughout the Upper Peninsula in March, 1979. The Osmonds had built a fourteen-foot, eleven-inch snowman in Ogden, Utah.

1. HOUGHTON
   Built by members of Delta Sigma Fraternity at Michigan Tech University

2. CALUMET
   Built by students at Sacred Heart Elementary School.

3. GREENLAND
   Built by a neighborhood group of youths.

6 LARGEST SKI AREAS

Based on the total number of runs in 1982.

1. CABERFAE (Cadillac) - 36
2. CANNONSBURG (Cannonsburg) - 32
3. SUGARLOAF (Cedar) - 24
4. ALPINE VALLEY (Milford) - 23
5. NUBS NOB (Harbor Springs) - 21
6. CRYSTAL MT. (Thompsonville) - 20

6 MOST ECONOMICAL SKI AREAS

Based on the 1982 weekend lift fee for areas with at least one chair lift.

1. MT. ZION (Ironwood) - $5.00
2. RIVERVIEW HIGHLANDS (Riverview) - $6.00
3. PORCUPINE MT. (Ontonagon) - $7.00
4. SNOWSNAKE (Harrison) - $8.50
5. MOTT MT. (Farwell) - $9.00
6. MONT RIPLEY (Houghton) - $9.50

4 MOST POPULAR STATE PARKS

Based on 1978 attendance figures.

1.	HOLLAND (Holland at U.S. 131)	1,695,926
2.	WARREN DUNES (I-94 at Sawyer)	1,322,651
3.	WATERLOO (I-94 at Chelsea)	887,613
4.	LUDINGTON (M-116 at Ludington)	810,252

4 LARGEST ROADSIDE PARKS

Based on the number of tables at Michigan Department of Transportation roadside parks. Michigan was the first state to establish roadside picnic tables.

1.	M-21 (4.5 miles west of Imlay City)	62
2.	M-15 (One mile south of Vassar)	30
3.	M-46 (Ten miles east of Richville)	30
4.	U.S. 127 (Seven miles south of Jackson)	28

11 OCCUPATIONAL VANITY PLATES

1.	PPMD	Urologist
2.	EYEGUY	Eye doctor
3.	EI EI O	Farmer
4.	SU EM	Attorney
5.	LOC M UP	Policeman
6.	TOT DOC	Pediatrician
7.	PASTOR	Minister
8.	BISHOP	Bishop

9.	TRY GOD	Minister
10.	2THAKE	Dentist
11.	I BILDM	Contractor

3 COUPLES' VANITY PLATES

1. REV and MRS REV   Minister and his wife
2. BRAND X and BRAND Y Mr. and Mrs. Brand
3. HIS CAR and HER CAR

14 REJECTED VANITY PLATE REQUESTS

Michigan Department of State registrars reject obviously obscene vanity plate requests and those that contain four-letter words. When in doubt, they even hold requests up to mirrors and consult foreign language instructors. The following requests have also been rejected:

1. REEFER
2. BRAS
3. POLICE
4. POLACK
5. G MAN
6. KKK
7. IMEASY
8. HELL
9. SCREWY
10. MR SEXY
11. SEXPAD
12. USMAIL
13. KRAUT
14. 6ULDV8

8 INTERESTING VANITY PLATES

1. GO AWAY
2. B HAPPY
3. XQUZMEE
4. PRESHS
5. I LUV U
6. 10S NE1
7. BOOZER
8. EZ EZ EZ

2 DULLEST HIGHWAYS

Based on an informal *Detroit Free Press* reader poll and published in their Travel Section, September 27, 1981.

1. M-28

Thirty-six miles between Seney and Shingleton in the Upper Peninsula.

2. M-57
Between Chesaning and U.S. 27.

9 FANTASTIC VOYAGES

1. AUGUST, 1969
Victor Jackson (East Lansing) sailed across Lake Michigan in a bathtub. The 32-year-old father of six made the 65-mile, 14½-hour journey in a household-type tub welded to a frame supported by four thirty-gallon oil drums. His craft, registered in Michigan as a one-passenger pleasure craft, was powered by a twenty-horsepower outboard motor.

2. JULY, 1967
On the thirtieth anniversary of Amelia Earhart's disappearance, Ann Pellegreno (Saline) recreated the famed aviatrix's flight. The thirty-year-old junior-high-school English teacher made the 28-day, around-the-world flight in the same model airplane as Earhart.

3. SUMMER, 1978
Lloyd Henry Roland (East Detroit) sailed his 42-foot sloop across the Atlantic Ocean alone. The 51-year-old former Merchant Marine made the 2,355-mile voyage from Nova Scotia to Ireland in twenty-two days.

4. OCTOBER, 1978
Acting on a sudden impulse, Thomas Brady Coles (Detroit) stowed away in the cargo hold of a jumbo jet at Detroit Metro Airport. Nine hours later, the 21-year-old arrived in London semi-conscious and half frozen.

5. WINTER, 1980
Richard Moore, Lorne Matthews and Ray Moore traveled from their hometown, Flint, to Alaska by snowmobile. The 6000-mile, 42-day trip set a world record.

6. JULY, 1979
Ted Anderson, 32, and Don Winegarden, 35, crossed Lake Michigan from Milwaukee to Muskegon in a seventeen-foot canoe. The 75-mile journey, which, because of navigational errors, turned out to be ninety, took the Manton men twenty-eight hours.

7. 1977
Karl Thomas (Troy) soloed a hot-air balloon cross-country in a record eighteen days. The 28-year-old, suspended in a five-by-five-foot wicker gondola, flew from Arcadia, California, to Jacksonville, Florida.

8. 1898

Augustus Moore Herring (Benton Harbor) may have flown the world's first airplane five years before the Wright brothers' famous flight. A reporter for the *Benton Harbor Evening News* reported the brief flight from Silver Beach (St. Joseph), but did not take an in-flight picture of the motorized chanute glider. In the absence of any conclusive proof that Herring's plane left the ground under its own power, Orville and Wilbur Wright were given credit for the first manned flight in 1903.

9. WINTER, 1973

Nine Michigan men snowmobiled from the Upper Peninsula to the Atlantic Ocean. The trip took eleven days.

5 UNIQUE MACKINAC BRIDGE CROSSINGS

1. JUNE, 1973

An Amish family, traveling from Maine to Colorado, crossed the bridge in a horse-drawn buggy. Bridge authorities closed one lane of the five-mile span for the one-hour crossing.

2. LABOR DAY, 1959

The first annual Labor Day bridge walk was held. More than 15,000 walkers joined Governor G. Mennen Williams as he set the first time record for governors, covering the 4½-mile distance in sixty-five minutes.

3. LABOR DAY, 1976

Twenty-six thousand, including a man in an Uncle Sam suit who crossed on stilts and two couples who were married , joined   Governor William G. Milliken in the bicentennial Labor Day bridge walk.

4. LABOR DAY, 1978

Farmers, protesting government policy on beef import quotas and standards, blocked the one open traffic lane and backed up automobile traffic for several miles as 30,000 walkers crossed.

5. LABOR DAY, 1971

Governor William G. Milliken set a record for governors by walking across the bridge in forty-six minutes, thirty seconds.

6 WAYS NOT TO CROSS THE MACKINAC BRIDGE

Each year more than two million vehicles cross the Mackinac Bridge. Some, however, don't quite make it. In 1980:

1. One out of every 80,000 had a collision, mostly rear-enders because the driver was distracted by the scenery.

2. One out of 27,000 ran out of gas.

3. One out of 45,000 had a flat tire.

4. One out of 71,000 received the wrong change.

5. One out of 10,000 had to be driven across because the driver was afraid.

6. Patrol cars stopped one out of 25,000 for not paying the toll.

8 OUTSTANDING BRIDGES

1. MACKINAC (Mackinaw City - St. Ignace) - Completed in 1958
    From cable anchor to cable anchor the bridge is the longest suspension type in the world. The American Institute of Architects has designated the bridge as one of the seven man-made wonders of the world.

2. OLD ZILWAUKEE BRIDGE (Saginaw)
    An infamous bottleneck on the 1,800 miles of I-75 from Tampa Bay, Florida, to Sault Ste. Marie, the drawbridge across the Saginaw River opens approximately nine hundred times each year to allow ships to pass through. Traffic has often backed up fifteen to twenty miles in each direction and the bridge has been blamed for more than a dozen fatal accidents in recent years. Ships have rammed the bridge twice.

3. HOUGHTON-HANCOCK - Completed in 1959
    The double-deck lift span has a four-lane highway on its upper level and a railroad track on its lower level. The bridge can be raised like an elevator up to one hundred feet to allow trains, autos, or a combination of both to cross the Portage Lake Waterway.

4. AMBASSADOR (Detroit - Windsor) - Completed in 1929
    The 1,850-foot suspension span crosses the Detroit River and the roadway runs 1⅓ miles between the American and Canadian terminals.

5. BLUEWATER (Port Huron - Sarnia) - Built in 1938
    Crossing over the St. Clair River, the bridge is the eleventh longest cantilever-type span in North America.

6. NEW ZILWAUKEE BRIDGE (Saginaw)
    When completed in late fall, 1983, the $81-million, 1½-mile-long, concrete structure will replace the old drawbridge. Towering thirteen stories above the Saginaw River, it will be the largest pre-cast concrete segment bridge in the world.

New Zilwaukee Bridge

International Bridge

7. INTERNATIONAL BRIDGE (Saulte Ste. Marie) - Built in 1962
The two-mile-long series of arch and truss bridges crosses the St. Mary's River and joins the United States and Canada.

8. MANISTIQUE BRIDGE (Manistique) - Built in 1918
Ripley's Believe It Or Not column once featured this structure because the water level is higher than the driving surface.

9 MAN-MADE WONDERS

1. PONTIAC SILVERDOME
2. RENAISSANCE CENTER
3. MACKINAC BRIDGE
4. GREENFIELD VILLAGE
5. GRAND HOTEL (Mackinac Island)
6. SOO LOCKS
7. DETROIT ZOO
8. FORT MICHILMACKINAC
9. DETROIT-WINDSOR TUNNEL

DETROIT'S 5 TALLEST BUILDINGS

1. PLAZA HOTEL	748 feet
2. CITY NATIONAL BANK BUILDING	557 feet
3. GUARDIAN	485 feet
4. RENAISSANCE CENTER	479 feet
5. BOOK TOWER	472 feet

6 MAJOR FINE ARTS CENTERS

1. INTERLOCHEN CENTER FOR THE ARTS
2. MIDLAND CENTER FOR THE ARTS
3. GRAND RAPIDS ART MUSEUM
4. KALAMAZOO INSTITUTE OF ARTS
5. MEADOWBROOK THEATRE
6. CRANBROOK ACADEMY OF ARTS

6 EMBARRASSING ERRORS AT THE FORD MUSEUM DEDICATION

In his days as the nation's thirty-eighth president, Gerald R. Ford was known as an amiable bumbler who meant well but always stubbed his toe. It was fitting, then, that at the dedication of the Gerald R. Ford Museum (Grand Rapids), September, 1981, the following happened:

1. President Reagan slipped and fell down the steps of *Air Force One* as he arrived for the dedication.

2. House Speaker "Tip" O'Neill paid tribute to Ford and his wife "Nancy." (Mrs. Ford is Betty; Mrs. Reagan is Nancy.)

3. When a reporter shouted, "Mr. President," Ford quickly replied while President Reagan's mouth dropped open.

4. President Reagan referred to Ford as "General Ford."

5. At an evening celebration, Bob Hope and Danny Thomas stumbled through a musical number five times before getting it right.

6. Sammy Davis Jr. blew the punch line to a joke.

15 WELL-KNOWN SUMMER THEATRES

1. CROSWELL OPERA HOUSE (Adrian)
2. THUNDER BAY SUMMER THEATRE (Alpena)
3. MICHIGAN REPERTORY (Ann Arbor)
4. BARN THEATRE (Augusta)
5. CLARK LAKE PLAYERS (Clark Lake)
6. TIBBITS SUMMER THEATRE (Coldwater)
7. GREENFIELD VILLAGE PLAYERS (Dearborn)
8. HILLBERRY SUMMER THEATRE (Detroit)
9. STAR THEATRE (Flint)
10. BOARS HEAD THEATRE (Grand Ledge)
11. HOPE SUMMER REPERTORY THEATRE (Holland)
12. BLACK SHEEP REPERTORY THEATRE (Manchester)
13. MACOMB SUMMER THEATRE (Mount Clemens)
14. RED BARN THEATRE (Saugatuck)
15. CHERRY COUNTY PLAYHOUSE (Traverse City)

7 MUSIC FESTIVALS

1. THORNAPPLE BLUEGRASS MUSIC FESTIVAL (Hastings) - June,

2. GILBERT and SULLIVAN FESTIVAL (Saugatuck) - June, July
3. BLUEGRASS FESTIVAL (Battle Creek) - July
4. MONTREAUX - DETROIT INTERNATIONAL JAZZ FESTIVAL (Detroit) - August
5. BLUEGRASS FESTIVAL (Dearborn) - August
6. MUSIC FESTIVAL (Swartz Creek) - September
7. BLUES FESTIVAL (Detroit) - September

17 PROMINENT FOOD FESTIVALS

1. MAPLE SYRUP FESTIVAL (Vermontville) - April
2. NATIONAL MUSHROOM FESTIVAL (Boyne City) - May
3. NATIONAL ASPARAGUS FESTIVAL (Shelby) - June
4. STRAWBERRY FESTIVAL (Belleville) - June
5. THIMBLEBERRY FESTIVAL (Keeweenaw Peninsula) - June
6. NATIONAL CHERRY FESTIVAL (Traverse City) - July
7. STRAWBERRY FESTIVAL (Chassell) - July
8. NATIONAL BLUEBERRY FESTIVAL (South Haven) - July
9. CHEESE FESTIVAL (Pinconning) - July
10. POTATO FESTIVAL (Munger) - July
11. BLUEBERRY FESTIVAL (Montrose) - August
12. MELON FESTIVAL (Howell) - August
13. BUFFALO BARBECUE (Stanwood) - August
14. PEACH FESTIVAL (Romeo) - August, September
15. FUDGE and FALL FESTIVAL (Mackinaw City) - September
16. WINE FESTIVAL (Paw Paw) - September
17. FOUR FLAGS AREA APPLE FESTIVAL (Niles) - September

11 HISTORIC FESTIVALS

1. FT. MICHILIMACKINAC PAGEANT (Mackinaw City) - May
2. MUZZLELOADERS FESTIVAL (Greenfield Village) - June
3. FOUNDERS FESTIVAL (Farmington-Farmington Hills) - July
4. LUMBERJACK FESTIVAL (Farwell) - August
5. YESTERYEAR HERITAGE FESTIVAL (Ypsilanti) - August
6. NEWAGO LOG FEST (Newago) - August
7. CARRY NATION FESTIVAL (Holly) - September

8. OLD CAR FESTIVAL (Greenfield Village) - September
9. HERITAGE FESTIVAL IN THE PARK (Adrian) - September
10. COLONIAL AUTUMN FESTIVAL (Lincoln Park) - September
11. ANTIQUE FESTIVAL (Saginaw) - September

27 PROMINENT ETHNIC FESTIVALS

1. TULIP FESTIVAL (Holland) - May
2. BAVARIAN FESTIVAL (Frankenmuth) - June
3. YUGOSLAVIAN FESTIVAL (Detroit) - June
4. GREEK FESTIVAL (Flint) - June
5. ITALIAN FESTIVAL (Flint) - June
6. FAR EASTERN and FRENCH FESTIVAL (Detroit) - June
7. INTERNATIONAL FESTIVAL (Flint) - June
8. INTERNATIONAL FREEDOM FESTIVAL (Detroit-Windsor) June, July
9. IRISH FESTIVAL (Bellaire) - June
10. GREEK FESTIVAL (Saginaw) - July
11. CZECHOSLOVAKIAN FESTIVAL (Wyandotte) - July
12. POLISH FESTIVAL DAYS (Bronson) - July
13. VENETIAN FESTIVAL (Charlevoix) - July
14. AFRO-AMERICAN FESTIVAL (Detroit) - July
15. NORTH COUNTRY FOLK FESTIVAL (Ironwood) - July
16. SCANDANAVIAN FESTIVAL (Detroit) - August
17. POLISH POLKA FESTIVAL (Wyandotte) - August
18. HUNGARIAN FESTIVAL (Burton) - August
19. POLISH POLKA FESTIVAL (Wyandotte) - August
20. IRISH FESTIVAL (Wyandotte) - August
21. DANISH FESTIVAL (Greenville) - August
22. UKRANIAN FESTIVAL (Detroit) - August
23. ETHNIC FESTIVAL (Saginaw) - August
24. ARAB WORLD FESTIVAL (Detroit) - August
25. LATIN-AMERICAN FESTIVAL (Detroit) - August
26. FESTIVAL OF INDIA (Detroit) - September
27. MEXICAN FESTIVAL (Detroit) - September

HONORABLE MENTIONS

12 WORLD'S LARGESTS

1. LARGEST DOG*
Thomas and Ann Irwin (Grand Rapids) own a 305-pound St. Bernard named "Benedictine." (Photo, back cover)

2. LARGEST PIE*
As part of Charlevoix's bicentennial celebration, residents baked a seven-ton cherry pie. The pie measured fourteen feet, four inches in diameter, was twenty-four inches deep, and contained 4,950 pounds of cherries.

3. LARGEST AIR SUPPORTED ROOF*
The ten-acre translucent fiberglass roof of the Pontiac Silverdome is supported by five-pounds-per-square-inch air pressure.

4. LARGEST ZUCHINNI*
In 1979 Douglas Andre (Millington) grew a 19.14-pound zuchinni.

5. LARGEST LIMESTONE QUARRIES (Rogers City)

6. LARGEST PORTLAND CEMENT PLANT (Alpena)

7. LARGEST GYPSUM QUARRY (Alabaster)

8. LARGEST KOHLRABI*
In 1979 Emil Krejci (Mount Clemens) grew a 36-pound kohlrabi.

9. LARGEST FRUIT MARKET (Benton Harbor)

---

* From the *1981 Guinness Book of World Records*, Sterling Publishing Company, Incorporated, Copyright 1980.

WORLD'S LARGEST CHERRY PIE

5,850	lbs.	Red Tart Cherries
3,850	"	Cherry Juice
4,750	"	Sugar
740	"	Cornstarch
360	"	Tapioca
180	"	Butter
90	"	Lemon Juice
20	"	Salt

CRUST

750	"	Flour
325	"	Shortning
325	"	Water
110	"	Milk
55	"	Baking Powder
15	"	Salt

ORIGINATOR: DAVE PHILLIPS
1976

Mixing the ingredients of the world's largest cherry pie. (Photo of pie courtesy of Aartvark Studio, Charlevoix.)

49

10. LARGEST BEAN ELEVATOR (Saginaw)

11. LARGEST COMMERCIAL BUILDING*
The Ford Parts Redistribution Center (Brownstone Township) covers 71.16 acres.

12. LARGEST CORN YIELD*
Roy Lynn, Jr. (Kalamazoo), harvested 352.64 bushels per acre in September, 1977.

6 WORLD'S LONGESTS

1. LONGEST CRAWL*
Jim Purol (Livonia) crawled (with one knee or the other in unbroken contact with the ground) twenty-five miles October 22-23, 1979.

2. LONGEST TOBOGGAN RUN
A 3000-foot run at Grayling sweeps tobogganists at speeds up to 100 miles per hour.

3. LONGEST PORCH
Mackinac Island's Grand Hotel porch measures 880 feet.

4. LONGEST *WHO'S WHO* ENTRY
The longest entry of the 66,000 included in *Who's Who In America* is that of Dr. Glen T. Seaborg (Ishpeming) whose all-time record listing is ninety-seven lines.

5. LONGEST SUSPENSION BRIDGE
The Mackinac Bridge measures 1.58 miles from cable anchorage to cable anchorage.

6. LONGEST REIGNING HEAVYWEIGHT CHAMPION*
Joe Louis held boxing's heavyweight championship for eleven years, eight months and seven days.

---

* From the *1981 Guinness Book of World Records*, Sterling Publishing Company, Incorporated, Copyright, 1980.

World's longest porch

3 WORLD'S HIGHESTS

1. HIGHEST ROCK CONCERT ATTENDANCE*
A record 76,229 paid to see *Led Zeppelin* perform at the Pontiac Silverdome April 30, 1977.

2. HIGHEST HOTEL*
The Detroit Plaza Hotel measures 748 feet from the back entrance to the top.

3. HIGHEST PRICE FOR A WORK BY A LIVING SCULPTOR*
The Cranbrook Academy (Bloomfield Hills) sold a 75-inch wooden carving by Henry Moore for $260,000 (March 1, 1972).

3 WORLD'S GREATESTS

1. GREATEST CAR SALESMAN*
Joe Girard (Detroit) sold 1,423 vehicles in 1973 and a lifetime total of 13,001.

2. GREATEST NET PROFIT
General Motors made $3.5 billion dollars in 1978.

3. GREATEST NET LOSS
Chrysler lost 1.1 billion in 1979.

10 GUINNESS WORLD RECORD HOLDERS*

1. JIM ELLIS (Montrose) ate three pounds, one ounce of grapes in 34.6 seconds (May 30, 1976).

2. JIM PUROL and MIKE PAPA (Detroit) crammed 135 cigarettes into their mouths and smoked them for five minutes (October 5, 1978).

3. DENNIS MARTZ (Detroit) ran up the stairs at the 73-story Detroit Plaza Hotel in eleven minutes, 23.8 seconds (June 26, 1978).

4. RICK KRAUSE (Eau Claire) spit a cherry stone sixty-five feet, two inches (July 5, 1980).

---

* From the *1981 Guinness Book of World Records*, Sterling Publishing Company, Incorporated, Copyright 1980.

5. KEVIN ST. ONGE (Dearborn) threw a standard playing card 185 feet, one inch (June 12, 1979).

6. WARREN KOPE (Troy) skipped a stone twenty-four times during Mackinac Island's stone-skipping contest (July 5, 1975). JOHN KOLAR (Birmingham) and GLENN LOY, JR. (Flint) tied the record on July 4, 1977.

7. WILLIAM VARGO (Swartz Creek) smoked 0.1 ounce of pipe tobacco for two hours, six minutes and thirty-nine seconds using only one match (August, 1975).

8. LUCILLE H. McCULLOUGH (Dearborn) had a perfect attendance record from her election to the Michigan House of Representatives 31st District in 1955 through 1980.

9. THE UNIVERSITY OF MICHIGAN built the most powerful microscope in the world with a magnifying power of 260 million-fold (1974).

10. JOE THOMAS (Detroit) has the highest known count of Anti-Lewis B, a rare blood antibody (August, 1970).

5 MISS AMERICA WINNERS

1. PATRICIA DONNELLY (Detroit) - 1939

2. NANCY FLEMING (Montague) - 1961

3. VONDA KAY VANDYKE (Muskegon) - 1964
    Though she won the Miss America title as Miss Arizona, Miss Van Dyke was born in Muskegon.

4. SHIRLEY WASHINGTON (Detroit) - 1969
    Won the Miss Black America title.

5. PAMELA ANNE ELDRED (Birmingham) - 1970

2 PROHIBITED PAGEANTS

1. A young entrepreneur who spent $2,100 to promote and stage a "Ms. Nude Michigan Beauty Pageant" gave up in late summer 1972 after Cobo Hall, Olympia Stadium, Tiger Stadium and several Detroit-area race tracks, theatres and hotels denied his request to hold the pageant in their facilities.

2. Amid Jewish protests in late fall, 1980, a Lansing-area nightclub scrapped plans for an Adolph Hitler-Eva Braun look-alike contest.

5 MALE PINUPS

1. *EVE'S 12* - 1973
   Evelyn Carter (Birmingham) created a calendar for women featuring a nude male pinup for each month. *Eve's 12*, as the 29-year-old housewife called her creation, was the first such calendar in the nation.

2. MIKE GAROFALO (Detroit) - 1973
   As "Mr. February" on the *Eve's 12* calendar, the 26-year-old heavy-equipment operator was voted the "Man of the Year" by thousands of women.

3 ANONYMOUS (Lansing) - December, 1980
   At an exhibition at Michigan State University's Student Gallery, a stark naked nineteen-year-old astrophysics student played Christmas carols and old standards on an electric piano.

4. MIKE DEERING (White Lake) - 1980
   The young brunet posed *au naturel* for the centerfold of *Playgirl* magazine.

5. *MEN OF MSU* (Lansing) - 1981-82
   The calendar, featuring Michigan State University male students in various states of dress, sold seven hundred copies during its first three days of publication. Not to be outdone, six weeks later an Ann Arbor promotional company published a similar calendar featuring scantily clad University of Michigan male physiques.

4 BEAUTY PAGEANT WINNERS

1. PATRICE GAUNDER (St. Joseph) - 1965 Junior Miss
2. PAMELA MARTIN (Birmingham) - 1968 Miss Teen U.S.A.
3. SHARON SEXTON (Detroit) - 1971 Miss Black Teenage America
4. KIMBERLEE FOLEY (Southfield) - 1976 Miss World-U.S.A.

2 DISABLED WINNERS

1. PAMELA YOUNG (Flint) - 1975 Miss Deaf America

2. MARGARET CHMIELEWSKI (Canton Township) - 1978 Miss Wheelchair America.

3 SOUND WINNERS

1. BILLY PAGE (Bellevue) - 1981
   The 25-year-old unemployed handyman who can perfectly mimic a fire or ambulance siren was featured on NBC's *Real People* television show.

2. CYNTHIA RAIM (Detroit) - 1977
   The 25-year-old pianist won the national Three Rivers Piano competition, the instrumental equivalent of winning a prestigious Metropolitan Opera audition.

3. CLYDE VAUGHN (Clio) - 1980
   The gospel singer won first prize in national competition for vocal soloists sponsored by the Music City Song Festival of Nashville, Tennessee.

2 DOMESTIC WINNERS

1. MRS. ROMAN WALLKO (Detroit) - 1963
   Won the Pillsbury National Bake-Off with her recipe for "Hungry Boys Casserole."

2. JANE MAXWELL PRITCHARD - 1956
   Named the national Mother of the Year.

7 BIG MONEY WINNERS

1. RICHARD KIPPEN (Detroit) - 1981
   When the motor-city attorney bought a $39 ticket on New York Air he learned he was the line's one-millionth passenger and was given $1 million worth of free trips.

2. KAY SCHEPKE (Troy) - 1981
   The 41-year-old bank teller won the $72,500 grand prize in the *Reader's Digest* sweepstakes.

3. CHERYL PEOPLES and ROBERT JOHNSON (Detroit) - 1981
   The young dancing couple won a $25,000 grand prize on the nationally televised *Dance Fever* show.

4. J. DOUGLAS JOHNSON (Flint) - 1968
    The 34-year-old tobacco salesman won the thirteenth Annual Gin Rummy Tournament in Las Vegas and collected $18,455.

5. PATTI VANLERBERGHE (Dimondale) - December, 1981
    The travel agent won $14,000 worth of prizes, including a washer, dryer, stereo, jewelry and cash, on *The Price Is Right* television show.

6. BARBARA GMEREK - 1979
    The eight-year-old won $10,000 in the New York Metropolitan Museum of Art's "Q-Tip Art Contest" by making a thirteen-inch working model of a ferris wheel.

7. ROY TACOMA (Falmouth) - 1981
    After this farmer had lost one hundred fifty head of cattle as a result of the 1970's PBB crisis (see page 161), oil was discovered on his property and he now has four producing oil wells pumping at a steady rate.

3 SPECIAL APPEARANCES

1. BURR GRAY (Muskegon) - 1980
    The 64-year-old president of Gray Mobile Homes joined Anwar Sadat, President Jimmy Carter and actor Patrick McNee as one of the Men's Fashion Guild of America's "Ten Best Dressed Men of 1980."

2. MIKE BUTLER (Grand Junction) - 1980
    The eighteen-year-old waiter won the 1980 Model of the Year Award in New York City.

3. JOHN COOTS (Pontiac) - 1979
    While covering the Special Olympics at Mount Pleasant, the mild-mannered reporter won a Clarke Kent look-alike contest.

3 NOTABLE SMOKERS

1. JANET MACAINSH (Howell) - 1981
    By telling how she kicked a 26-year smoking habit, the 46-year-old mother of eight won an all-expense-paid trip to Hollywood including dinner with television star Larry Hagman. The University of Michigan executive secretary won the American Cancer Society's "Larry Hagman Quit Smoking Letter Writing Contest" by detailing how she wore a rubber band around her wrist and snapped it each time she felt like lighting up.

2. PAUL SPANIOLA (Flint)

The pipe and tobacco shop owner has won the world's pipe-smoking championship five times since the contest started in 1949. Contestants light 3.3 grams of tobacco with one match and see how long they can keep their pipes smoking.

3. WILLIAM VARGO (Swartz Creek)

The autoworker holds the world's pipe-smoking record, puffing his regulation 3.3 grams of tobacco for two hours, six minutes and thirty-nine seconds in 1975. He has also won the world's pipe-smoking championship four times.

2 SPECIAL SCHOLARS

1. GREG HUGHES (Farmington)

The serious student compiled a thirteen-year perfect attendance record from the time he started kindergarten in Detroit to graduation in 1978 from North Farmington High School.

2. MOLLY BRENNAN (Waterford) - 1981

The Michigan State University senior was one of only thirty-two American recipients of the prestigious Rhodes Scholarships to England's Oxford University.

2 AWARDED PRISONERS

1. CHARLES CLARK (Detroit) - 1972

Governor William G. Milliken presented a check for $10,000 to Clark who had spent thirty years in prison for a crime he did not commit. In 1937 Clark, then a restaurant waiter, was found guilty of a hold-up murder at a Hamtramck store. He was acquitted at a retrial in 1968 when it was discovered that Clark had been pointed out to the chief witness before she identified him in a police line-up.

2. LLOYD TISI (Warren) - 1974

The Michigan Jaycees selected the convicted murderer as one of Michigan's five top young men of 1974 for translating over 50,000 pages of printed material into Braille. He has also gained a nationwide reputation for producing a series of maps of Michigan college campuses in Braille.

5 WHO HAVE RECENTLY WRITTEN TO ANN LANDERS

1. CRAMPED IN MICHIGAN — November 12, 1981
    "Cramped" wrote to complain about having to store her adult children's "junk" in her garage when they no longer lived at home. Ann's advice: Give them thirty days' notice to pick it up; anything left after that should be given to charity.

2. ROYAL OAK COMPLAINT — August 5, 1980
    "Complaint" expressed her irritation at Ann's "confidential" replies to anonymous writers whose problems aren't published. "Complaint" found it irksome to see the answers without knowing the problem. Ann's reply: Some people's problems are so unique they may be recognized.

3. BENT OUT OF SHAPE IN BENTON HARBOR - November 1, 1979
    "Bent" was upset that Ann didn't express much sympathy to a 26-year-old who got pregnant by a man who falsely claimed he was single and had a vasectomy. Ann's reply: A 26-year-old woman should know better than to get sexually involved with someone she knows little about.

4. OFF MY CHEST IN DEARBORN - June 5, 1978
    The teenager wrote because she felt terrible after calling her mother names during a fight. Ann's advice: Tell your mother you love her by taping this column to the refrigerator.

5. BAY CITY - July 22, 1977
    When her husband, whom she had divorced twelve years prior, died, "Bay City" wondered if she should or could refer to herself as his widow. Ann's advice: No, because he wasn't her husband.

4 FEATURED FAMILIES

1. THE DESSERS (Ada) - September 27, 1980
    Because of the number of children and their many activities, the family of eighteen was featured on the national television show, *30 Minutes*. Sixteen persons spent four days filming the family's daily activities and interviewing them.

2. THE LONGS (Rockford) - 1978
    A New York ad agency selected the Longs as one of fifteen "average American families" and treated them to an all-expense-paid, four-day trip to New York City. There, the couple participated in a research project designed to discover how young, suburban, middle-class families allocate

their money.

3. THE HERMANS (Southfield) - 1981

CBS made a TV movie, *The Victor Herman Saga*, about the Michigan man who left Detroit for Russia with his parents in 1931 so they could work in the Gorky Ford plant. Herman spent the next forty-five years in Russia, eighteen of them in prison and exile in Siberia. He was finally allowed to return to Detroit in 1976 only after divorcing his Russian wife, Galina, so she could avoid government censure. She and their two daughters joined him a year later in Southfield where they have made their home.

4. THE FITZPATRICKS (Flint) - 1977

The fictional Irish-American working-class television family and show by the same name were cancelled after seven months of low ratings. The show revolved around the activities of the family and their steelworker father, even though Flint has no steel mills, only auto factories.

2 RECENTLY AWARDED HEROES

1. DONNA LEE SLACK (West Bloomfield) - 1981

President Ronald Reagan presented a Young America Medal for Bravery to the teenager for her rescue of three children while baby-sitting at a home demolished by a 1976 tornado.

2. KENNETH SMITH (Troy) - 1981

The 31-year-old truck driver received the Carnegie Hero Fund Medal for pulling two injured state troopers from their wrecked, burning patrol car minutes before it exploded in a ball of flame.

2 WHO RECEIVED THE
CONGRESSIONAL MEDAL OF HONOR TWICE

One hundred six Michigan men have received the Congressional Medal of Honor, the nation's highest decoration for bravery above and beyond the call of military duty. Two Michigan men have received the medal twice.

1. SECOND LT. THOMAS W. CUSTER

The brother of famous General George Armstrong Custer received his medals for acts of heroism during the Civil War.

2. CAPT. FRANK D. BALDWIN (Constantine)

The soldier received his medals for acts of heroism during the Civil War and later for bravery during the Indian wars.

12 SILVER BUFFALO AWARD WINNERS

The Silver Buffalo Award is the highest of national Boy Scout service awards given to honor outstanding commitment to service to young people.

1. GERALD R. FORD (Grand Rapids) - 1975
2. WALLACE WILSON (Detroit) - 1974
3. CLARENCE "BIGGIE" MUNN (Lansing) - 1967
4. ZENON HANSEN (Lansing) - 1962
5. WYETH ALLEN (Ann Arbor) - 1961
6. ROBERT GIBSON (East Lansing) - 1958
7. JOHN LORD (Detroit) - 1958
8. EDGAR GUEST (Detroit) - 1951
9. FRANK CODY (Detroit) - 1938
10. FIELDING H. YOST (Ann Arbor) - 1935
11. GRIFFITH OGDEN ELLIS (Detroit) - 1931
12. MILTON A. McRAE (Detroit) - 1926

7 PULITZER PRIZE WINNERS

1. LEE HILLS (*Detroit Free Press*) - Reporting, 1956
2. BRUCE CATTON (Petoskey) - History for the book, *A Stillness At Appomattox*, 1954
3. WILLIAM M. GALLAGHER (*The Flint Journal*) - News Photography, 1953
4. CARL M. SAUNDERS (*Jackson Citizen Patriot*) - Editorial, 1950
5. *DETROIT FREE PRESS* - Meritorious Public Service, 1945
6. MILTON BROOKS (*Detroit News*) - News Photography, 1942
7. W. C. RICHARDS, D. D. MARTIN, J. S. POOLER, F. O. WEBB, J. N. W. SLOAN, (*Detroit Free Press*) - Reporting, 1932

4 GREAT SCIENTISTS BORN IN MICHIGAN

From Isaac Asimov's *Biographical Encyclopedia of Science and Technology*, published by Doubleday and Company, incorporated, copyright 1964.

1. HENRY FORD (Dearborn)
The industrial pioneer who, by initiating mass production and assembly-line techniques, placed the automobile within reach of every American's budget and, thus, revolutionized the American way of life.

2. THOMAS H. WELLER (Ann Arbor)
    A microbiologist who won the Nobel Prize in Medicine and Physiology.

3. GLENN T. SEABORG (Ishpeming)
    A physicist who won the Nobel Prize in chemistry for discovering trans-uranium elements.

4. CLAUDE SHANNON (Gaylord)
    A mathematician who did fundamental work in binary methods essential to computer design.

10 FAMOUS PEOPLE BORN IN MICHIGAN

1. CHARLES LINDBERGH (Detroit)
    Aviator who made the first solo flight across the Atlantic Ocean.

2. GEORGE CUSTER (Monroe)
    Civil War general and Indian fighter who, with 225 soldiers, was killed on the banks of the Little Big Horn River in Montana.

3. JOHN MITCHELL (Detroit)
    Attorney General of the United States under President Richard M. Nixon. Mitchell was later convicted and jailed for his role in the Watergate scandal, the first U.S. Attorney General ever to serve a prison sentence.

4. POTTER STEWART (Jackson)
    Supreme Court of the United States Justice from 1958 to 1981.

5. THOMAS DEWEY (Owosso)
    Two-time presidential candidate who lost to Franklin D. Roosevelt and Harry S Truman.

6. RALPH BUNCHE (Detroit)
    Statesman who received the Nobel Peace Prize in 1950 for his work in the United Nations.

7. CHARLES COLLINGWOOD (Three Rivers)
    Television commentator and newsman.

8. AVERY BRUNDAGE (Detroit)
    Former long-time World Olympic executive.

9. PERLE MESTA (Sturgis)
Social figure and former U.S. ambassador to Luxembourg.

10. WILLIAM EDWARD BOEING (Detroit)
Founder of Boeing Aircraft.

4 MICHIGAN ASTRONAUTS

1. JAMES McDIVITT (Jackson)
The Air Force Colonel was the first Michigan man chosen for astronaut training. On March 23, 1965, he teamed with Virgil Grissom and John Young for the Gemini-Titan 3 mission, the first manned spacecraft to change its orbital path.

Two months later, McDivitt piloted a Gemini IV space capsule while Edward White took the first American space walk. In March, 1969, McDivitt commanded the successful Apollo-Saturn 9 mission on a ten-day flight around the moon, the first manned flight of the lunar landing module.

2. JACK LOUSMA (Grand Rapids and Ann Arbor)
Lousma is a veteran of one of the country's space spectaculars — the nearly two-month-long, 1973 Skylab II mission. As pilot, he and commander Alan Bean and crew member Owen Garriott spent a record 59½ days in flight, orbited the earth 858 times, and traveled 24.4 million miles in orbit. Lousma and Garriott also made a record six-hour, 31-minute space walk.

3. ROGER CHAFFEE (Grand Rapids)
On January 27, 1967, while simulating what would have been his first venture into space, Chaffee, along with veteran astronauts "Gus" Grissom and Edward White II, died in a flash fire aboard the Apollo I module.

4. ALFRED M. WORDEN (Jackson)
During a 1971 mission, the Air Force Major piloted the Apollo 15 command module around the moon while Colonel David Scott and Lt. Colonel James B. Irwin spent sixty-six hours on the moon's surface.

6 NOTABLE CENTENARIANS

1. CLARA BARTELS (Grand Rapids)
The New Zealand native, who moved to Michigan in 1881, became the oldest immigrant ever naturalized in Michigan during 1973 ceremonies. She was one hundred years old at the time.

2. JOHN D. MORTON (Detroit)
The longest-living United Auto Workers (UAW) pensioner died in 1975

at the age of 101.

3. DR. ZACHARY VELDHUIS (Hamilton)
The oldest practicing veterinarian in Michigan died at age 105. Both Wayne State University and Hope college claim him as their longest-living alumnus.

4. MRS. ALVIN E. EWING (Grand Haven)
The longest-living graduate of Hillsdale College celebrated her one-hundredth birthday in 1970.

5. MONROE RUTTY (Saugatuck)
Rutty worked along the west coast of Michigan as a logger until a 1907 accident caused him to lose his memory. Though only forty-seven at the time, he was moved into the Ottawa Home For The Aged where he spent the next fifty-eight years not knowing who he was. In 1965 a nephew recognized Rutty from a picture and story published on his 105th birthday. Rutty died at age 111 in 1971.

6. BERNICE WOOD (Indian River)
The oldest member of the Michigan Eastern Star celebrated her 103rd birthday in 1978.

3 LONGEST-SERVING GOVERNORS

1. WILLIAM G. MILLIKEN (1969-1982)
2. G. MENNEN WILLIAMS (1949-1960)
3. GEORGE ROMNEY (1963-1969)

2 SUPREME COURT JUSTICES

Two Supreme Court Justices of the United States appointed from Michigan. (Note: See also page 61. Although Justice Potter Stewart was born in Jackson, Michigan, he resided in Ohio at the time of his appointment.)

1. HENRY B. BROWN
Appointed by President Benjamin Harrison in 1890 and served until his retirement in 1906.

2. FRANK MURPHY
Appointed by Franklin D. Roosevelt in 1940 and served until his death in 1949.

14 CABINET MEMBERS

Fourteen Michigan men who have served in the Cabinets of Presidents of the United States.

1. W. MICHAEL BLUMENTHAL (1977)
   Secretary of the Treasury, President Jimmy Carter.

2. GEORGE ROMNEY (1969)
   Secretary of Housing and Urban Development, President Richard M. Nixon.

3. WILBUR J. COHEN (1968)
   Secretary of Health, Education and Welfare, President Lyndon B. Johnson.

4. ROBERT McNAMARA (1961 and 1963)
   Secretary of Defense, President John F. Kennedy.

5. FREDERICK MUELLER (1959)
   Secretary of Commerce and Labor, President Dwight D. Eisenhower.

6. CHARLES WILSON (1953)
   Secretary of Defense, President Dwight D. Eisenhower.

7. FRANK MURPHY (1939)
   Attorney General, President Franklin D. Roosevelt.

8. ROY CHAPIN (1932)
   Secretary of Commerce and Labor, President Herbert Hoover.

9. EDWIN DENBY (1921)
   Secretary of the Navy, President Warren G. Harding.

10. TRUMAN NEWBURY (1908)
    Secretary of the Navy, President Theodore Roosevelt.

11. RUSSELL A. ALGER (1897)
    Secretary of War, President William McKinley.

12. ZACHARIAH CHANDLER (1875)
    Secretary of the Interior, President U. S. Grant.

13. LEWIS CASS (1857)
    Secretary of State, President James Buchanan.

14. ROBERT McCLELLAND (1853)
Secretary of the Interior, President Franklin Pierce.

10 PRESIDENTIAL CANDIDATES
WHO WON IN MICHIGAN BUT LOST THE ELECTION

WON IN MICHIGAN	YEAR	WON THE ELECTION
1. GERALD R. FORD (R)	1976	Jimmy Carter (D)
2. HUBERT HUMPHREY (D)	1968	Richard M. Nixon (R)
3. THOMAS DEWEY (R)	1948	Harry S Truman (D)
4. WENDELL WILLKIE (R)	1940	Franklin D. Roosevelt (D)
5. CHARLES E. HUGHES (R)	1916	Woodrow Wilson (D)
6. THEODORE ROOSEVELT (Progressive)	1912	Woodrow Wilson (D)
7. BENJAMIN HARRISON (R)	1892	Grover Cleveland (D)
8. JAMES G. BLAINE (R)	1884	Grover Cleveland (D)
9. JOHN C. FREMONT (R)	1856	James Buchanan (D)
10. LEWIS CASS (D)	1848	Zachary Taylor (Whig)

5 MEMORABLE MAP OMISSIONS

1. Rand McNally left Warren (then population 185,000) off its *1977 Road Atlas and Travel Guide.*

2. In 1974 the Michigan Bicentennial Commission published Michigan's bicentennial emblem which omitted a large portion of the western Upper Peninsula. The committee re-designed the emblem after protests.

3. The State Highway Commission omitted Davison (population 5,000) from its official 1972 map.

4. The Huron-Clinton Metropolitan Authority printed 400,000 maps in 1967 that omitted Garden City, Ferndale, Madison Heights and Hazel Park.

5. In 1974 a map sent by the Commerce Department as an out-of-state promotion left off the entire Upper Peninsula.

2 CONSPICUOUS MAP ADDITIONS

In 1978 State Highway Commission Chairman and University of Michigan alumnus Peter Fletcher added the following two towns to the section of Ohio that appeared south of Michigan's border on the official 1978

University of Michigan football partisanship knows no bounds as demonstrated by the two towns added to the 1978 official State Highway Commission map by a U of M graduate.

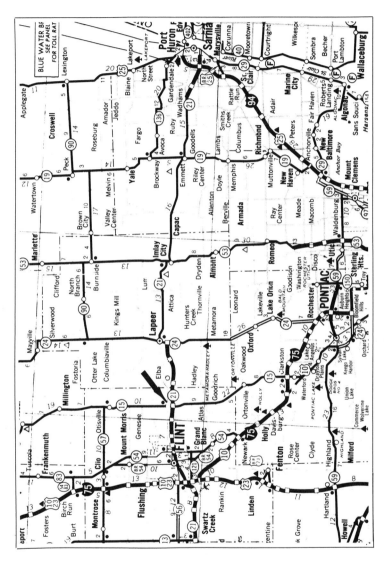

Davison residents displayed bumper stickers that read, "What's a map without Davison?" when their community was omitted from the 1972 State Highway Commission map

State Highway Department maps.

1. GO BLU
2. BEAT OSU

11 ALL AMERICAN CITIES

Eleven cities who have won the National Municipal League's annual "All-America City" awards for community improvement through citizen action.

1. GRAND RAPIDS - 1949, 1960 and 1961
2. KALAMAZOO - 1951 and 1969
3. FLINT - 1953
4. PORT HURON - 1955
5. ANN ARBOR - 1966
6. DETROIT - 1966
7. ROYAL OAK - 1967
8. SAGINAW - 1968
9. ALBION - 1973
10. PONTIAC - 1974
11. HARBOR SPRINGS - 1975

We're Number One
12 AREAS IN WHICH
MICHIGAN RANKS FIRST IN THE NATION

1. SNOWMOBILE FATALITIES
2. PRODUCTION OF PICKLING CUCUMBERS
3. COLLEGE FOOTBALL ATTENDANCE
4. SALT PRODUCTION
5. CASES OF RUBELLA (MEASLES)
6. PRODUCTION OF BLUEBERRIES
7. SUPPLIER OF BIRDS EYE MAPLE
8. NUMBER OF STATE PARKS AND PREPARED CAMPSITES
9. PRODUCTION OF RED TART CHERRIES
10. AUTOMOBILES ASSEMBLED
11. COMMERCIAL PEAT PRODUCTION
12. PRODUCTION OF DRY EDIBLE BEANS

8 SECOND BESTS

Seven areas in which Michigan ranks second in the nation.

1. MILES OF SHORELINE (3,121 miles; only Alaska has more)
2. FINGERPRINT COLLECTION (Michigan State Police; only the FBI's is larger)
3. PAY TO LOCAL GOVERNMENT EMPLOYEES
4. PRODUCTION OF RHUBARB
5. AMOUNT OF TIME KIDS SPEND IN SCHOOL
6. UNION MEMBERSHIP
7. AVERAGE HOURLY EARNINGS
8. NUMBER OF DOG SHOWS

5 THIRDS

1. PAY TO STATE GOVERNMENT EMPLOYEES
2. PRODUCTION OF APPLES
3. PRODUCTION OF ASPARAGUS
4. PRODUCTION OF CELERY
5. PRODUCTION OF MUSHROOMS

10 FOURTHS

Ten areas in which Michigan ranks fourth in the nation.
1. BOWLING LEAGUES
2. PRODUCTION OF PRUNE PLUMS
3. NATIONAL FOOTBALL LEAGUE ATTENDANCE
4. PRODUCTION OF CARROTS
5. RATE OF INCARCERATION OF WOMEN
6. MILK COWS
7. LICENSED HUNTERS AND FISHERMEN
8. PRODUCTION OF SWEET CHERRIES
9. PROPERTY TAXES
10. RECREATIONAL VEHICLE PRODUCTION

4

JUSTICE   FOR   ALL

5 MOST CRIMINOUS CITIES

Five Michigan cities of over 10,000 population with the most reported major crimes per one hundred residents for the year 1979.
1. BENTON HARBOR   23.2
2. HIGHLAND PARK   17.0
3. MUSKEGON   12.8
4. FLINT   12.4
5. KALAMAZOO   11.3

5 SAFEST CITIES

The five safest cities of over 10,000 population based on the number of major crimes (murder, manslaughter, rape, robbery, assault, burglary, theft, auto theft and arson) per one hundred residents for the year 1979.
1. EAST LANSING   2.2
2. GROSSE POINTE WOODS   2.8
3. BEVERLY HILLS   2.9
4. CLAWSON   2.9
5. TRENTON   3.0

4 NUDE CRIMES AND MISDEMEANORS

1. LANSING - April 17, 1980
    Three nude sisters, bodies smeared with mustard and hair full of pickle relish, hopped into a delivery van while the driver was gone and drove the truck a short distance before stopping in front of a police station where officers gave them blankets and arrested them.
    Identifying themselves as Goliath, Mary and Jesus and later as Her-

cules, Zorro and Charlie's Angels, the three, ages twenty-six to thirty, claimed they had been overcome with frenzy after fasting and watching a religious television program. After removing their clothes because of the unbearable heat, they covered themselves with mustard as "a salve against sin."

A judge sentenced them to eight days in jail for joyriding and indecent exposure.

2. FLINT - November 1, 1979

A naked woman entertained Genesee County jail inmates by posing nude in a window across the street from the building. To inmates' cheers, which could be heard two blocks away, the woman kicked an officer and refused to be covered with a blanket as she was arrested for disorderly conduct.

3. BAY CITY - 1977

Contestants in a Bay City Miss Nude contest danced in evening gowns, bathing suits and finally nude. As the panel of two barbers, two disc jockeys and a music agent announced the winner, police arrested and removed her and three other contestants. The three hundred men, who had paid $10 apiece to watch the contest, stamped their feet and booed.

4. CENTERLINE AND LANSING - 1974

During the "streaking" craze, hundreds of nude dashers technically broke the law but few were caught or arrested.

One judge, however, did fine a 22-year-old man $75 for streaking through a Centerline restaurant. The defendant claimed he didn't really want to streak but friends had stripped him and pushed him out the bathroom door.

Another, who was nabbed after running up the center aisle of the House chamber in Lansing while lawmakers were deep in debate, swore he was not politically motivated.

2 CASES OF "WOOD RUSTLING"

1. October 1, 1979 - September 20, 1980

Department of Natural Resources' officers arrested eighty-six people for the unauthorized cutting of timber on state lands.

With home heating costs soaring, wood rustlers steal several thousand cords each year from state lands and the arrests by the DNR, plagued by budget and personnel cutbacks, barely scratch the surface of the problem.

2. November, 1971

The Michigan Agriculture Department warned farmers to look out for walnut-tree rustlers who were systematically stealing the valuable trees and selling them to cabinet and furniture makers.

6 UNIQUE THEFTS

1. PETOSKEY - April 29, 1980

An elderly Newberry woman had $12,000 stolen from her bra two days after entering a Petoskey-area hospital.

Since 1928 the woman, who had feared banks because of the depression, had tucked bills into four pouches, two made of nylon stockings and two crocheted, and fastened them inside her bra. Only one pouch, containing $1,000, was left after the robbery.

2. GRAND RAPIDS - October 23, 1981

Police charged a 23-year-old suburban man with stealing panties during a break-in at a Kentwood apartment building. Residents of the building, in which the arrested man lived, had previously reported seventeen similar thefts of women's underwear and nightgowns.

3. BESSEMER - August 26, 1889

Reimund (Rheinhardt) Holzhey, while robbing a stagecoach between Gogebic Station and Lake Gogebic, killed a passenger. The robber was sentenced to life imprisonment for the murder during, what turned out to be, the last stagecoach robbery in Michigan.

4. YPSILANTI - January 16, 1980

A nineteen-year-old bank vault teller stole $421,000 from the National Bank of Ypsilanti where he worked. The teller was convicted of the largest bank theft recorded in Michigan after his partner returned the money and testified in return for immunity.

5. BAY CITY - October 29, 1981

Though the owner's house was only fifty yards away, an unknown thief stole 1,600 chickens from the Monitor Hatchery without being noticed.

6. ROSEVILLE - November, 1981

Over a two-week period, a St. Clair Shores man, posing as a mourner, stole gold rings from the fingers of three corpses in a local mortuary.

4 BODY SNATCHERS

In the late 1800's, though society and the law objected, medical colleges began teaching anatomy by requiring their students to dissect human cadavers. But, because of difficulties in legally obtaining bodies, many schools, most prominently the University of Michigan, depended on professional grave robbers and body snatchers to meet the ever-increasing need.

When any one of a number of collaborators, mostly doctors or morticians, told a body snatcher of the death of a likely subject—usually paupers buried in rural cemeteries—he and a confederate set out, always at night, to the burial site to "resurrect" the body before it began decomposing. There, they would dig out a three-foot square at the head of the grave, remove the front end of the coffin, place a five-foot-long iron hook under the chin of the cadaver and remove the body.

If the grave robbers could reach a college by wagon before daylight, they would personally deliver the body to a medical building janitor. For longer deliveries they would ship the bodies by rail in "pickling barrels." In fact, many such barrels, labeled "turpentine," arrived at the University of Michigan from all over the country and the school became the center of what the public believed to be a vast network of body snatchers.

In 1881 the Michigan legislature passed a law that allowed state medical schools to obtain cadavers legally and, by the end of the century, ghoul traffic had stopped.

Four of Michigan's well-publicized body snatchers:

1. DR. HENRI LE CARON
The 1872 graduate of Detroit Medical College financed his medical studies by robbing Ontario cemeteries and selling the bodies to the University of Michigan. As the leader of a gang of body snatchers that sold bodies to schools throughout the Midwest, authorities caught him exhuming two bodies in Toledo in 1878. He was arrested but escaped from a prison hospital where he had been confined after producing fake smallpox eruptions.

2. DR. CHARLES G. CRUIKSHANK
Police arrested the Howell doctor in 1880 and charged him with stealing a body and selling it back to his alma mater, the University of Michigan.

3. JAMES McGUIRE
In 1880 the Macomb County body snatcher was convicted and sentenced to a five-year term in the state prison.

4. ALLAN DURFEE
The Grand Rapids undertaker confessed that, instead of burying body, he had performed a mock funeral and then sold the cadaver. He skipped town before his trial.

2 RECENT GRAVE ROBBINGS

1. PONTIAC - June, 1981

An eighteen-year-old Pontiac man and two juvenile accomplices took two skulls from crypts at the Oak Hill Cemetery. The man then played practical jokes with the skulls such as putting them in his family's refrigerator, on his sister's bed or on top of gravestones.

A County Circuit Court judge sentenced the man to one to ten years in prison.

2. GAINES TOWNSHIP - November, 1981

Six high-school students dug up a grave in a small rural cemetery, opened the coffin and removed a skull.

4 RARE OFFENSES

1. MAN ATTACKS CAR - 1980

A 27-year-old Benton Harbor man, who got a little carried away practicing his karate moves, absent-mindedly stepped backward into the street and was struck by a car. Adding insult to minor injuries, police ticketed the hospitalized man for jaywalking.

2. BILLBOARD BANDITS - 1971

Over a two-month period, unknown culprits, who objected to unsightly billboards along Michigan highways, used axes and chain saws to cut down more than eighty of the offending signs.

3. SUICIDE IS MURDER - 1981

Based on a unique 61-year-old Michigan Supreme Court ruling, a county prosecutor in February charged a Port Huron man with murder for allegedly providing his friend with the shotgun he used to commit suicide.

Seven months later, a Mt. Morris Township man was charged with murder for giving a .357 magnum pistol to a young dental assistant who then shot herself.

4. ROAD WORK(H)ER SUSPENDED - 1976

The Wayne County Road Commissioner suspended a male road worker who, in the process of undergoing a sex change operation, wore jeans and a woman's blouse instead of the regulation male work uniform.

After agreeing to wear a modified version of the required uniform, the transsexual was again suspended when she, formerly he, worked in a halter top on an eighty-degree day.

6 MOST COMMON NON-CRIMINAL OFFENSES

Based on 1978 figures.
1. VANDALISM   167,043
2. DISORDERLY CONDUCT   73,860
3. SEX OFFENSES AGAINST FAMILY OR CHILDREN   68,865
4. NON-AGGRAVATED ASSAULTS   53,029
5. DRIVING UNDER THE INFLUENCE OF ALCOHOL   36,776
6. FRAUD   33,054

7 MOST COMMON CRIMES

Based on 1978 figures.
1. THEFT   279,621
2. BURGLARY   130,716
3. CAR THEFT   47,995
4. ASSAULT   28,661
5. ROBBERY   20,192
6. RAPE   3,614
7. MURDER   908

6 CONVICTED PUBLIC OFFICIALS

1. CHARLES DIGGS

The U.S. Representative was charged with illegally inflating his staff's salaries and accepting kickbacks from them to pay his personal, business and congressional expenses. On October 7, 1978, he was convicted on twenty-nine counts of payroll padding and mail fraud and sentenced to three years in prison. The House of Representatives also censured Diggs, who resigned May, 1980, and he agreed to pay back $40,031.

2. JOHN B. SWAINSON

The State Supreme Court justice and former governor was implicated in an alleged conspiracy to accept $30,000 from a bail bondsman in return for arranging a new trial for a burglar. The FBI had monitored contacts between the bondsman and burglar and between Swainson and the bondsman. In November, 1975, Swainson was convicted on three counts of lying to a grand jury about those conversations but was found not guilty of bribery and conspiracy.

3. DANIEL W. WEST

The Detroit representative to the Michigan House had just been elected for a second term in 1964 when investigators discovered he actually was a convicted felon and forgerer who had assumed the credentials of a deceased attorney by the same name. In December, 1964, a federal grand jury indicted West on 117 counts of voter registration fraud and income tax fraud but he fled, reportedly to Canada, before his trial.

4. ROBERT F. LEONARD

On November 23, 1979, a U.S. District Court jury convicted the Genesee County prosecutor of embezzling $34,000 in federal money from a secret fund used to pay informers, taking $33,450 in stolen money out of state, and evading taxes. Leonard was sentenced to five and a half years in prison and fined a total of $14,000.

5. ARTHUR CARTWRIGHT

The state senator was charged in March, 1978, with eight felonies for allegedly cheating taxpayers by padding his Senate expense accounts. Two months later he pleaded guilty to a misdemeanor, admitted that he collected $45.80 for a meal that cost $4.16 and resigned his Senate seat.

6. MONTE GERALDS

The state representative was convicted of embezzling $24,000 from a Bloomfield Hills heiress and using the money to help finance an office building.

In May, 1978, he was placed on two years probation, directed to pay back the money and ordered to do four hundred hours of volunteer work at a family counseling center.

He later became the first representative ever expelled from the Michigan House of Representatives.

4 MEMORABLE CASES OF PROSTITUTION

1. SAULT STE. MARIE - 1979

A small, working-class pleasure spot at the edge of town became Michigan's first taxpaying bordello when the understaffed police department, frustrated in their attempts to close it down, asked the State Treasury Department to add the madam owner's name to the state tax rolls.

The madam agreed to pay fifteen thousand dollars in back taxes and began skimming 4.6% from the nightly earnings of her four or five workers. But, instead of economically squeezing her out of business as the officials had hoped, the move elevated the woman to folk-hero status almost overnight.

2. DETROIT - 1980

Prostitutes, including many out-of-town entrepreneurs, did a thriving business during the week-long National Republican Convention. The high-class hookers, who earned two hundred dollars an hour and up, dressed conservatively and paraded through bars and hotels looking for moneyed men.

Republican delegates, however, most of whom were with wives and families and many of whom were women, were not the primary customers. Members of the news media, who outnumbered delegates two to one, who had been in Detroit without families for over a month and who enjoyed generous expense accounts, were the prime targets.

3. DETROIT - 1970

Even though prostitution is illegal in Michigan, it's a crime to steal money a prostitute earned for her services. So ruled the State Court of Appeals when it upheld the conviction of two Detroit men who had purchased ten dollars worth of favors from two prostitutes, then stole it back.

4. MUSKEGON - 1876

As part of the July 4th centennial celebration, "Big Delia," a six-foot, two-inch, 225-pound, tobacco-chewing madam and her employees, built a huge pavilion, hired two bands, invited their sisters from Chicago and Milwaukee, provided free beer and threw a free party for more than a thousand lumberjacks.

Drinking And Driving
3 RIGHTS

Michigan has an Implied Consent Law. Under this law any person who drives a motor vehicle on a public highway is considered to have given their consent to be tested to determine the alcoholic content of their blood. If arrested for drunk or impaired driving, you have the right:

1. To take or refuse a chemical blood test for blood-alcohol content.

2. To have a second chemical test given by a person of your own choosing within a reasonable time after the police test.

3. To demand that only a breath test be given.

Drinking And Driving
4 PENALTIES

1. You can be charged with impaired driving if your blood-alcohol content is between 0.07% and 0.10%.

2. You can be charged with driving under the influence of liquor if your blood-alcohol content is 0.10% or more.

3. Your license may be suspended if you refuse to take a breath test.

4. You can be arrested for having an open container of liquor, beer or wine in the passenger area of your car.

6 CREATIVE EXCUSES FOR SPEEDING

Six imaginative excuses offered to Michigan police officers who have stopped drivers for speeding. (As submitted to a contest sponsored by the Michigan Fraternal Order of Police.)

1. My wife is going to get pregnant tonight and I want to be there when she does.

2. My car is so light the wind must have blown it over the speed limit.

3. One man said he had the right to speed to make up for lost time in a construction zone. He argued unsuccessfully that his average speed was 55 m.p.h.

4. I have to go to the bathroom (the most common excuse).

5. I was speeding to keep up with the cars behind me.

6. I was speeding to get away from my mother-in-law.

2 POISONINGS

1. OKEMOS - 1978

Police accused a mother whose three children were beaten out for top seats in their school orchestra of breaking and entering the home of a music teacher while carrying a sack of poisonous chemicals.

Police suspected, but did not accuse, the 47-year-old microbiologist of also being responsible for more than one hundred similar chemical dumping incidents over a three-year period. Twenty families, all music instructors or pupils, had reported that such potentially lethal chemicals as powdered mercury, arsenic, lead and zinc were scattered throughout their homes while they attended music recitals or similar events.

No serious injuries or illnesses resulted and the suspected jealous mother, though claiming she was not responsible, pleaded guilty to a misdemeanor and agreed to undergo five years of psychiatric counseling.

2. ANN ARBOR - 1975

Fifty-two patients in the intensive-care unit of the Ann Arbor Veterans Administration Hospital mysteriously quit breathing during the summer of

1975 and twelve died. Two nurses were accused of injecting Pavulon, a powerful muscle relaxant, into the patients' intravenous tubes to induce the breathing failures.

The nurses were indicted on several murder and lesser charges but, by the time the case came to trial, each was charged with two murders, seven poisonings and conspiracy. The jury returned a verdict of guilty on three poisoning charges and conspiracy but the verdict was overturned and the nurses acquitted because of circumstantial evidence and alleged improprieties by the prosecutor. All charges were subsequently dropped and no other suspects charged.

5 SKYJACKINGS

1. OCTOBER 9, 1971

Holding a cocked gun to a flight attendant's head, a 31-year-old Pontiac ex-convict hijacked a plane at Detroit's Metro Airport and forced it to fly to Cuba.

The Eastern Airline flight, with thirty-three passengers, six crew members and five attendants, landed in Cuba where uniformed men escorted the skyjacker away.

2 NOVEMBER 12, 1972

Three Michigan men, wanted for multiple rape charges, hijacked a Southern Airways DC-9 in Birmingham, Alabama. Then, in a bizarre 29-hour escapade, the hijackers forced the pilot to land in Cleveland, Toronto and Orlando, collected $2 million in ransom money (including $500,000 from the city of Detroit) and attempted to call then President Nixon. The hijackers also wounded the co-pilot and threatened to crash the plane into the Oak Ridge, Tennessee, nuclear reactor before finally landing in Cuba.

The three spent eight years in Cuban jails before being sent back in October, 1980, on the "freedom flights," in which thirty-eight Americans were released from Cuban prisons. Upon their return, the three were arrested immediately by federal marshalls.

3. JUNE 6, 1975

A convicted hog thief and rubber-check artist flew to freedom from the yard of Southern Michigan Prison (Jackson) in a hijacked helicopter.

A friend had chartered a helicopter and forced the pilot at knife-point to swoop over the prison walls and land out of guards' firing range on a grassy spot marked by a red handkerchief.

The prisoner, hiding between two buildings, darted aboard and flew six miles to Munith where he switched to a car. Police captured him thirty hours later in a bar at Leslie, Michigan.

4. JUNE 23, 1972

A 28-year-old, unemployed Wyandotte veteran commandeered a plane to St. Louis, Missouri, where he demanded a $502,200 ransom, a parachute and a shovel. The hijacker, who allowed eighty of the ninety-three passengers to disembark, forgot to take the ransom money aboard so forced the plane to land again at St. Louis. When a security car rammed the plane, he switched to another, took off and bailed out over Indiana. FBI agents caught him and he was convicted of extortion and hijacking.

5. AUGUST 25, 1970

A Nahma army enlisted man hijacked a plane over Indiana and forced the pilot to fly him to Cuba.

4 IRANIAN HOSTAGES FROM MICHIGAN

On November 4, 1979, Iranian militants overran the U.S. embassy compound in Teheran and took fifty-two American citizens prisoner. A rescue attempt ended in tragedy when a helicopter collided with a support plane in the Iranian desert, killing eight servicemen. The hostages endured a total of 444 days of despair, trauma, uncertainty, torture and extreme mental stress before being released January 20, 1981.

Four from Michigan are;

1. CHARLES JONES (Detroit)

The 39-year-old career teletype operator for the International Communications Agency was the only remaining black hostage at the embassy after thirteen women and black hostages "who were not involved in spying" were released.

For Jones, this was his third brush with danger. He had previously been rescued from the roof of the American embassy in Saigon when that city fell to the North Vietnamese and, two years later, had to be evacuated from Cairo when the six-day war broke out. Jones said he would rather have died in captivity than see the U.S. give in to the Iranians' demands.

2. JOSEPH SUBIC (Redford Township)

The 23-year-old military policeman and Army staff sergeant was known as a super patriot "G.I. Joe" to his school friends and quit high school to join the army.

A cheering Michigan State Senate honored Subic for his courage during his captivity. But, because of his appearance in an Iranian propaganda film, Subic was only one of twenty military hostages who did not receive a commendation medal.

3. ROBERT ODE (Manistee)

A native of Manistee, Ode joined the foreign service as a career diplomat in 1947 and retired to Falls Church, Virginia, but was on a special 45-day assignment to the Teheran embassy.

Ode's captors took his shoes and he went barefoot and wore the same clothes for the entire period of captivity. Speaking at Olivet College's 1981 graduating ceremonies, the oldest of the hostages said that the ill-fated rescue attempt was a mistake.

4 JOHN GRAVES - Detroit

The Detroit-born public affairs officer, who formerly taught at Detroit schools and Wayne State University, was an eighteen-year veteran of the foreign service at the time of his capture.

2 FAMOUS MISSING PERSONS

1. JIMMY HOFFA

On July 30, 1975, former Teamsters president Jimmy Hoffa disappeared from the parking lot of a suburban Detroit restaurant. Government officials and the FBI theorized that Hoffa was the victim of a contract murder at the hands of one-time Teamster allies and some organized crime figures he had once welcomed into the nation's largest labor union.

None of the suspected figures in the case has been indicted. One has been executed by unknown gunmen and five have refused to answer grand jury questions under the Fifth Amendment.

2 JAMES DALLAS EGBERT, III

As a sophomore at Michigan State University, the sixteen-year-old computer science whiz vanished from the campus August 15, 1979, and the search for him attracted massive national publicity.

Investigators spent several days searching eight miles of sweltering steam tunnels beneath the university believing that Egbert may have been hiding or even killed playing a live version of a fantasy game called *Dungeons and Dragons*.

Sales of the game, in which players roll dice to overcome various barriers, risk death and escape from a "dungeon master," rose briskly with publicity over the disappearance.

A private investigator found Egbert, unharmed, one month later in Texas.

5 INFAMOUS MURDERS

1. BATH - 1927

Andrew Kehoe, school board treasurer for the small town of Bath (Clinton County), silently suffered as his power, influence and prominence in the community began to slip away. His defeat in an election for justice of the peace, the frequent hospitalization of his wife Nellie for severe headaches and a notice of foreclosure on his farm increased his frustration, despair and sense of betrayal.

In a desire to punish Bath and his enemies, he spent a month painstakingly wiring and precisely placing hundreds of pounds of explosives under the newly constructed schoolhouse.

On May 16, 1927, he killed his wife Nellie. During the night of May 17, he connected a timing device to the deadly circuit and set the clock for 9:45 a.m. The next morning, after setting fire to his farmhouse with his wife's body inside, Kehoe drove a dynamite-loaded truck to a street near the school filled with over three hundred students and teachers. As a tremendous blast tore the school apart, Kehoe simultaneously exploded his truck, killing himself, the school's superintendent and three bystanders. In all, forty-five people, including thirty-eight students and teachers, died in Michigan's worst mass murder.

2. ANN ARBOR/YPSILANTI - 1967-1969

On August 7, 1967, the mutilated, battered remains of a nineteen-year-old Eastern Michigan University student, who had disappeared a month earlier, were found on a rubbish dump near Ypsilanti. The gruesome discovery was only the first of what would become seven macabre, grisly, "co-ed murders" in the area in the next two years.

The next five victims included:

—July 5, 1968 — A twenty-year-old Eastern Michigan University co-ed whose slashed body was kept in a cellar for several days before being dumped in a field.

—March, 1969 - A 23-year-old University of Michigan law student shot twice in the head and left on a grave.

—March, 1969 - A sixteen-year-old high-school dropout and frequent runaway who was sexually abused, whipped and slashed before being killed by a blow to the head.

—April, 1969 - A thirteen-year-old junior-high schoolgirl was garrotted with an electric cord, slashed and stabbed in the basement of a farmhouse and her body dumped on a road two-and-a-half miles away.

—June, 1969 - A 21-year-old University of Michigan co-ed was raped, slashed and shot in the head and her body dumped in a field.

Through these six brutal slayings, police couldn't determine whether the killings were connected or how many killers were involved.

Finally, in July, 1969, a chance remark by the seventh victim shortly before her murder began a chain of events that eventually resulted in the arrest and first-degree murder conviction of Eastern Michigan University student John Norman Collins.

Collins, who is serving a life sentence at Southern Michigan Prison, has yet to confess to that seventh murder let alone any of the other six. Though police claim to have evidence that ties Collins to the other six killings, the murders remain officially unsolved.

3. OAKLAND COUNTY - 1967-1977

Between February 15, 1976, and January 2, 1977, a mysterious killer ritualistically abducted and slew two boys and two girls, ages ten to twelve, from Detroit's affluent northern suburbs.

Each abduction occurred shortly after a snowfall and the killer kept the victims secluded but alive before smothering or shooting them. The killer also manicured the children's fingernails and immaculately cleaned the young victims before dumping their bodies along roadsides or in parking lots.

A task force, which at its peak included two hundred investigators from fifty police agencies, stopped its investigation in late 1978. The identity of the killer is still a mystery.

4. GRAND RAPIDS - 1970-1976

In an apparently random, motiveless manner, a deranged killer, over a six-year period, stabbed or strangled seven young women in the Hill District, a neighborhood of stately but deteriorating homes near downtown Grand Rapids.

The county prosecutor, after convening a grand jury probe, concluded that, because there was no evidence of sexual assault, robbery or any other motive, the murders were the result of a single "kook." Police disagreed, theorizing that different killers committed the murders. All went unsolved.

5. RENO, NEVADA - November, 1980

A 51-year-old former Berrien Springs woman suddenly veered her black Continental onto the bustling sidewalk in the heart of the casino district and plowed through the mass of pedestrians for more than a block, killing six tourists and injuring twenty-six more.

The woman, who had taught at two rural Cass County schools for eight years, was convicted in March, 1982, of six counts of first-degree murder and sentenced to die in Nevada's gas chamber.

2 TEACHERS MURDERED
IN FRONT OF THEIR CLASSES

1. ROBERT BRAUER (Ferris State College) - March, 1980

A student, who had failed an exam, walked to the front of a classroom and, in front of thirty students, shot a 34-year-old accounting professor to death.

The assailant, the son of the college's assistant dean of the School of General Education, was acquitted of murder by reason of insanity.

2. BETTYE McCASTER (Burt Elementary School, Detroit) - November, 1976

The estranged husband of the 45-year-old teacher entered her classroom and, in front of twenty-nine first- and second-grade students, fired five shots into her head. He was sentenced to life imprisonment with recommendation of no parole.

3 ABUSED WIVES FOUND INNOCENT OF MURDERING THEIR HUSBANDS

1. FRANCINE HUGHES (Ingham County) - March, 1977

The thirty-year-old woman, whose husband allegedly beat and choked her repeatedly, poured gasoline under the sleeping man's bed and set the house afire. A jury found the mother of four not guilty of first-degree murder by reason of temporary insanity. Feminists lauded the case as a landmark to a wife's right to self-defense.

2. JEANETTE SMITH (Kalkaska) - May, 1978

The 47-year-old woman, who claimed her husband had abused her for years, stabbed him to death after he allegedly threatened to kill her. An Otsego County Court jury acquitted her of second-degree murder.

The trial turned Mrs. Smith into a celebrity. She appeared on several television shows including an ABC-TV documentary on spouse abuse but, shortly after, attempted suicide.

3. PATRICIA GROSS (Port Huron) - September, 1978

The 27-year-old woman, who testified that her husband had beaten her, kicked her with steel-toed boots and threatened their three children, shot the man seven times with a rifle. She was acquitted of murder by self-defense.

6 NOTABLE EXECUTIONS

1. FIRST LEGAL EXECUTION

Acting under the laws of France, Daniel de Gresolon Sieur du L'Hut, commandant of Fort Michilimackinac in 1684, executed an Indian convicted of murdering two Frenchmen.

2. FIRST WHITE MAN EXECUTED

Bartellemy Pichon, a deserter of the French army occupying Detroit in 1707, was captured, tried for treason, found guilty and sentenced to "have his head broken till death follows by eight soldiers."

3. FIRST WOMAN EXECUTED

In 1763 an English trader named Clapham purchased two Panis Indian slaves, a man and a woman, and took them by canoe from Detroit to Sandusky. En route, the two murdered Clapham and stole all his belongings. The man escaped but the woman was caught, tried and publicly hanged in Detroit.

4. ONLY BLACK WOMAN EXECUTED

In June, 1776, a Canadian Frenchman and Ann Wyley, a black woman, were convicted of stealing a small sum of money from a warehouse but found innocent of trying to set fire to it.

A notorious "hanging judge," however, ordered them executed and they were hanged March 26, 1777, in Detroit.

5. LAST EXECUTION UNDER STATE LAW

Stephen G. Simmons was publicly hanged in Detroit for murdering his wife in a drunken fury. Officials erected seats for spectators and a military band provided music. As a result of this carnival-like atmosphere, public opinion turned against executions and the Michigan legislature abolished capital punishment in 1846, the first state in the nation to do so.

6. LAST EXECUTION

Though capital punishment had been abolished by law for almost one hundred years in Michigan, on July 8, 1938, Anthony Chebatoris was hanged in Milan for murdering a bystander while robbing the Chemical State Savings Bank in Bay City. He was executed under a stringent federal law, the National Bank Robbery Act, that had been enacted to quell a national rampage of bank robberies. Chebatoris was the first person to be sentenced to death in the U.S. under this act and the last person executed in Michigan.

2 NOTORIOUS GANGS

1. PURPLE GANG

This vicious gang plagued Detroit during the Prohibition years, killing hundreds during Detroit's "bootleg wars." The gang sold illegal whiskey and protection to operators of "blind pigs" and also loaned killers to other gang leaders such as Chicago's Al Capone.

After three key members were convicted of slaying three Chicago hoodlums, the gang was absorbed by a larger national crime syndicate.

2. BLACK LEGION

In 1932 native Michiganians organized recently transplanted, predominantly uneducated, southern factory workers into an underground society of guns, bizarre initiation rites, dire oaths, midnight meetings and group vengeance. Calling themselves the United Brotherhood of America, but better known as the "Black Legion," the group carried out a four-year series of brutal murders, attempted murders, beatings and terrorism of those who opposed their anti-Jew, anti-black, anti-communist and anti-Catholic philosophy.

Investigators accidentally discovered the society in 1936 when four of sixteen members, arrested for the brutal murder of a young Detroit WPA worker, confessed. Their revelations led investigators to a vast network of Black Legion members that had spread throughout the factories of Detroit. State officials were shocked to learn that government workers, state and public utility board members, police and fire department officers and other educated native Michiganians led the society.

Investigations, arrests, trials and efforts to weed members out of government bodies persisted for three years until the Legion was completely destroyed in 1939.

2 MAJOR INTERRACIAL RIOTS

1. DETROIT - June 20, 1945
During a blistering heat wave, blacks and whites began fighting on a bridge connecting Belle Isle and the mainland. The altercation incited whites to invade black neighborhoods where they smashed windows and beat residents. Shooting, stoning, knifing, bludgeoning, arson and looting continued for twenty-four hours and left thirty-five dead and seven hundred injured before federal troops quelled the riot.

2. DETROIT - July 23-30, 1967
Shortly after 4:00 a.m. on July 23, police raided a bar illegally serving liquor after hours and arrested seventy-three customers and the bartender. Rumors spread through a gathering crowd that police had beaten some of those arrested and someone threw a brick through a window starting a week of rioting, looting and burning that reached a scale unknown in the twentieth century. The riot left forty-three dead, two thousand injured, five thousand homeless and caused $500 million in damage.

2 WORST PRISON RIOTS

1. SOUTHERN MICHIGAN PRISON (Jackson) - May, 1981
Overcrowding and an unauthorized "shakedown" by rebellious guards triggered a takeover of the world's largest walled prison by eight hundred inmates. The week-long riot resulted in twenty-four injuries and $5 million in damage and triggered violence at three other Michigan penal institutions.

86

2. SOUTHERN MICHIGAN PRISON (Jackson) - April, 1952

Two thousand, six hundred inmates took eleven guards hostage and caused two million dollars damage in a four-day riot. Guards killed one prisoner and wounded another during the disturbance which ended when the state guaranteed to meet the prisoners' demands.

13 MICHIGAN PRISONS

1. STATE PRISON OF SOUTHERN MICHIGAN (Jackson) - 5,500 inmates

2. STATE HOUSE OF CORRECTION AND BRANCH PRISON (Marquette) - 850 inmates

3. MICHIGAN INTENSIVE PROGRAM CENTER (Marquette) - 89 inmates, all maximum security and behavior problems

4. MICHIGAN REFORMATORY (Ionia) - 1,490 inmates

5. RIVERSIDE CORRECTIONAL FACILITY (Ionia) - 570 inmates

6. MICHIGAN TRAINING UNIT (Ionia) - 780 inmates

7. MUSKEGON CORRECTIONAL FACILITY (Muskegon) - 583 inmates

8. KINROSS CORRECTIONAL FACILITY (Kinross) - 645 inmates

9. MICHIGAN DUNES CORRECTIONAL FACILITY (Holland) - 333 inmates

10. PHOENIX CORRECTIONAL FACILITY (Plymouth) - 304 inmates

11. CASSIDY LAKE TECHNICAL SCHOOL (Chelsea) - 238 inmates

12. HURON VALLEY WOMEN'S FACILITY (Ypsilanti) - 406 inmates

13. HURON VALLEY MAXIMUM SECURITY PRISON (Ypsilanti) -388 inmates

4 MUSEUMS THAT WERE ONCE JAILS

1. LUCE COUNTY HISTORICAL MUSEUM (Newberry)
2. ALLEGAN COUNTY HISTORICAL MUSEUM (Allegan)
3. HISTORICAL MUSEUM OF CHEBOYGAN COUNTY (Cheboygan)
4. LEELANAU COUNTY HISTORICAL MUSEUM (Leland)

8 OLDEST COUNTY JAILS STILL IN USE

Based on the year built.
1. KEEWEENAW - 1886
2. DICKINSON - 1889
3. MARQUETTE - 1924
4. MONROE - 1929
5. WAYNE - 1929
6. GENESEE - 1930
7. IRON - 1936
8. GRATIOT - 1939

4 SMALLEST COUNTY JAILS

Based on lock-up capacity.

1. MONTMORENCY - 2
2. KALKASKA - 4
3. LUCE - 5
4. KEEWEENAW - 8

11 INTERESTING ATTORNEY GENERAL'S OPINIONS

1. It is legally possible for the Upper Peninsula to withdraw from Michigan and form a separate state. (January 22, 1976)

2. A woman's surname does not automatically change when she marries, she is not required to adopt her husband's name and she may resume her maiden name at any time without court or legal action. (July 15, 1975)

3. Funeral homes or burial establishments may not serve food or beverages. (November 13, 1970)

4. Parents may not educate their children at home unless a certified teacher is present and can provide instruction of the quality offered in schools. (September 30, 1979)

5. Putting sound monitors and television cameras at entrances to public rest rooms to curb illegal activity doesn't violate people's rights as long as the cameras are not pointed at the stalls. (August 13, 1980)

6. The State Corrections Department cannot make a profit from the production of license plates. (February 25, 1976)

7. The use of hypnosis to cure morbid fears, unwanted habits and obesity legally constitutes the practice of medicine and can only be done under a doctor's direction. (March 24, 1976)

8. Church employees and those working for church-run schools are not entitled to unemployment benefits. (January 21, 1979)

9. Medical and osteopathic physicians may legally practice acupuncture but dentists and chiropractors may not. (February 21, 1975)

10. Hair transplants by the use of skin grafts to the scalp constitutes surgery and may only be performed by licensed doctors. (February 28, 1975)

11. Any salesperson who arranges, styles, combs, dresses or curls the hair of a customer in fitting a wig or hairpiece must be licensed by the State Board of Cosmetology. (February 8, 1973)

9 ATTORNEY GENERAL'S OPINIONS
THAT WERE PROBABLY IMPORTANT TO SOMEONE

1. The state is not obligated to pay for a prison inmate's sex change operation. (April 28, 1976)

2. A state law banning three-quart milk containers is unconstitutional. (January 19, 1975)

3. County officials do not have the authority or power to hire a rain-maker. (May 19, 1972)

4. Bullfighting in Michigan is allowable but bulls cannot be injured and matches must end bloodlessly. (September 23, 1978)

5. Counties may not operate spay and neuter clinics for dogs and cats. (August 1, 1978)

6. People who wave signs in the galleries of the State House and Senate after legislative leaders have warned against it can be ejected. (December 12, 1980)

7. The family of a deceased person cannot file a death certificate or prepare, remove or dispose of a body without the supervision of a funeral director or medical examiner. (July 23, 1973)

8. A hunter wearing a hip-mounted firearm under a jacket is violating the concealed weapons law even if he has a permit to carry the weapon. (July 4, 1979)

9. City and village charters may ban convicted felons from holding office. (February 7, 1980)

8 UNUSUAL LAWSUITS

1. BAY CITY - September, 1980
   A 32-year-old man was convicted and sent to prison for life for kidnapping a Bay City woman at gunpoint from her home, repeatedly raping her in a field, raping her again back at her home and shooting at her as she ran screaming for help.
   He filed suit naming the victim as a defendant, claiming she conspired with authorities to violate his civil rights by allegedly tampering with the mug book used to identify him.

2. MOUNT CLEMENS - December, 1979
   A Windsor man filed a property settlement suit against his male lover, a Mount Clemens man, claiming an unfair division of property was made when the two ended their four-year relationship.

3. LAPEER - March, 1973
   A Lapeer man sued the owner of a goat for $225,000 claiming that his father had died as a result of injuries suffered from repeated butting by the animal.

4. DETROIT - April, 1977
   A 225-pound lion mauled a young deaf girl in front of thirty classmates, according to a $1.5-million lawsuit filed by her parents. The owner of a private zoo had brought the animal to the school gym and, according to the suit, allowed it to roam unrestrained among the children.
   The girl made a sudden gesture and the lion grabbed her with his jaws around the upper part of her body. It took four adults twenty seconds to pry the jaws apart. The incident was captured on school video tape and aired that night on television news broadcasts.

5. DETROIT - July, 1980
   A New Haven woman sued her parents for allegedly having her falsely diagnosed as mentally retarded and committed to a home for the mentally retarded because she suffered from a birth defect. She remained in the home until she was seven when an observant nurse noticed that she was of normal intelligence. The $33-million suit also charged that her parents then refused to take her back so she was placed in a foster home.

6. FLINT - September, 1975
   A Flint salesman and ex-convict was serving time in Tennessee State Prison for larceny when Paramount Pictures filmed the movie, *Framed*, at the prison. In a $100,000 lawsuit, the man claimed that, without his knowledge or permission, the film featured him in several close-up shots.
   When he moved to Michigan to start a new life, employers, friends and neighbors saw him in the movie which, he claimed, subjected him to mental

suffering, shame and humiliation.

7. DETROIT - November, 1977

A Detroit woman filed a $1-million lawsuit against Detroit's Crittendon Hospital claiming that they, eight years earlier, had given her the wrong baby to take home.

8. PONTIAC - December, 1981

A man, who was charged with negligent homicide after driving his car sixty miles per hour down the wrong side of the highway, striking another car head-on and killing its two occupants, sued the dead couple's estate. He claimed that the driver should have seen him coming and should have swerved out of the way.

5 FANTASTICALLY LARGE AWARDS
LEVIED AGAINST MICHIGAN AUTOMAKERS

1. SANTA ANA, CALIFORNIA - February, 1978

A jury ordered Ford Motor Company to pay $128 million to a youth burned when his Pinto exploded after being hit in the rear. At the time, the judgment, $125 million of which was punitive damages, was the largest in U.S. legal history.

2. WASHINGTON, D.C. - June, 1979

A Federal Court jury ordered General Motors to pay $6.5 million to a woman who broke her neck when her 1975 Buick Electra suddenly began to shake, left the road and hit several trees. Witnesses testified that the car's universal joint (part of the drive shaft) broke causing her to lose control of the brakes and steering.

3. SACRAMENTO, CALIFORNIA - February, 1980

In an out-of-court settlement, General Motors agreed to pay $5.25 million to a teenage girl who was badly burned when her Chevy Nova caught fire after a rear-end collision. The suit claimed that the fuel system was defective.

4. ANCHORAGE, ALASKA - June, 1980

A Superior Court jury awarded $4.6 million to a man who claimed that he was paralyzed when a defective rear brake system in his 1972 Caprice caused the car to spin off a road and crash into a tree.

5. MILWAUKEE, WISCONSIN - December, 1976

A jury decided that a young woman's Cadillac had defects that caused a disabling accident and awarded her $3.3 million. Her attorney contended that a defective differential gear had reduced traction on wet pavement, causing her car to hydroplane and veer out of control.

7 AWARDS FOR UNUSUAL REASONS

1. DETROIT - June, 1979

A Macomb Circuit Court jury awarded $250,000 to a Sicilian-American woman whose husband had questioned her chastity on their wedding night.

The husband claimed that he had soured on the marriage months before the wedding and decided to get out of it by telling his family that his wife was "not right." The couple had immigrated from the same village in western Sicily and the woman claimed that, when word of her alleged "infidelity" spread throughout both families, she became a social outcast.

2. FLINT - October, 1974

A Galesburg man was awarded $50,000 for injuring his back when he slipped on fat at a Flint Kentucky Fried Chicken establishment while delivering a load of chicken. The firm argued unsuccessfully that any fat on the floor must have come from the chickens he was delivering.

3. BLOOMFIELD HILLS - October, 1978

A woman kept in bondage and beaten for thirteen years by her legal guardians was awarded $1.5 million by a judge who termed her treatment a "shocking example of human serfdom."

According to the suit, the woman was released from the Lapeer State Hospital to live with her guardians, worked for them for thirteen years, and was paid only $1,630 which her guardians coerced into signing over to them.

Her guardians also allegedly choked her, forced her to sleep in an unheated garage in the winter and tied a live chicken to her head if she complained.

4. TROY - July, 1979

A Troy man, not a lawyer, filed his own lawsuit against the city of Troy for $1.2 million, alleging that Troy police had kicked and beaten him. He won the suit by default when real lawyers, the Troy City Attorney and his staff forgot to file a required written brief on time.

5. DETROIT - December, 1977

A Detroit man was awarded $2,067,696 after party-goers threw a couch out the fourteenth-floor window of a Detroit hotel in December, 1975, and hit him on the head.

6. CLINTON - June, 1977

A Clinton man, who lost an arm when a modified tractor engine exploded at a county-fair tractor-pulling contest, was awarded $1.5 million.

7. MUSKEGON - February, 1980

A Fruitport Township man was overcome by carbon monoxide gas when he entered an oven at the Anaconda Wire and Cable Company in 1974. When rescuers revived him, he had permanently and totally lost his memory and received $200,000 in an out-of-court settlement.

11 FANTASTICALLY LARGE AWARDS

1. FLINT - 1981

A child, who suffered brain damage when doctors at Hurley Medical Center abandoned her at birth as hopelessly premature, could get as much as thirteen million dollars in an out-of-court settlement. Under the agreement, the child's family received an immediate $400,000 plus monthly payments to the child or her estate until the year 2018.

2. HARTFORD - 1981

A ten-year-old boy, whose right arm had to be amputated after he touched a power line while climbing a tree, could receive more than twelve million dollars under terms of an out-of-court agreement. The agreement called for a rural electric cooperative to make monthly payments, which start at $1,500 and increase 5.25% a year, for the rest of the boy's life.

3. DETROIT - 1979

A Chicago Marine private, left paralyzed from the chest down after an alleged beating by Detroit police officers, was awarded $10.4 million by a Wayne County Circuit Court jury.

4. DETROIT - 1981

A U.S. District Court awarded $5.75 million to the parents of a Troy man mistakenly killed in 1979 by police officers while he guarded his van against burglars.

5. DETROIT - 1979

A sewer construction worker, who suffered permanent back injuries when struck by a train of small cars used to haul coal, was awarded $4.2 million. The suit claimed that the cars were improperly switched to a track where the man was working in 1970.

6. DETROIT - 1981

A Wayne County Circuit Court jury awarded $4 million to a Dearborn woman who charged that a urologist at a Detroit hospital had performed unneeded surgery and caused her to lose a kidney.

7. DETROIT - 1979

A Detroit woman, who lost most of her right leg and intestines through radiation damage suffered during cancer treatment, won $3.5 million from a Grosse Pointe x-ray clinic.

8. BAY CITY - 1981

A man, who was accidentally shot in the spine and paralyzed by a state trooper, was awarded $3.5 million in compensatory damages.

9. DETROIT - 1981

A young Lansing man, who was allegedly improperly treated for carbon monoxide poisoning at a Wayne County hospital, was awarded $3.1 million.

10. DETROIT - 1980

The widow and seven-year-old son of a man killed in 1973 when he was crushed by an 18,000-pound load of steel were awarded $2.8 million from the company that hauled the steel. The man, then twenty, was crushed when a chain used to hoist the steel coils broke.

11. MICHIGAN - 1979

The Velsicol Chemical Company reached an out-of-court settlement with seventy Michigan farm families who sued the company in the aftermath of the PBB disaster. (See page 161.) The families, who waived current personal-injury claims but who reserved the right to sue for long-term health damages, were awarded $2.6 million.

Previously the firm and their insurers had settled PBB-related property claims for $40 million.

FIRST 2 CRIME VICTIMS WHO WERE COMPENSATED

Under a law passed October 1, 1977, crime victims in the state of Michigan may be compensated. Victims must report the crime within forty-eight hours and file a claim with the Crime Victims Compensation Board in Lansing within thirty days.

In a ceremony on the Capitol steps December 28, 1977, Governor William G. Milliken presented checks to the first two victims to be compensated under the law.

1. ALLAN SANBORN (Flint)

The 21-year-old man received $377 for medical expenses. He lost two teeth and suffered facial injuries when assaulted by a gang after a football game.

2. MR. and MRS. CHARLES NICHOLS (Lansing)

The couple, whose daughter was murdered, received $1,500 for burial expenses.

5

THE WAY WE WERE

FIRST 4 WHITE MEN TO VISIT MICHIGAN

1. ETIENNE BRULE - 1622
   The twenty-year-old Frenchman explored the Lake Superior area in search of fur and mineral resources. He lived with the Huron Indians until they boiled and ate him in the fall of 1629.

2. JEAN NICOLET - 1634
   As an agent of French Governor Samuel de Champlain, the explorer reached the Sault in 1634 during his search for a route to the Orient.

3. ISAAC JOQUES - 1641
   The Jesuit missionary and his companion, Raymbault, visited the Rapids at the foot of Lake Superior which they named Sault de Sainte Marie.

4. CHARLES RAYMBAULT - 1641
   Joques' fellow traveling missionary.

FIRST 3 BOOKS IN THE WORLD
TO MENTION MICHIGAN

The first three books to mention Michigan were French and all were published in Paris.

1. *THE SAVAGES* by Samuel de Champlain (1603)
   The author mentions Lake Superior and the Indian copper mines of the Upper Peninsula. He didn't visit Michigan but got his information from Indians he met on the St. Lawrence River.

2. *HISTORY OF CANADA* by Gabriel Sagard-Theodat (1636)
    Contains reports of Etienne Brule's visit in 1622.

3. *REPORT* by Barthelemy Vimont (1644)
    Includes a sketch of the life of Jean Nicolet and his passage through the Straits of Mackinac in 1634.

3 COUNTRIES THAT HAVE CLAIMED
OR HELD MICHIGAN

1. FRANCE
    France claimed all of Michigan in 1671.

2. ENGLAND
    In 1760 Fort Ponchartrain (Detroit) surrendered to British troops. In 1763 the Treaty of Paris formally ceded Michigan to England. In a second Treaty of Paris (1783) which ended the Revolutionary War, Michigan was included within the boundaries of the new Republic of America but, because of the lucrative fur trade, the British didn't leave until 1796.
    During the War of 1812, both Detroit and Mackinac surrendered to the British and stayed under their control for nearly a year.

3. SPAIN
    In 1781 a Spanish raiding expedition seized the British Fort St. Joseph at Niles and the flag of Spain flew over the outpost for several days.

5 EARLIEST PERMANENT SETTLEMENTS

1. SAULT de SAINTE MARIE - 1668
    Founded by Father Jaques Marquette, it is the third oldest remaining settlement in the United States.

2. ST. IGNACE - 1671

3. MACKINAC - 1675

4. ST. JOSEPH - 1679

5. PORT HURON - 1686

10 OLDEST COUNTIES

Based on date of incorporation.

1.	WAYNE	1815
2.	MONROE	1817
3.	MACOMB	1818
4.	OAKLAND	1820
5.	ST. CLAIR	1821
6.	WASHTENAW	1826
7.	LENAWEE	1826
8.	CASS	1829
9.	ST. JOSEPH	1820
10.	KALAMAZOO	1830

7 OLDEST INCORPORATED CITIES AND VILLAGES

Based on date of incorporation.

1.	CITY OF DETROIT	1806
2.	CITY OF MONROE	1837
3.	VILLAGE OF CENTREVILLE	1837
4.	VILLAGE OF CONSTANTINE	1837
5.	CITY OF GRAND RAPIDS	1850
6.	CITY OF ANN ARBOR	1851
7.	CITY OF ADRIAN	1853

14 OLD BUILDINGS

Fourteen of Michigan's oldest existing buildings as listed in *The National Register of Historic Places.*

1. ROBERT STUART HOUSE (Mackinac Island - 1817
2. JOHN JOHNSTON HOUSE (Sault Ste. Marie) - 1822
3. ELMWOOD SCHOOLCRAFT HOUSE (Sault Ste. Marie) - 1826
4. ST. JOSEPH'S ROMAN CATHOLIC CHURCH (Detroit) - 1828
5. WARD HOLLAND HOUSE (Marine City) - 1830
6. MISSION CHURCH (Mackinac Island) - 1830
7. CASWELL HOUSE (Troy) - 1832
8. TROMBLE HOUSE (Bay City) - 1835
9. GOVERNOR JOHN S. BARRY HOUSE (Constantine) - 1835
10. MARANTETTE HOUSE (Mendon) - 1835

President's House

Berrien County Courthouse

Ward Holland House

Robert Stuart House

Caswell House

John S. Barry House

Mission Church

John Johnston House

Lapeer County Courthouse

11. ORRIN WHITE HOUSE (Ann Arbor) - 1836
12. LAPEER COUNTY COURTHOUSE (Lapeer) - 1839
13. BERRIEN COUNTY COURTHOUSE (Berrien Springs) - 1839
14. PRESIDENT'S HOUSE (Ann Arbor) - 1839

2 CASTLES

1. CURWOOD CASTLE (Owosso)
Author James Oliver Curwood built this castle in 1922-23 and wrote several novels there.

2. CASTLE FARMS (Charlevoix)
Albert and Anna Loeb, mail-order merchants of farm equipment built the once flourishing replica of a French country estate in 1918.

2 MICHIGAN KINGS

1. JAMES JESSE STRANG
During their westward migration, a Mormon colony settled on Beaver Island (upper Lake Michigan) in 1846. Six years later their leader, James Jesse Strang, defied the United States Government and proclaimed himself king of the island.
King Strang maintained the only absolute monarchy in America until he was assassinated in 1856.

2. BENJAMIN PURNELL
A group of people claiming to be descendants of the scattered tribes of Israel founded a colony in Benton Harbor in 1903 and was led for many years by King Benjamin Purnell. His bearded followers still maintain the House of David which he founded.

9 MICHIGAN HISTORICAL FIELD MUSEUMS

The Michigan Historical Museum, located a few steps from the state Capitol in Lansing, offers insights and learning experiences in Michigan's history through artifacts, photographs, audio visual materials and other exhibits. The museum also has eleven field branches.

1. SANILAC PETROGLYPHS (New Greenleaf)

A thousand-year-old series of figures carved by Indians into a sandstone outcrop along the north branch of the Cass River.

Curwood Castle

Castle Farms

2. BRICK WATER TOWER (Kalamazoo)

3. THE MANN HOUSE (Concord)

A Victorian era (1884) house perfectly preserved.

4. HISTORIC FAYATEE TOWNSITE (Manistique)

5. FORT WILKINS (Copper Harbor)

Built in 1844 to defend the Copper Country from attacks by Chippewa Indians.

6. INDIAN MUSEUM (Manistique)

Situated on the shore of Indian Lake, this small museum depicts the Indian way of life in the Upper Peninsula as it was four hundred years ago.

7. FATHER JACQUES MARQUETTE MEMORIAL (St. Ignace)

An outdoor memorial to the early missionary and explorer.

8. HARTWICK PINES LUMBERING MUSEUM (Grayling)

Exhibits feature the stories of loggers, rivermen, millhands, and entrepreneurs of Michigan's white pine lumbering era.

9. WALKER TAVERN (Intersection of U.S. 12 and M-50 in Lenawee County)

A perfectly restored tavern and barn that served as a stopping point for Detroit to Chicago travelers in the 1830's and 1840's.

8 ITEMS IN THE CAPITOL CORNERSTONE

During ceremonies on October 2, 1873, forty-three items were placed in a hermetically sealed glass casket which was enclosed in a massive copper box and placed in the cornerstone of the new Capitol building in Lansing. Eight of the more interesting items were:

1. A package containing the contents of the cornerstone of the Territorial Capitol erected in Detroit in 1823.

2. *Transactions* of the Michigan State Medical Society for 1873.

3. A Lansing City Directory.

4. The pen used in the signing of the first constitution of the State of Michigan in 1835.

5. Gold, nickel, silver and copper coins minted in 1873.

6. A collection of copper cents from 1794 to 1857.

7. A *Report on Crime and Pauperism in Michigan* for 1873.

8. A United States postcard.

On November 8, 1978, state officials opened the copper box and found the glass liner smashed and full of wet ashes. Of the forty-three items, only the coins survived.

FIRST 6 NEWSPAPERS

1. *MICHIGAN ESSAY* OR *IMPARTIAL OBSERVER*
Father Gabriel Richard published only one known issue in Detroit in 1809. The issue was printed partially in French and partially in English.

2. *DETROIT GAZETTE*
Michigan's first successful newspaper was published weekly from 1817 to 1830 at a subscription cost of $4 per year.

3. *MONROE SENTINAL*
Started weekly publication in 1825.

4. *ANN ARBOR WESTERN EMIGRANT*
Published from 1829 to 1834.

5. *OAKLAND CHRONICLE*
The Pontiac weekly was launched in 1830 but merged with the *Detroit Free Press* the following year.

6. *DEMOCRATIC FREE PRESS AND MICHIGAN INTELLIGENCER*
This predecessor of the *Detroit Free Press* was first published in 1831 and became Michigan's first daily newspaper.

6 OLDEST RADIO STATIONS

1. WWJ (Detroit) - 1920
   By commercially broadcasting regular programs in 1920, WWJ became the first such station in the country.

2. WFDF (Flint) - 1922

3. WJR (Detroit) - 1922

4. WKZO (Kalamazoo) - 1923

5. WEXL (Royal Oak) - 1923

6. WOOD (Grand Rapids) - 1924

6 OLDEST COLLEGES

1. UNIVERSITY OF MICHIGAN - 1817
Opened in Detroit as the *Catholepistemiad*, it was the first university established by any of the states. In 1821 the name was changed to the University of Michigan and, in 1841, the school moved to its present site, Ann Arbor.

2. KALAMAZOO COLLEGE - 1833
Founded by Baptists in 1829, the college was chartered in 1833.

3. ALBION COLLEGE - 1835
Founded by Methodists.

4. HILLSDALE COLLEGE - 1844

5. OLIVET COLLEGE - 1844
Founded by Congregationalists.

6. EASTERN MICHIGAN UNIVERSITY - 1849
Created to train teachers.

ORIGINAL NAMES OF 6 COLLEGES

1. MICHIGAN AND HURON INSTITUTE (Kalamazoo College)

2. SPRING ARBOR ACADEMY (Albion College)

3. MICHIGAN CENTRAL COLLEGE (Hillsdale College)

4. YPSILANTI NORMAL COLLEGE (Eastern Michigan University)

5. MICHIGAN AGRICULTURAL COLLEGE (Michigan State University)

6. MICHIGAN COLLEGE OF MINES (Michigan Technological University)

FORMER NAMES OF 8 CITIES

1. ABA (Warren)
2. LOGAN (Adrian)
3. FORT MIAMI (St. Joseph)
4. FREMONT (Alpena)
5. MILTON (Battle Creek)
6. LEONARD (Big Rapids)
7. FORT PONCHARTRAIN (Detroit)
8. FORT ST. JOSEPH (Port Huron)

7 CITIES NAMED AFTER WOMEN

From *Dictionary of Michigan Place Names*, by Theodore Foster, published by the Michigan State University Library.

1. ANN ARBOR (Washtenaw County)
   When pioneers John Allen and Elisha Rumsey settled among the lush groves of Washtenaw County in 1823, they named their settlement after their wives, both of whom were named Ann.

2. COOPER (Kalamazoo County)
   Horace Comstock named the town for his wife's family name. She was the niece of James Fennimore Cooper.

3. ALLENDALE (Ottawa County)
   When organized, the first name on the town's assessment rolls was Agnes B. Allen, daughter-in-law of Revolutionary War hero Ethan Allen.

4. ADA (Kent County)
   Named after the daughter of one of the town's founders, Sidney Smith.

5. DAGGETT (Menominee County)
   When the post office was established in 1880, the postmaster selected his wife's family name.

6. ELMIRA (Otsego County)
   Named for Elmira Eldridge, one of the pioneer women of the community.

7. MARENISCO (Gogebic County)
   The village manufactured the name out of the letters of the name of the wife of the village's founder, Mary Enid Scott.

4 TOWNSHIPS NAMED AFTER WOMEN

1. BUEL TOWNSHIP (Sanilac County)
Named in honor of Mrs. Mary L. Buel who operated a hotel and accepted shingles from sawmill workers as payment for meals.

2. ALMIRA TOWNSHIP (Benzie County)
Named after the township's first woman settler, Almira Burl.

3. HELENA TOWNSHIP (Antrim)
Named for Helena Thayer, wife of Lucius Thayer, one of the early settlers of the township.

4. MARION TOWNSHIP (Livingston County)
Named after Marion Harris, wife of the township's first elected supervisor.

6 SHIPS NAMED "MICHIGAN"

1. 1762
The sloop *Michigan* withstood Chief Pontiac's forces at Detroit in a 1763 battle.

2. 1816
The topsail schooner that patrolled the Great Lakes for eleven years met an undignified death when showmen bought the ship, loaded it with a camel, an elk, a bear, and a variety of dogs, sold tickets to spectators and sent the entire lot over Niagara Falls.

3. 1833
The most advanced luxury passenger steamer and largest Great Lakes vessel of its time.

4. 1844
The gunboat *U.S.S. Michigan* was the Navy's first iron warship and guarded the Great Lakes for eighty years.

5. 1906
The second *U.S.S. Michigan* was one of the first "battle wagons" built by the Navy.

6. 1976
The Navy named a Trident missile-carrying submarine the *U.S.S. Michigan.*

Three U.S.S. Michigans. Top left: 1906 "battle wagon;" Bottom left: Missile-carrying submarine under construction; Above: 1844 16-gun steamer, the only national war vessel to ever sail the Great Lakes. (Photos courtesy of the U.S. Navy.)

8 PLACES NAMED IN AN UNUSUAL MANNER

1. FENTON (Genesee County)
    The name of the community was decided by a card game between Robert Leroy, Norman Rockwell and William Fenton, each of whom wanted the community named after them. Fenton won the card game so the main streets were named after the losers. The game continued with winners naming streets after members of their families.

2. BLOOMER TOWNSHIP (Montcalm County)
    At a dance held in the winter of 1851-52, several ladies astonished the gathering by appearing in bloomer dresses. The township was organized in 1852 and bloomer evidently was still on everyone's mind.

3. MICHIGAN: THE WOLVERINE STATE
    There is no evidence that wolverines were ever commercially trapped in the state or roamed the state in very great numbers. The nickname most probably came from the fact that wolverine pelts, trapped in upper Canada and relayed through Michigan to eastern cities, bore the name "Sault Ste. Marie, Michigan," on the shipping labels.

4. DAY TOWNSHIP (Montcalm County)
    At the first meeting of the township held to select a name, someone suggested that a name be considered "another day."

5. COLON (St. Joseph County)
    When the early settlers needed a name for their settlement on the St. Joseph River, someone randomly flipped open a dictionary and dropped his finger onto the middle of the page.

6. VENICE TOWNSHIP (Shiawassee County)
    At the time of the township's naming, most of the land was swamp and the large number of drainage ditches suggested the name of the famous Italian canal city.

7. EMPIRE (Leelanau County)
    In 1865 the schooner *Empire* became icebound in the harbor and was forced to spend the winter there. The post office opened the same winter and adopted the ship's name.

8. AETNA TOWNSHIP (Mecosta County)
    Named to commemorate the eruption of the volcano of the same name in Sicily two years before the township's organization.

2 TOWNSHIPS NAMED AFTER STOVES

1. COVINGTON (Baraga County)
A committee to select a name for the newly organized township gathered around a stove with the maker's name and "Covington, Kentucky," stamped on it.

2. NOVESTA (Tuscola County)
The township board gathered around a stove to select a name. The trade name on the stove was "Vesta No."

3 UNIQUE GHOST TOWNS

1. FAYETTE (Delta County)
Michigan's only completely restored ghost town has been reborn as a state park. Established in 1867 as a facility to smelt local iron ore into pig iron for delivery to foundries, the town prospered into the 1890's before dying out. Today, nineteen structures, including several public and commercial buildings, residences and furnaces, are visible.

2. PEQUAMING (Baraga County)
Henry Ford purchased the entire town in 1923 and used local timber in the manufacture of his "woodies." As control of the Ford Motor Company shifted to his grandson, Henry Ford II, in the 1940's, the empire Henry had built in Pequaming and other Upper Peninsula sites was slowly sold, scrapped or given away.

3. SINGAPORE (Allegan County)
Once an active lumbering town, the entire town was covered with drifting sand when protective trees were removed. For awhile, the roof of the town's tallest building, a three-story boarding house, stuck up from the sand until vandals burned it. The town is now completely buried under Lake Michigan sand.

2 ABANDONED GOLD MINES

These two mines, located northwest of Ishpeming, were worked in the 1880's and 1890's but closed after producing nearly $1 million in gold.

1. ROPES MINE
2. MICHIGAN MINE

4 WORKING MILLS

Four water-powered flour and grist mills still in use or with original machinery extant.

1. ATLAS MILL (Crossroads Village, Flint)
Built in 1836, this mill is the oldest surviving mill in Michigan. The entire mill, including the original shafting and gearing, was moved from Atlas to Historical Crossroads Village in 1975 and restored.

2. NEW TROY MILL (New Troy)
Though now powered by electricity, most of the 1867 gearing and belt system is intact in this still active mill.

3. FLEMING CREEK MILL (Ann Arbor)
The Washtenaw County Historical Society intends to fully restore this 1873 grist mill and once again grind flour there. Also located on the same site is a water-powered cider mill erected in 1887.

4. BELLEVUE MILL (Bellevue)
Built in 1852.

7 NATIONAL TRANSPORTATION FIRSTS THAT TOOK PLACE IN MICHIGAN

1. FIRST CONCRETE ROAD
Laid on Woodward Avenue between Six and Seven Mile Roads (Detroit) in 1909 at a cost of $13,537.

2. FIRST AIRPLANE TO EXCEED 200 M.P.H.
Was piloted by Lt. Lester James Maitland at a national airplane meet at Selfridge Field (Mount Clemens) October 14, 1922.

3. FIRST PASSENGER AIRLINE SERVICE
In 1926 Stout Air Services began operating between Grand Rapids and Detroit.

4. FIRST GLIDER TO LAND IN NORMANDY ON D-DAY
Was made by the Gibson Refrigerator Company (Greenville). Greenville's children purchased the glider for the U.S. Army by selling $72,000 worth of war bonds.

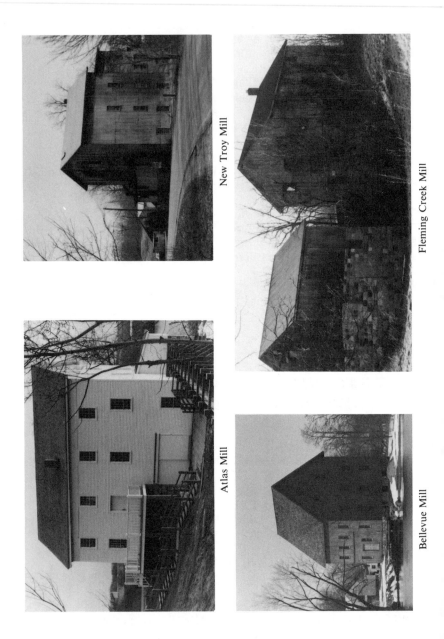

New Troy Mill

Fleming Creek Mill

Atlas Mill

Bellevue Mill

5. FIRST AIRPORT TO RECEIVE AN A1-A RATING
   The Pontiac Municipal Airport received the Department of Commerce's highest rating February 11, 1930.

6. FIRST ELECTRICAL UNDERWATER RAILWAY TUNNEL
   Port Huron to Sarnia opened in 1891.

7. FIRST STEEL RAILROAD TRACKS
   Were made in Ironwood, 1885.

FIRST 3 RAILROADS

1. ERIE & KALAMAZOO - 1837
   Michigan's first rail service ran thirty-five miles between Adrian and Toledo at a top speed of ten m.p.h. The railroad was also the first in the country to be built west of the Allegheny Mountains.

2. MICHIGAN SOUTHERN - 1843
   Monroe to Hillsdale.

3. MICHIGAN CENTRAL - 1846
   Detroit to Kalamazoo valley.

FIRST 3 MAJOR ROADS

1. In 1816 the state's first road was started leading from Detroit to Pontiac and Saginaw. This military road later became parts of Woodward Avenue, M-1, U.S. 10 and I-75.

2. In 1825 a military road was built to link Detroit and Chicago.

3. In 1827 a stagecoach-working road was completed through the Black Swamp to link Detroit and Ohio.

6 NATIONAL AUTO FIRSTS

1. FIRST AIR-CONDITIONED CAR - 1939
   Manufactured by the Packard Motor Car Company (Detroit).

2. FIRST AUTOMOBILE WITH LEFT-HANDED STEERING - 1907
   Manufactured by the Northern Motor Car Company (Detroit).

3. FIRST PLASTIC AUTOMOBILE - 1941
   Manufactured by the Ford Motor Company (Detroit).

4. FIRST MASS-PRODUCED AUTOMOBILE
   Oldsmobile, which from 1901 to 1903 had sold ten thousand—more than sold by all other manufacturers combined.

5. FIRST CLOSED CAR
   The 1922 Hudson's Essex was the first serious all-weather automobile.

6. FIRST CAR WITH TAILFINS
   1948 V-8 Cadillac.

3 NATIONAL AUTO FIRSTS THAT DIDN'T HAPPEN IN MICHIGAN

1. FIRST AUTOMOBILE PATENT
   George Baldwin Selden (Rochester, New York) filed patent #549,160 on May 8, 1879.

2. FIRST AUTOMOBILE COMPANY
   The Duryea Motor Wagon Company (Springfield, Massachusetts) incorporated September 21, 1895, six years before the Olds Motor Works incorporated in Detroit.

3. FIRST AUTOMOBILE REGULARLY MADE FOR SALE
   The *Duryea* manufactured in Springfield, Massachusetts, in 1892.

3 MEMORABLE FIRST AUTOMOBILE TRIPS

1. FIRST LONG DISTANCE AUTO TRIP - 1901
   To prove that the automobile should be viewed as an important means of transportation, Roy Chapin, a young Oldsmobile engineer, drove from Detroit to New York in 7½ days at an average speed of fourteen miles per hour.

2. FIRST TRANSCONTINENTAL AUTO RACE - 1905
   Dwight B. Huss (Detroit) set the first transcontinental time record, leaving New York City in his Oldsmobile *Old Scout* on May 8 and arriving in Portland, Oregon, on June 21.

3. FIRST TRIP USING INTERCHANGEABLE PARTS - 1908

At a racetrack near London, Detroit Cadillac mechanics stripped three new cars down to the last piston ring, shuffled the parts, reassembled them with only wrenches, screwdrivers, hammers and pliers, then ran the cars five hundred miles around the track without a breakdown.

11 NATIONAL SPORTS AND ENTERTAINMENT FIRSTS THAT HAPPENED IN MICHIGAN

1. FIRST RADIO ORCHESTRA (Detroit) - May 28, 1922

2. FIRST BLACK-OWNED TELEVISION STATION
WGDR-TV, Channel 62 (Detroit), went on the air July, 1975.

3. FIRST STATE FAIR
The Michigan State Fair was established in 1849.

4. FIRST SALARIED GAME AND FISH WARDEN
William Alden Smith (Grand Rapids) was hired on March 15, 1887, at an annual salary of $1,200.

5. FIRST REGULARLY SCHEDULED NIGHT BASEBALL GAME
Grand Rapids and Zanesville of the Central League played under the lights at Grand Rapids July 8, 1909. Grand Rapids won 11-10.

6. FIRST ROSE BOWL WINNER
The University of Michigan beat Stanford, 49-0, in 1902.

7. FIRST COLLEGE TEAM TO PLAY ENTIRE SEASON ON ARTIFICIAL TURF
Michigan State, whose home stadium had artificial turf as did the stadiums of the four opponents they played on the road in 1970.

8. FIRST SKI CLUB
Marquette, 1863.

9. FIRST CURLING CLUB
The Orchard Lake Curling Club organized in 1831-32.

10. FIRST PINBALL MACHINE
Manufactured in Detroit, 1910.

11. FIRST NATIONAL BILLIARD CHAMPIONSHIPS
Held at Fireman's Hall (Detroit) April 12, 1858.

2 INTERNATIONAL ENTERTAINMENT FIRSTS THAT TOOK PLACE IN MICHIGAN

1. FIRST INTERNATIONAL BILLIARD CHAMPIONSHIP
Played in Detroit April 12, 1859, between John Seereiter (Detroit) and Mike Phelan (New York City) with Phelan winning the $15,000 purse.

2. FIRST INTERNATIONAL DART MATCH
Played by phone in 1979 between members of the Wolverine Dart Association (Detroit) and the Manchester (England) Beech Hall Social Club.

9 NATIONAL BUSINESS FIRSTS THAT OCCURRED IN MICHIGAN

1. FIRST PHONE NUMBERS
Detroit phone customers of 1879 were the first in the nation to be assigned numbers.

2. FIRST PEDESTRIAN MALL
The first community in the country to close off city streets and turn them into a permanent pedestrian mall was downtown Kalamazoo in 1959.

3. FIRST COMMERCIAL HYDROELECTRIC POWER PLANT
Organized in Detroit March 2, 1880.

4. FIRST DENTAL DRILL
Was patented by G. F. Green (Kalamazoo) January 26, 1875.

5. FIRST STEEL INGOTS BY BESSEMER PROCESS
Made in 1864 by Eber Brock Ward (Wyandotte).

6. FIRST CORPORATION TO EARN $1 BILLION A YEAR
General Motors, 1955

7. FIRST AUTO DEALERSHIP
Bill Metzger, co-founder of the Cadillac Motor Car Company (Detroit), opened a dealership on Woodward Avenue in 1898. He sold his first car, a Waverly Electric, a year later to a wealthy Detroit furrier.

8. FIRST PRODUCTION OF MORE THAN ONE MILLION PASSENGER CARS OF ONE MAKE IN ONE YEAR
Chevrolet, 1949 (Detroit).

Kalamazoo pedestrian mall.

9. FIRST NEWSPAPER PRINTED ON A TRAIN

Thomas Edison printed a seven-by-eight-inch, one-page paper called the *Weekly Herald* and distributed it on a train run between Port Huron and Detroit. The first known issue is dated February 3, 1862.

8 NATIONAL EDUCATION FIRSTS
THAT HAPPENED IN MICHIGAN

1. FIRST STATE-SPONSORED UNIVERSITY

University of Michigan, established in Detroit in 1817 and moved to Ann Arbor in 1841.

2. FIRST COLLEGE TO ELIMINATE GRADES

In 1934 Olivet College dispensed with the normal system of grades, credits and hours.

3. FIRST UNIVERSITY SUPPORTED BY A DIRECT PROPERTY TAX

University of Michigan, March 15, 1867.

4. FIRST HONORS COURSE

Offered by the University of Michigan in 1882.

5. FIRST UNIVERSITY HOSPITAL

Opened at the University of Michigan, 1869.

6. FIRST PUBLIC SCHOOL CLASS FOR EPILEPTIC CHILDREN

Detroit, 1935.

7. FIRST ORGANIZED SCHOOL SAFETY PATROLS

1931.

8. FIRST STATE-SUPPORTED AGRICULTURAL COLLEGE

Michigan Agricultural College (later named Michigan State University), 1857.

4 NATIONAL LAW AND ORDER FIRSTS
THAT TOOK PLACE IN MICHIGAN

1. FIRST STATE TO ABOLISH THE DEATH PENALTY

The Michigan legislature abolished the state's death penalty in 1846.

2. FIRST FIREWORKS LEGISLATION

March 29, 1929.

3. FIRST LICENSED POLICE RADIO NETWORK

In 1929 the Michigan State Police installed the first licensed police radio network in the nation and the world. Six years earlier, Detroit police utilized an unlicensed, experimental station, KOP.

4. FIRST HIGHWAY CENTERLINE

In 1911, after noticing an accidental streak of paint down the center of a road, Wayne County Road Commissioner Edward Hines ordered a four-inch white stripe painted down the center of a narrow bridge on Seven Mile Road (Detroit) as a guide for motorists.

33 STATE FIRSTS

1. AIRMAIL SERVICE - 1920

2. AUTOMOBILE COMPANY
The Olds Motor Works (Detroit) incorporated in 1901.

3. BANK
Bank of Detroit, 1806.

4. BOOK PRINTED
Printed in 1809 by Father Gabriel Richard (Detroit).

5. CITY
Detroit, 1802.

6. COLLEGE
University of Michigan, 1817.

7. COMMERCIAL RADIO BROADCAST
WWJ (Detroit), 1920.

8. COMMERCIAL TELEVISION BROADCAST
WWJ-TV (Detroit), 1947.

9. COMMUNITY TO FLUORIDATE ITS WATER
Grand Rapids, January 25, 1945.

10. COMPULSORY ELEMENTARY EDUCATION - 1871

11. EIGHTEEN-YEAR-OLD TO SIGN A CONTRACT
Donald Beadow (Detroit) signed a contract with an entertainment agency at the stroke of midnight when the new Age of Majority law took effect January 1, 1972.

12. ELECTRIC TROLLEYS
   Port Huron, 1886.

13. INTERRACIAL RIOT - 1943

14. LIGHTHOUSE
   The Presque Isle lighthouse, built in 1870, was the first lighthouse on any of the Great Lakes.

15. LOTTERY
   First ticket sold November 13, 1972.

16. MOVIE HOUSE
   Casino Theatre (Detroit), 1905.

17. NEWSPAPER
   Michigan Essay, 1809.

18. PRIMARY ELECTION - 1910

19. POET
   Arent Schuyler de Peyster, commander of the British garrison at Michilimackinac, 1774-1779.

20. PROFESSIONAL BASKETBALL GAME - 1957

21. RAIL SERVICE
   Erie and Kalamazoo Railroad between Toledo and Adrian, 1836.

22. ROADSIDE PICNIC TABLE
   Located on Grand River Avenue just outside of Saranac (Ionia County).

23. SALES TAX - 1933

24. SECRET BALLOT - 1891

25. SKYJACKING - January 22, 1971
   A man holding a hatchet and claiming to have a bomb in a briefcase hijacked a Boeing 727 carrying forty-five passengers in Michigan skies and forced it to land at Detroit Metropolitan Airport before flying to Cuba.

26. SOFT DRINK
   Vernors, concocted by Detroit pharmacist James Vernor in 1861 and sold regularly from 1886.

27. STATE INCOME TAX - 1967

Still surrounded by the original walls, Michigan's first prison is now used as a National Guard Armory.

28. STATE PARK
   Mackinac Island, 1895.

29. STATE PRISON
   Michigan State Prison (Jackson).

30. STEAMBOAT VISIT
   Walk-In-The-Water came to Detroit in 1820.

31. SYMPHONY CONCERT
   Detroit Symphony Orchestra, 1914.

32. TELEGRAPH COMMUNICATIONS - 1847

33. UNION
   Detroit Mechanics Society, 1818.

15 MICHIGAN WOMEN · FIRST IN THE STATE

1. FIRST CERTIFIED FEMALE MASTER AUTO MECHANIC
   Janis Syrovy (Ann Arbor), 1977.

2. FIRST WOMEN TO VOTE
   Miss Mary Wilson (Battle Creek) and Mrs. Nanette B. Gardner (Detroit) somehow managed to vote in the 1871 election.

3. FIRST FEMALE UNIVERSITY OF MICHIGAN STUDENT
   Madelon Stockwell (Kalamazoo) in 1870. The University of Michigan was the first major university in the nation to admit women.

4. FIRST FEMALE BUILDING INSPECTOR
   Alicia Worthly (Troy), 1974.

5. FIRST MICHIGAN WOMAN TO JOIN THE COASTGUARD
   Donna Jean Godfrey (Redford Township), March, 1974.

6. FIRST LICENSED FEMALE PILOT
   Mary Elizabeth Von Mach (Detroit), 1927.

7. FIRST FEMALE TOLL COLLECTOR AT THE MACKINAC BRIDGE
   Mary Otto, 1975.

8. FIRST WOMAN SETTLER
Marie Therese Guyon de Cadillac, 1701.

9. FIRST POLICEWOMAN
Daisey Godfrey (Detroit), 1849.

10. FIRST LICENSED WOMAN DRIVER
Marie Comstock (Detroit), 1900.

11. FIRST FEMALE AUTO SALESPERSON
Lillian Reynolds Wagner (Detroit), 1915.

12. FIRST FEMALE LEGISLATOR
Eva M. Hamilton (Grand Rapids) elected to the state Senate in 1921.

13. FIRST WOMAN LT. GOVERNOR
Matilda Dodge Wilson (Rochester), 1940.

14. FIRST WOMAN ON MICHIGAN TELEVISION
Fran Harris (Detroit), 1946.

15. FIRST FEMALE CIVIL WAR SOLDIER
Sarah Emma Edmonds enlisted as Franklin Thompson and concealed her sex for two years while fighting with the 2nd Michigan Infantry in four major campaigns.

6 MICHIGAN WOMEN - FIRST IN THE NATION

1. FIRST FEMALE TRAFFIC HELICOPTER REPORTER
Jo Jo Shutty MacGregor (West Bloomfield), as the first female traffic helicopter reporter in the country, reported traffic conditions for CKLW radio (Detroit) from 1974 to 1977.

2. FIRST WOMAN TO PLAY IN THE UNITED STATES MARINE CORPS BAND
Sgt. Ruth Johnson (Saginaw), October, 1973.

3. FIRST FEMALE GENERAL IN THE U.S. MARINE CORPS
Gen. Margaret Brewer (Durand).

4. FIRST FEMALE BACTERIOLOGIST
Arylyle Noble (Orchard Lake) who joined Parke, Davis and Company in Detroit after graduating from Smith College in 1911.

5. FIRST FEMALE FEDERAL JUDGE
   Cornelia Kennedy (Detroit) nominated by President Nixon and appointed in 1970.

6. FIRST FEMALE CO-PILOT FOR A U.S. AIRLINE
   Barbara J. Barrett (Ypsilanti), 1972.

MICHIGAN IN 6 WARS

The number of Michigan men and women who have served in the last six wars.

1. CIVIL WAR (1861-1865) - 92,220
   Including the Fourth U.S. Cavalry from Michigan who, in 1865, surrounded the fleeing remnants of the Confederate Army and captured Jefferson Davis, president of the Confederacy.

2. SPANISH AMERICAN WAR (1898) - 7,500
   The role of Michigan regiments in this conflict was limited to building roads in Cuba as the soldiers were sent into the semi-tropical weather with wool winter uniforms and Civil War rifles.

3. WORLD WAR I (1917-1918) - 175,300
   Including the 399th Infantry Regiment who, after being stationed at Archangel on the Arctic Ocean for a year, adopted the name "polar bears."

4. WORLD WAR II (1941-1945) - 658,100

5. KOREAN CONFLICT (1950-1953) - 210,000
   The Michigan National Guard sent the first American unit into action in Korea.

6. VIETNAM (1964-1973) - 400,000

NUMBER OF MICHIGAN MEN AND WOMEN KILLED IN 6 WARS

1. CIVIL WAR - 14,350
   Only 4,200 died as a result of battles. The rest died from disease and illness.

2. SPANISH AMERICAN WAR - 701

Only three were killed in action; 698 died from dysentery, yellow fever, malaria and other illnesses.

3. WORLD WAR I - 5,000

4. WORLD WAR II - 10,265

5. KOREAN WAR - 2,500

6. VIETNAM WAR - 2,500

6

NATURE'S WAY

5 EARTHQUAKES

Michigan, generally, is protected from earthquakes by its location and the fact that, unlike California, Michigan rests on a solid rock base. Still, earthquakes, most too small to be noticed except on instruments, rumble through the state every fifteen to twenty years. Five of Michigan's largest quakes:

1. JULY 27, 1980 - 2:54 p.m.
   The upper tail of a quake centering in Kentucky rumbled through Michigan. The quake noticeably rocked cars in Allegan, Coldwater, Flint, Hastings and Mount Pleasant; dishes and windows were broken in Detroit; and, during the fifth inning of a baseball game, the top levels of Tiger Stadium began swaying noticeably.

2. MAY 2, 1976
   A tremor registering 3.75 on the Richter Scale shook ten southern Wayne County communities between Trenton and Rockwood.

3. AUGUST, 1947
   A fairly strong shock occurred in Branch County which felled some chimneys.

4. JULY 26, 1905 - 6:30 p.m.
   The pressure of an earthquake that moved through the vast network of underground mine caverns created an air blast which exploded through the Calumet-Lake Linden area smashing windows, toppling chimneys and causing telephone poles to sway violently.

5. DECEMBER 16, 1811
   One of the series of earthquakes known collectively as the "New Madrid Earthquake" reached out of the Mississippi Valley into Michigan. Indians who were camped near Orchard Lake reported that the waters bub-

bled and rolled causing great numbers of turtles to rise to the surface which the Indians collected and ate.

7 CITIES HIT BY METEORITES

1. ALLEGAN - 1889
   Accompanied by thunderous rumbling sounds, a seventy-pound meteorite crashed into the streets of Allegan on July 10 with such force that it buried itself 1½ feet in the ground.

2. ROSE CITY - 1921
   On the evening of October 17 at about 11:00 p.m., a bright meteor exploded in the skies over Rose City. A resident found a thirteen-pound fragment forty feet from his house the next day.

3. GRAND RAPIDS - 1883
   A contractor uncovered Michigan's first scientifically authenticated meteorite, a 114-pound specimen lying about three feet below the surface.

4. KALKASKA - 1947
   A farmer struck a meteorite while cultivating a field.

5. IRON RIVER — 1889
   While helping his father clear land, a six-year-old boy found a three-pound meteorite.

6. REED CITY - 1895
   A farmer found a 43-pound meteorite in his field.

7. SENECA - 1923
   A farmer uncovered a 25-pound meteorite while cultivating corn.

8 MICHIGAN WEATHER EXTREMES

1. HIGHEST TEMPERATURE (Mio) - July 13, 1936
   112°.

2. LOWEST TEMPERATURE (Vanderbilt) - February 9, 1934
   -51°.

3. GREATEST DAILY RAINFALL (Bloomingdale) - September 1, 1914
   9.78 inches.

4. GREATEST MONTHLY RAINFALL (Battle Creek) - June, 1883
   16.24 inches.

5. GREATEST ANNUAL RAINFALL (Adrian) - 1881
   64.01 inches.

6. GREATEST DAILY SNOWFALL (Ishpeming) - February 23, 1922
   29 inches.

7. GREATEST MONTHLY SNOWFALL (Calumet) - January, 1950
   115.3 inches.

8. GREATEST SEASONAL SNOWFALL (Tahquamenon Falls) - 1976-77
   332.8 inches.

4 MOST DEADLY TORNADOES

Four tornadoes that have killed the greatest number of Michigan people.

1. Michigan's worst tornado hit the Beecher area north of Flint June 8, 1953, killing 116, injuring nearly nine hundred and destroying or damaging more than five hundred homes and businesses.

2. On Palm Sunday (April 11), 1965, three tornado systems ripped through central and southern Michigan killing forty-nine and injuring 732. President Johnson declared ten Michigan counties disaster areas as nearly 2,500 buildings were destroyed or damaged for a total of nearly $51 million. The third worst tornado on record in the United States also moved through Indiana, Illinois and Ohio killing a total of 271, injuring three thousand and causing over $600 million in damage.

3. In 1897 Oakland County was struck by a tornado in which forty-seven died.

4. A twister struck Grand Rapids and Standale on April 3, 1956, leaving nineteen dead, 307 injured and causing $11 million in damage.

4 MEMORABLE WINTER STORMS

1. The worst blizzard in Michigan occurred January 26, 1978, when up to two feet of snow fell and was whipped by sixty-to seventy-five-mile-per-hour winds into ten-foot drifts. The storm killed twenty and left 400,000 stranded along Michigan's highways. Hundreds of schools closed including Michigan State University for only the third time in its 125-year history. Fif-

Michigan's deadliest tornado hit the Beecher area near Flint on June 8, 1953. Below: Flint's National Guard Armory served as a temporary morgue for many of the 116 killed. (Photos courtesy of The Flint Journal.)

Michigan's worst ice storm crippled much of the Lower Peninsula for days and left more than half a million residents without power for weeks.

ty out of Michigan's eighty-three counties declared snow emergencies and President Carter declared Michigan a national disaster area.

2. On January 27, 1967, twenty-two inches of snow fell which paralyzed most of lower Michigan for a week and caused twenty deaths. Several roofs of large buildings collapsed under the weight and almost every school in southern lower Michigan was closed. Passengers on several buses spent the night in their seats as they joined thousands of other motorists stranded on drift-filled highways.

3. The state record snowfall in a single snowstorm is 46.1 inches which fell on Calumet from January 15 to January 20, 1950.

4. The most damaging ice storm in Michigan history struck March, 1976, over the Lower Peninsula. Twenty-eight counties were designated as disaster areas and the storm caused an estimated $18 million in agricultural damage. Six hundred thousand residents were without power, some for as long as two weeks, as they waited for Consumers Power and Detroit Edison to replace more than four thousand miles of power lines.

5 DESTRUCTIVE FLOODS

1. The state record for maximum amount of rain to fall in a five-minute storm is 1.2 inches which occurred in Detroit on July 19, 1967. On that same date, five inches of rain fell in ninety minutes from a thunderstorm over Royal Oak. The losses from these brief storms totalled over $10 million from flooding caused by storm drainage system failures.

2. Twenty-one counties were declared disaster areas when several major rivers in southern lower Michigan covered roads, washed out crops and caused $60 million in damage late April, 1975. Residents of several cities were evacuated and the national guard, state police and Red Cross had to rescue hundreds trapped by the high water. Particularly hard hit was the Lansing area where the Red Cedar river crested at twelve feet and filled Lansing streets with bobbing furniture and cars submerged up to their roofs.

3. A rare tidal wave, reaching as high as seven feet, damaged boats and flooded basements along the Keeweenaw Bay shoreline on June 30, 1968. The wave was caused by an extremely strong low-pressure cell that moved very rapidly over the Bay from L'Anse.

4. On September 30 and October 1, 1981, a thick band of storms swept across lower Michigan from Grand Rapids to Detroit dropping as much as nine inches of water on some parts of the state. The storm wiped out more than $5 million in crops, drowned $1 million worth of cars at a Farmington Hills dealership, knocked out power to 100,000 residents and submerged

homes and businesses. One man died near Lansing when a fierce current of swirling water sucked him out of his stalled pickup.

5. Swollen by several torrential downpours, rivers throughout lower Michigan crested at record heights April 5-7, 1947, and flooded thousands of streets, homes and businesses. Several communities were virtually isolated because of flooded roads and the three main highways linking Detroit to Chicago were impassable. Overloaded drain systems in Detroit shot manhole covers into the air and gushed six-foot geysers.

4 COUNTIES IN THE GREAT LAKES STATE WITH NO WATER ACREAGE

1. GRATIOT
2. MACOMB
3. SANILAC
4. SHIAWASSEE

4 COUNTIES WITH THE MOST WATER

Based on total water area in acres.

1. CHEBOYGAN	46,720
2. CHIPPEWA	45,440
3. MACKINAC	42,880
4. ROSCOMMON	33,280

3 COUNTIES WITH THE MOST LAKES

1. MARQUETTE	835
2. LUCE	571
3. IRON	528

11 LARGEST LAKES

Measured in acres.

1. HOUGHTON (Roscommon County)	20,044
2. TORCH (Antrim County)	18,566
3. BURT (Cheboygan County)	18,114

4. CHARLEVOIX (Charlevoix County)	17,388
5. MULLET (Cheboygan County)	16,210
6. GOGEBIC (Ontonagon and Gogebic Counties)	13,029
7. PORTAGE (Houghton County)	11,726
8. CRYSTAL (Benzie County)	10,423
9. MANISTIQUE (Luce and Mackinac Counties)	10,298
10. BLACK (Cheboygan and Presque Isle Counties)	10,047
11. HIGGINS (Roscommon County)	10,022

3 LONGEST RIVERS

1. GRAND	300 miles
2. MANISTEE	200 miles
3. MENOMINEE	180 miles

3 NOTABLE RIVERS

1. AU SABLE
   Swiftest moving Michigan river drops 609 feet.

2. DETROIT
   Widest Michigan river at 2,200 feet and also handles more boat traffic than any other river in the world.

3. SAGINAW RIVER
   Michigan's shortest river at twenty miles.

8 PICTURESQUE WATERFALLS

There are at least one hundred fifty named waterfalls in Michigan as well as several unnamed ones. Eight of the most scenic:

1. OCQUEOC FALLS (Onaway)
   The only waterfalls on public property in the Lower Peninsula.

2. CHAPEL FALLS (Melstrand)

3. MUNISING FALLS (Munising)

4. SLATE RIVER FALLS (L'Anse)

5. AGATE FALLS (Agate)

133

Munising Falls

Ocqueoc Falls

6. BOND FALLS (Paulding)

7. GORGE FALLS (Bessemer)

8. TAHQUAMENON (Paradise)

6 NATURAL WONDERS

1. SLEEPING BEAR DUNES (Glen Haven)
   A 57,000-acre, desert-like expanse of sand, the Dunes, with a five-hundred-foot crest, is the largest hill of live shifting sand in the United States.

2. HARTWICK PINES (Crawford County)
   Within its 8,200 acres are eighty-five acres of virgin white pine, one of the last remaining stands of the magnificent timber that once covered Michigan.

3. MACKINAC ISLAND
   Now a two-thousand-acre state park, the island was worshipped as a shrine by the Indians because of its entrancing beauty, towering heights, magnificent rock formations and sweeping vistas.

4. PICTURED ROCKS (Munising)
   Twenty miles of multi-colored, weather-carved, high-rise stone cliffs along the south shore of Lake Superior is the legendary home of Hiawatha.

5. TAHQUAMENON FALLS (Paradise)
   The largest falls east of the Missisippi River, with the exception of Niagara Falls.

6. LAKE OF THE CLOUDS (Porcupine Mountains)

3 MOUNTAIN RANGES

1. PORCUPINE (Ontonagon County)
2. KEEWEENAW (Houghton and Keeweenaw Counties)
3. HURON (Marquette County)

4 INTERESTING GEOGRAPHIC POINTS

1. HIGHEST POINT IN UPPER PENINSULA
   Mt. Curwood, 1,980 feet above sea level.

2. HIGHEST POINT IN LOWER PENINSULA
   Near Cadillac, 1,712 feet above sea level.

3. LOWEST POINT IN MICHIGAN
   Lake Erie, 572 feet above sea level.

4. GEOGRAPHIC CENTER
   Wexford, five miles NNW of Cadillac.

3 TOWNS THAT LIE ON THE 45TH PARALLEL

Exactly halfway between the equator and north pole.
1. ATLANTA (Montmorency County)
2. SPRATT (Alpena County)
3. HETHERTON (Otsego County)

4 SMALLEST COUNTIES

Based on land area in square miles.

1. BENZIE	316
2. LEELANAU	345
3. CHARLEVOIX	414
4. BAY	447

4 LARGEST COUNTIES

Based on land area in square miles.

1. MARQUETTE	1,828
2. CHIPPEWA	1,580
3. ONTONAGON	1,316
4. SCHOOLCRAFT	1,181

10 NATURAL LANDMARKS

The U.S. Department of Interior has designated ten Michigan outdoor sites as "natural landmarks," preserving these areas as illustrations of the nation's environmental history.

1. GRAND MERE LAKES (Berrien County)
2. WARREN WOODS (Berrien County)
3. STANGMOOR BOG (Schoolcraft County)
4. NORTHERN HARDWOODS NATURAL AREA (Marquette)
5. DEAD STREAM SWAMP (Roscommon and Missaukee Counties)
6. TOBICO MARSH (Bay City)
7. BEECH-MAPLE WOODLOT (Michigan State University)
8. NEWTON WOODS (Cass County)
9. HAVEN HILL NATURAL AREA (Oakland County)
10. BLACK SPRUCE BOG (Jackson)

6 STATE SYMBOLS

1. STONE
   Petoskey - adopted in 1965.

2. GEM
   Isle Royale Greenstone.

3. FISH
   Trout - adopted in 1965.

4. BIRD
   Robin Redbreast - adopted in 1931.

5. FLOWER
   Apple Blossom - adopted in 1897.

6. TREE
   White Pine - adopted in 1955.

5 CHAMPION TREES

Michigan is the leader in national champion trees with ninety-four located throughout the state. A champion tree of each species is based on the total mass of the tree as measured by circumference, height and crown spread. Five of Michigan's tallest national champions:

1. AMERICAN BEECH (Three Oaks) - 161 feet
2. BLACK CHERRY (Washtenaw County) - 132 feet
3. THORNLESS HONEYLOCUST (Washtenaw County) - 130 feet
4. BALSAM POPLAR (Champion) - 128 feet
5. RED MAPLE (Armada) - 125 feet

4 SPECIAL CHRISTMAS TREES

1. A 19½-foot concolor fir from Mayville was used as President and Mrs. Gerald Ford's 1974 Christmas tree in the White House "Blue Room," the first time ever a Michigan Christmas tree was inside the White House. Edward Cole (Mayville), who had won the Grand National Championship for Christmas tree growers, selected the tree.

2. In 1971 Disney World used a seventy-foot-tall, 22-foot-diameter blue spruce from Paradise in a gigantic, five-ton, $15,000 Christmas display at their Orlando Park.

3. A 65-year-old, 52-foot white spruce from the Hiawatha National Forest was used as the 1981 White House Capitol Rotunda Christmas tree. The tree, with thirty-foot branch spread, was decorated with 2,500 lights, five thousand hollow plastic ornaments and six hundred stained glass discs. The tree twinkled from the Capitol end of the national mall from December 16 until January 2 when it was ground into mulch for Capitol lawns and gardens.

4. A 41-foot-tall balsam fir from the Ottawa National Forest stood on Capitol Hill as the 1975 national Christmas tree.

5 UNIQUE TREES

1. MOON TREE
On April 22, 1976, Governor William G. Milliken planted an unusual two-foot sycamore seedling on the state Capitol grounds. The tree was grown from a seed carried to the moon by Apollo 14 astronauts.

2. MILLWHEEL TREE (Owosso)
About 150 years ago someone leaned an old millwheel against a nearby tree and forgot about it. The tree grew and took the wheel in, covering about one-fourth of the rim with its trunk.

3. SLEEPER NATURAL GRAFT TREE (Caseville)
A falling white-pine branch split and lodged itself in the fork of a red pine. A natural graft resulted and the large red pine now has a large white

Above: Millwheel tree

Below: Sleeper Natural Graft. White pine branch (dark) naturally grafted itself and grew from a red pine trunk (light). (Photo courtesy of Jan Dufty.)

pine branch.

4. MONARCH
The giant, three-hundred-year-old white pine stands in the Hartwick Pines State Park (Crawford County) as a magnificent example of the virgin timber that once covered Michigan. The tree, 155 feet high and 4½ feet in circumference, could provide all the lumber needed to build a five-room house.

5. PRESIDENT'S TREE
On January 14, 1977, President Gerald R. Ford planted a six-foot easter white pine from the Proud Lake Recreation Area (Oakland County) on the White House grounds.

5 MOST COMMON TREES

UPPER PENINSULA	LOWER PENINSULA
1. MAPLE	1. MAPLE
2. BIRCH	2. BEECH
3. HEMLOCK	3. BIRCH
4. ASPEN	4. ASPEN
5. SPRUCE	5. PINE

6 POISONOUS PLANTS

Our absent-minded habit of chewing on a stem of grass or twig as we stroll through Michigan's woods could be fatal if one of the following plants is chosen:

1. BUTTERCUP
All parts of the plant are poisonous.

2. ACORNS
Eating many can gradually poison the kidneys.

3. CHERRIES
Twigs and foliage are poisonous.

4. JIMSON WEED
The juice of the prickly, fleshy fruit can kill.

5. NIGHTSHADE
Berries, especially unripe, are poisonous.

6. ELDERBERRIES
All parts of the plant are toxic.

9 MONSTER VEGETABLE RECORDS

The Michigan Department of Natural Resource's *Michigan Natural Resources* magazine has, for the past four years, sponsored a Monster Vegetable contest to see who can grow the largest vegetables in Michigan each season. Monster records for nine selected vegetables as of 1981:

1. BEET	5 pounds, 12 ounces
2. CABBAGE	18 pounds
3. CARROT	3 pounds, 8 ounces
4. CELERY	10 pounds, 12 ounces
5. POTATO	4 pounds, 2½ ounces
6. PUMPKIN	224 pounds, 8 ounces
7. RADISH	8 pounds, 14 ounces
8. TOMATO	2 pounds, 12 ounces
9. ZUCCHINI	20 pounds

6 FRUIT TREE POPULATIONS

Numbers of fruit trees in Michigan as of 1978.

1. GRAPES	7,900
2. CHERRIES	3,680
3. APPLES	3,100
4. PEACHES	1,200
5. PEARS	710
6. PRUNES AND PLUMS	700

4 LIVESTOCK POPULATIONS

As of 1978.

1. CHICKENS	6,350,000
2. COWS	1,250,000
3. PIGS	810,000
4. SHEEP	121,000

3 COUNTIES WITH THE MOST CATTLE AND CALVES

As of January 1, 1978.

1. SANILAC   82,000
2. HURON   72,000
3. ALLEGAN   49,000

3 COUNTIES WITH THE MOST CHICKENS

Hens and pullets of laying age as of December 1, 1977.

1. OTTAWA   1,107,000
2. HURON   855,000
3. ALLEGAN   411,000

3 COUNTIES WITH THE MOST SHEEP AND LAMBS

As of January 1, 1978.

1. WASHTENAW   30,500
2. JACKSON   8,000
3. LENAWEE   7,200

5 COUNTIES WITH THE MOST PIGS

As of January 1, 1980.

1. CASS   150,000
2. OTTAWA   55,000
3. LENAWEE   49,000
4. BRANCH   44,100
5. ST. JOSEPH   44,000

13 ANIMAL JAYWALKERS

In Ionia County during 1971, the following animals were killed on their 114 miles of highways. Ionia is the only county that has ever compiled such statistics.

1. RACCOONS	445
2. SQUIRRELS	163
3. TURTLES	140
4. OPOSSUMS	137
5. SKUNKS	82
6. DEER	77
7. CATS	67
8. DOGS	66
9. WOODCHUCKS	57
10. MUSKRATS	49
11. RABBITS	45
12. FOXES	22
13. PHEASANTS	16

6 COUNTIES WITH NO VETERINARIANS

As of 1978.
1. KEEWEENAW
2. LAKE
3. LEELANAU
4. MISSAUKEE
5. ONTONAGON
6. OSCODA

8 ENDANGERED SPECIES

Eight species of wildlife in grave danger of becoming extinct or threatening to become extinct and whose habitat is in Michigan.

1. EASTERN TIMBER WOLF
2. PINE MARTEN
3. ARCTIC PEREGRINE FALCON
4. KIRTLAND'S WARBLER
5. COOPER'S HAWK
6. SOUTHERN BALD EAGLE
7. BARN OWL
8. LAKE STURGEON

3 WHALES

The fossilized remains of whales have been discovered in three separate areas of Michigan. Geologists speculate that the large mammals swam up the Mississippi River 8,000 to 10,000 years ago, entered the Great Lakes and Grand River, and became stranded in shallow water.

The fossils were found near:

1. FLINT
2. OSCODA
3. TECUMSEH

3 ALBINO ANIMALS

1. In June, 1974, nine-year-old Gail Cornish (Warren) found an albino toad in her backyard. A few days later four-year-old Joey Strain found another albino toad a few blocks from the first. Both toads had bulging pink eyes and skin so transparent their organs were visible.

2. In May, 1980, a pure white donkey was born on the Bruce Thorington farm (Holly). The extremely rare donkey was not classified as a true albino because it had blue instead of pink eyes.

3. *The Flint Journal* featured a photograph of an albino squirrel in its April 30, 1975, edition.

4 UNIQUE PETS

1. In December, 1980, several city and county officials asked a Bay City couple to get rid of their nine-month-old, 150-pound pet lion after a Consumers Power employee encountered the sleeping animal in the meter room. The couple also owned a boa constrictor and two monkeys.

2. Dan Miller and John Nemeth (Alma) own the largest private reptile collection in Michigan, housing more than seventy snakes in the basement of their tropical fish business.

3. In July, 1973, fourteen-year-old Alfred Wheatley (Flint) found a five-legged frog in his backyard. The unusual reptile had two front legs and three in back.

4. A Sawyer Air Force Base (Marquette) airman was bitten by his pet cobra when he reached into its cage in March, 1980. While on a flight to Milwaukee where the nearest anti-venom serum was stored, the man stopped breathing and became paralyzed but lived.

2 EXTRAORDINARY DOG LOVERS

1. PEARL KEELEY (Lansing) - January, 1982
The 69-year-old, who shared her dwelling with ninety-two dogs, was evicted when her landlord claimed she owed four years back rent.

2. DELORES FISHER (Flint) - June, 1978
By Flint City Council directive, a wrecking crew demolished the woman's house that had held more than forty dogs. The woman had moved to California and the Council claimed the abandoned house was a health hazard.

4 SPECIAL DOGS

1. ASHLEY (Detroit) - August, 1980
When Mt. St. Helens (Washington) erupted in a volcanic explosion May 18, 1980, the Associated Press transmitted the photo of a pathetic-looking cockapoo who had nearly been smothered by the volcano's ashes and had undergone a hysterectomy.

Dorothy and Bill Walenczak, who were the first of hundreds to respond, adopted the dog.

2. ZEKE THE WONDER DOG (Lansing)
In July, 1978, the Michigan Legislature approved a resolution honoring the frisbee-catching dog who had entertained fans across the country during halftimes at Michigan State University football games. The resolution was attached to a frisbee and tossed to Zeke.

3. MIKE (Sawyer)
According to Michigan State University veterinarians, the part-English terrier, part-mutt, who lived to be twenty-six, was Michigan's longest-living dog.

4. BONAMIE BONAPARTE (Byron)
The twelve-year-old poodle, owned by Rebecca Jo Hartley, is a pool hustler. The dog, who has been featured on several television shows, takes a cue ball between its front paws and knocks the colored balls into pockets by firing the cue ball between its hind legs.

1,688 ITEMS CAUGHT BY "MR. BUTLER"

Dr. G. W. Bradt, who managed the Rose Lake Wildlife Experiment Station (East Lansing) in the late 1940's, recorded the following items brought home over a period of eighteen months by his house cat, Mr. Butler.

1.	MEADOW MICE	1,200
2.	HOUSE, DEER, AND JUMPING MICE	400
3.	ENGLISH SPARROWS	554
4.	SHREWS	15
5.	BARN RATS	6
6.	MEADOWLARKS	4
7.	RABBITS	4
8.	THIRTEEN-LINED SPERMOPHILES	3
9.	FLICKER	1
10.	ROBIN	1

THE FACTS OF LIFE

10 CREATIVE "I DO'S"

. CATHY BURK and JOHN (CHICO) MARTINEZ - June 25, 1979

During a ninety-second, 3,500-foot free fall over Ann Arbor's Tecumseh Airport, the bride, who wore a wedding dress under her jump-uit, married her former skydiving instructor. Seventeen friends fell in a diamond formation after the skydiving minister performed the quick ceremony.

. BERTIL HJALMER CLASON (Detroit) and SIGRID SOPHIA MARGARET CARLSON (Stockholm, Sweden) - December 2, 1933

Judge John Watts (Detroit) married the couple in America's first transatlantic telephone wedding ceremony.

. PAM WITHERELL and HOWARD MALCOLM, JR. - August 27, 980

The couple skated to the center of the Lowell American Legion roller ink and pronounced their vows during a ceremony described by the minister as, "not spectacle but worship." Then, as rays of light bounced rom a colored, mirrored ball, the couple skated their first lap as husband nd wife.

. PENNY AMOS and ROBERT COOLEY - June 15, 1968

The two members of a Detroit diving club gurgled their vows at the bottom of Higgins Lake in Michigan's first underwater wedding.

. VERNA COGER and JERRY ROOT; ANNA MATER and LAURENCE PLATO - September 7, 1976

Miss Coger and Mr. Root couldn't decide whether to marry in her Upper Peninsula town of Newberry or his Lower Peninsula city of Battle Creek, so they compromised and got married in the middle of the Mackinac Bridge while 26,000 crossed during the annual Labor Day walk.

Laurence Plato, the best man, liked the idea so much he asked Miss

Mater if she would like to marry him there also. She did and a double wedding took place.

6. TINA BROWN and BRIAN GRIESER - August 19, 1979
   As members of the Franzen Brothers Circus, the aerial ballerina and her assistant were married in a center ring animal cage at the Genesee County Fair. The couple squeezed the ceremony between their 5:15 p.m. elephant ride and 6:30 p.m. high wire act.

7. MARSHELLA A. GRIFFITH and DAVID PFEIFFER - June 22, 1980
   The lifelong trucker and his bride were married in a forty-foot moving van in Davison Township.

8. SHARON PALACIOS and JOHN HUGGETT - March 28, 1971
   The flying student and her instructor were married over Flint's Bishop Airport in a 1943, five-seat, stagger-wing airplane.

9. BRENDA REAGER and TOM MATLES - August 10, 1970
   Dressed in American flag costumes they designed themselves, the young couple were married at the Goose Lake Rock Festival (Jackson) while the rock group Tea Garden and Van Winkle performed for the audience of two hundred thousand.

10. RICHARD T. SMITH and KAREN SOMMERS (Lansing) - September 11, 1971
   The groom took his wife's last name because of the many problems he had experienced with his own extremely common name.

3 LOVING YEARS

Three years since 1940 with the largest increases in numbers of marriages.

1. 1945 to 1946	48,329 to 78,808	an increase of 30,409
2. 1964 to 1965	73,911 to 81,247	an increase of 7,336
3. 1967 to 1968	84,363 to 90,984	an increase of 6,621

Here Comes The Bride
7 STATES MICHIGAN BRIDES
MOST OFTEN COME FROM

In 1977 2,137 brides who resided in other states held their wedding ceremonies in Michigan. The seven states these brides most often came from were:

1.	OHIO	440
2.	INDIANA	336
3.	WISCONSIN	282
4.	ILLINOIS	192
5.	CALIFORNIA	126
6.	FLORIDA	93
7.	MINNESOTA	62

Where You Lead, I Will Follow
8 STATES MICHIGAN GROOMS MOST OFTEN COME FROM

In 1977 4,478 non-resident men arrived in Michigan to be married. The eight states these bridegrooms most often came from were:

1.	OHIO	685
2.	INDIANA	483
3.	WISCONSIN	408
4.	ILLINOIS	398
5.	CALIFORNIA	278
6.	FLORIDA	217
7.	NEW YORK	172
8.	TEXAS	132

Why In Hell Not?
3 REASONS FOR GETTING MARRIED IN HELL

Hell, Michigan, located fifty miles west of Detroit, is a popular place to visit especially in late fall when it freezes over. Some couples also get married there.

. One couple, each twice divorced, said they had been through hell twice already and might as well start there for the third.

. A young woman drove her Detroit fiance to the Hell Justice of the Peace on a bitter four-degree-below-zero day after the man had claimed it would be a cold day in hell before he married her.

. A Nebraska couple arrived in Hell on April 1. The woman then compelled her prospective husband to make good on his promise to marry her on April Fool's Day in hell.

2 MOST WEDDED CITIES

The two cities with the highest percentage of married persons, fourteen years and older, in the total population, as per the 1970 census.

1. STERLING HEIGHTS
   76.6% of all males and 75.9% of all females are married.

2. TAYLOR
   73.9% of all males and 72.7% of all females are married.

3 "I DON'TS"

Three years since 1940 with the largest increases in the number of divorces.

1. 1945 to 1946	21,133 to 29,158	an increase of 8,025
2. 1971 to 1972	31,790 to 35,505	an increase of 3,715
3. 1968 to 1969	25,400 to 28,347	an increase of 2,947

9 GROUNDS FOR DIVORCE

Since the passage of Michigan's "no fault" divorce law, January 1, 1972, couples no longer need claim legal grounds to obtain a divorce. Prior to that law, however, a spouse had to claim one of several available legal grounds in order for the court to grant a divorce. For example, 23,375 divorces were granted in 1967 for the following causes:

1. CRUELTY	22,486
2. DESERTION	472
3. FRAUD	169
4. NON-SUPORT	146
4. BIGAMY	25
6. DRUNKENNESS	17
7. ADULTERY	16
8. CONVICTION OF A CRIME	13
9. ALL OTHER REASONS	31

5 MOST PREGNANT YEARS

Five years since 1940 with the most recorded live births.

1. 1957	211,642
2. 1956	206,068
3. 1958	202,690
4. 1959	198,301
5. 1955	196,294

4 CHILDLESS YEARS

Four years since 1940 with the fewest recorded live births.

1. 1940	99,106
2. 1941	107,498
3. 1945	111,557
4. 1944	113,586

5 UNIQUE BIRTHS

1. On July 31, 1979, a Benton Harbor woman gave birth to a five-pound, six-ounce girl that had developed in the body cavity where her intestines are located instead of in her womb. According to physicians, chances of such a birth are too rare to estimate scientifically since most such babies die within three months of conception.

2. On Tuesday, February 20, 1978, Mrs. Marietta Barbour (Lansing) completed the first half of a two-day state bar examination which she had to pass in order to practice law. At six a.m. Wednesday the *magna cum laude* graduate of Cooley Law School gave birth, six weeks prematurely, to twin girls and missed the second day of the exam she had spent two months cramming for.

3. On November 28, 1979, twin sisters from Clio gave birth six hours apart at two different hospitals. Each had a daughter.

4. Pamela Rose (Flint Township) gave birth to a thirteen-pound, one-half-ounce boy at Flint's Hurley Hospital February 2, 1979.

5. Mrs. Joseph Demenuir (Detroit) gave birth to her twentieth child August 27, 1968. The baby, a girl, evened the family at ten boys and ten girls, the oldest being twenty-six.

2 SIGNIFICANT SURROGATE BIRTHS

1. A young Detroit couple who couldn't have a child of their own artificially

inseminated a female friend with the husband's sperm and, fourteen months after the surrogate mother gave birth, legally adopted the child. The childless couple and the surrogate mother had to perform the insemination themselves because no doctor would handle the case. The surrogate lived with the adoptive parents from the time she became pregnant until the March 29, 1979, adoption, the nation's first of a child born to a surrogate mother.

2. In a test case, a Detroit judge refused to determine the legal parentage of a 5½-pound baby girl born November 22, 1981, to a twenty-year-old woman who had acted as a surrogate for a childless Dearborn Heights couple. As a result, the child's birth certificate listed the surrogate as the mother, listed no father but recorded the baby's last name as that of the biological father. The judge refused to name the biological father as the legal father saying it was up to the legislature to decide the fate of surrogate motherhood in Michigan.

5 REMARKABLE MULTIPLE BIRTHS

1. Mrs. Tom Bogus (Grand Rapids) gave birth to triplets, three boys, on her husband's birthday, December 12, 1981. Doctors said that conception of triplets without the use of fertility drugs has 9,000 to 1 odds and having them on the father's birthday would happen once in only 3,285,000 deliveries.

2. On December 9, 1977, Eliza and Cornelius Jackson (Flint) became parents of their third set of twins. Each set had alternated with a single child.

3. Pamela Pulter (Dearborn) gave birth to quadruplets, three girls and a boy, on November 25, 1968.

4. Margaret Guinnane (Highland Park) gave birth to quadruplets, all boys, on October 22, 1960.

5. Sharon Drozdowicz (Monroe) gave birth to quadruplets, two boys and two girls, April, 1978.

Young Moms
5 MOST PUBESCENT BIRTH YEARS

The five years since 1925 with the most births by girls ages ten to fourteen.

1. 1973		569
2. 1972		503
3. 1974		501

4. 1970	489
5. 1971	472

4 YEARS IN WHICH "MATURE" MOTHERS HAD THE MOST CHILDREN

The four years since 1925 when mothers ages forty-five to forty-nine had the most children.

1. 1925	379
2. 1927	332
3. 1928	315
4. 1931	302

4 YEARS IN WHICH "MATURE" MOTHERS HAD THE FEWEST CHILDREN

The four years since 1925 when mothers ages forty-five to forty-nine had the fewest children.

1. 1976	47
2. 1974	50
3. 1977	51
4. 1975	54

160 YEARS OF GROWTH

Michigan's population for selected years from 1820 to 1980.

1. 1820	9,000
2. 1840	212,000
3. 1860	749,000
4. 1880	1,637,000
5. 1900	2,421,000
6. 1920	3,668,000
7. 1940	5,256,000
8. 1960	7,823,000
9. 1980	9,258,000

5 MOST POPULOUS COUNTIES

Based on the official 1980 census.

1. WAYNE	2,337,240
2. OAKLAND	1,011,793
3. MACOMB	694,600
4. GENESEE	450,000
5. KENT	444,506

6 LEAST POPULOUS COUNTIES

Based on the official 1980 census.

1. KEEWEENAW	1,963
2. OSCODA	6,858
3. MONTMORENCY	7,492
4. LAKE	7,711
5. BARAGA	8,484
6. SCHOOLCRAFT	8,575

7 LARGEST CITIES

Based on the official 1980 census.

1. DETROIT	1,203,339
2. GRAND RAPIDS	181,843
3. WARREN	161,134
4. FLINT	159,611
5. LANSING	130,414
6. ANN ARBOR	107,316
7. LIVONIA	104,814

5 MOST ELDERLY COUNTIES

The five counties with the largest percentage of the population over sixty-five years of age.

1. LAKE	21.7%
2. ALCONA	19.0%
3. KEEWEENAW	18.3%
4. GOGEBIC	18.2%
5. ROSCOMMON	18.0%

7 MOST YOUTHFUL COUNTIES

The seven counties with the smallest percentage of the population over sixty-five years of age.

1. WASHTENAW		6.1%
2. ISABELLA		6.2%
3. MACOMB		6.2%
4. MIDLAND		6.6%
5. EATON		6.9%
6. LAPEER		6.9%
7. LIVINGSTON		6.9%

Elbow To Elbow
5 MOST DENSELY POPULATED COUNTIES

The five most densely populated counties measured by persons per square mile.

1. WAYNE	4,407
2. MACOMB	1,303
3. OAKLAND	1,047
4. GENESEE	692
5. KENT	480

Room To Move
5 LEAST DENSELY POPULATED COUNTIES

The five least densely populated counties measured by persons per square mile.

1. KEEWEENAW	4
2. SCHOOLCRAFT	7
3. LUCE	8
4. ONTONAGON	8
5. OSCODA	8

3 MOST RAPIDLY SHRINKING COUNTIES

Based on the percent population decline from 1970 to 1980.

1. KEEWEENAW	2,264 to	1,963	13.3% decrease
2. WAYNE	2,670,368 to	2,337,240	12.5% decrease
3. CHIPPEWA	32,412 to	29,029	10.4% decrease

155

5 COUNTIES WITH THE SMALLEST FAMILIES

Based on the average number of persons per household as reported in the official 1980 census.

1.	KEEWEENAW	2.34
2.	IRON	2.45
3.	ROSCOMMON	2.49
4.	GOGEBIC	2.52
5.	LAKE	2.53

5 MOST RAPIDLY SHRINKING CITIES AND VILLAGES

Based on the annual rate of population change from 1970 to 1980.

1.	COPPER CITY	Decreased 3.9% per year
2.	ECORSE	Decreased 2.8% per year
3.	RIVER ROUGE	Decreased 2.8% per year
4.	HIGHLAND PARK	Decreased 2.5% per year
5.	HARPER WOODS	Decreased 2.5% per year

On The Move
6 STATES WE MOST OFTEN MOVE TO

The six states Michiganians most often permanently moved to between 1965 and 1970.

1.	FLORIDA	65,642
2.	CALIFORNIA	60,484
3.	OHIO	43,743
4.	ILLINOIS	37,220
5.	INDIANA	26,215
6.	TEXAS	20,173

Not Welcome
260 WHO WERE ASKED TO LEAVE

Four days after Iran took fifty-two Americans hostage in November, 1979, President Carter ordered all Iranian citizens living in the United States to report to U.S. Immigration offices throughout the country. All Michigan colleges, universities and immigration offices conducted interviews. As a result, 260 Iranians were found to be here illegally and were given thirty days to leave for violating the terms of their visas.

5 COUNTRIES WITH THE MOST ALIENS PERMANENTLY RESIDING IN MICHIGAN

As reported in 1977 under the alien address program.

1.	CANADA	28,112
2.	UNITED KINGDOM	11,055
3.	GERMANY	7,300
4.	ITALY	6,835
5.	POLAND	6,340

5 LEADING SOURCES OF NEWCOMERS

Based on the number of people who permanently moved to Michigan from other states from 1960 to 1970.

1.	OHIO	58,350
2.	CALIFORNIA	50,127
3.	ILLINOIS	50,381
4.	INDIANA	36,433
5.	NEW YORK	23,761

5 FASTEST GROWING CITIES AND VILLAGES

Based on the annual rate of population change from 1970 to 1980.

1.	WIXOM	Increased 13.0% a year
2.	WOODHAVEN	Increased 12.5% a year
3.	TUSTIN	Increased 9.0% a year
4.	SOUTH LYON	Increased 8.1% a year
5.	AU GRES	Increased 8.1% a year

3 FASTEST GROWING COUNTIES

Based on the percent population increase from 1970 to 1980.

1.	KALKASKA	5,372 to	10,952	103.9% increase
2.	LIVINGSTON	58,967 to	100,289	70.1% increase
3.	ROSCOMMON	9,892 to	16,374	65.5% increase

8 COUNTIES WITH THE LARGEST FAMILIES

Based on the average number of persons per household as reported in the official 1980 census.

1. LAPEER	3.23
2. LIVINGSTON	3.15
3. CLINTON	3.14
4. MONROE	3.09
5. TUSCOLA	3.05
6. OTTAWA	3.04
7. SHIAWASSEE	3.03
8. MACOMB	3.00

Living Room
8 NUMBERS OF ROOMS IN MICHIGAN HOUSES

Number of Michigan homes having:

1. 5 ROOMS	785,664
2. 6 ROOMS	613,550
3. 4 ROOMS	425,856
4. 7 ROOMS	298,317
5. 8 OR MORE ROOMS	253,245
6. 3 ROOMS	189,383
7. 2 ROOMS	56,425
8. 1 ROOM	30,619

No Place Like Home
3 UNIQUE DWELLINGS

1. BEDFORD TOWNSHIP (Michigan) - TOLEDO (Ohio)

Wayne and Josephine Wilmoth own and live in a house which straddles the Ohio-Michigan border. The state line, which cuts through their dining room at an angle then doglegs out through a mirror, divides the house into one-third Michigan and two-thirds Ohio. They eat in their Michigan kitchen but, since they sleep in their Ohio bedroom, they are technically classified as Ohio residents.

Though the Wilmoths like their unusually placed home, it has caused them a few problems. For example, Ohio Fuel would not deliver natural gas since part of the fuel would go into Michigan and the Ohio Attorney General had to intervene. The Wilmoths also pay taxes to both states but more to Michigan because of the higher rates.

2. MUSKEGON

For the past ten years Russell Kinfield, a retired science teacher and University of Michigan graduate (class of 1928), has lived in a bus that sits, without tires, overlooking old U.S. 31 north of Muskegon. His "front door" still opens with a bar that extends to the driver's seat and, inside, his home still resembles a bus more than a house. The lifelong bachelor cooks on a hot plate and gets water from a nearby well.

3. YPSILANTI

In 1929 Harry Bennett, right-hand man to auto magnate Henry Ford, built a fabulous impregnable mansion high above the Huron River. Designed to protect him from numerous enemies he had made during thirty years as Ford Motor Company's head of security, Bennett's castle contains two-foot-thick walls, several secret doors, tunnels and escape routes, lion and tiger dens, hundreds of floodlights and two massive gun towers which he manned with machine-gun-carrying guards.

4 COUNTIES WITH THE MOST MOBILE HOMES

As of 1970.

1. WAYNE	5,601
2. OAKLAND	4,653
3. GENESEE	3,793
4. MACOMB	3,720

5 COMMON APPLIANCES

Five common appliances and conveniences found in Michigan homes in 1979.

1. TELEVISION SET	2,574,714
2. WASHER	2,090,041
3. DRYER	1,550,489
4. FREEZER	774,500
5. DISHWASHER	464,917

6 PHONEY YEARS

The number of telephones in Michigan homes for six selected years. For the past nine years Southfield has ranked second in the world in number of phones per person with an average of 1.5 phones per person. Number one is Washington, D.C., with 1.6 phones per person.

1. 1950	2.1 million
2. 1955	2.7 million
3. 1960	3.2 million
4. 1965	4.1 million
5. 1970	5.1 million
6. 1977	6.8 million

Waste Not

4 COUNTIES WITH THE MOST SEPTIC TANKS OR CESSPOOLS

1. OAKLAND	78,813
2. GENESEE	50,267
3. KENT	38,973
4. KALAMAZOO	33,386

16 WORST TOXIC WASTE DUMPS

In July, 1981, the Michigan Departments of Natural Resources, Agriculture, and Public Health jointly issued a list of what they considered to be the sixteen worst toxic waste dumps out of more than sixty-five located throughout the state. The rankings, based on such factors as potential environmental and human hazards, were submitted to the Environmental Protection Agency as Michigan's priority list for cleanup under a $1.6-billion federal grant.

1. GRATIOT COUNTY LANDFILL

2. STORY CHEMICAL COMPANY (Muskegon County)

3. BERLIN AND FARRO LIQUID INCINERATION COMPANY (Genesee County)

4. G & H LANDFILL (Oakland and Macomb Counties)

5. TAR LAKE (Antrim County)

6. LITTLEFIELD TOWNSHIP DUMP (Emmet County)

7. STEVENS LANDFILL (Monroe County)

8. WILLOW RUN AREA (Washtenaw County)

9. S.C.A. INDEPENDENT LANDFILL (Muskegon County)

10. ROSE AND SPRINGFIELD TOWNSHIP DUMPS (Oakland County)

11. BURROWS SANITATION (Van Buren County)

12. CEREAL CITY LANDFILL (Calhoun County)

13. SOUTHWEST OTTAWA COUNTY LANDFILL

14. SPARTA LANDFILL (Kent County)

15. WEST K. L. AVENUE LANDFILL (Kalamazoo County)

16. HAMLIN ROAD LANDFILL (Macomb County)

4 CONSPICUOUS INSTANCES
OF CHEMICAL POLLUTION

1. THE PBB CRISIS

During the summer of 1973 ten to twenty bags of poly-brominated biphenyl (PBB), a fire retardant, were mistaken for a feed supplement and mixed with batches of cattle and poultry feed at the Farm Bureau Services feed plant in Climax, thus setting off one of the nation's worst chemical disasters. The suspected carcinogen spread through Michigan's food supply to the point that the bodies of almost every one of Michigan's residents contains some PBB.

In addition to being a possible cancer-causing agent, PBB is suspected of raising havoc with the body's immunity systems and possibly causing aching joints and severe fatigue. Studies, however, have shown no significant short-term health problems definitely traced to PBB and data on long-range effects are still incomplete and contradictory.

The potential human health tragedy of the disaster was compounded by massive financial losses to farmers whose herds had to be destroyed, and bungling, reluctance to act, passing of responsibility, and arguing on the part of state government agencies and institutions.

2. HOOKER MONTAGUE DUMP

From 1957 to 1972 the Hooker Chemical and Plastics Corporation routinely dumped massive amounts of toxic wastes into an isolated dump on its 880-acre factory site near Whitehall. The forty thousand yards of toxic material, enough to fill a 24-acre field ten feet deep, included thousands of barrels of C-56, a deadly chemical used in the manufacture of pesticides.

Over the years the C-56 and other chemical residues seeped into the groundwater, contaminating several wells and polluting nearby White Lake. At one point almost 1,300 pounds of toxins seeped into the lake each day.

In 1977 the firm stopped production of C-56 and eventually paid over $300,000 in pollution fines. Two years later, in an out-of-court settlement, Hooker agreed to clean up the dump site at an estimated cost of $13 million and provide safe drinking water for nearby residents.

3. CURENE

In 1978 Department of Natural Resources officials found Curene, a suspected cancer-causing agent, in roadside dust, parking lots, sandboxes and gardens throughout the town of Adrian where it was produced. Workers at the Anderson Development Company, which produced the plastics hardener, also carried Curene home on their clothing and the substance turned up in their urine. Repeated washings did not destroy the yellowish powder and it eventually contaminated the city's water treatment plant.

Researchers from the National Institute of Occupational Health and Safety feared, after tests on animals, that Curene could promote bladder cancer in humans. And, a 1980 federal study showed that birth defects in Adrian were significantly higher than state or national averages.

State officials ordered Anderson to remove the contaminated soil and repave parking lots but company officials, who maintained that the dangers of Curene were exaggerated, said they could not afford it.

4. WURTSMITH AIR FORCE BASE

TCE, a cancer-causing chemical used by the Air Force to degrease aircraft parts, drained from buried storage tanks at Wurtsmith Air Force Base and contaminated the Oscoda-area groundwater.

A base resident exposed the contamination October, 1977, after persistently complaining of foul-smelling water. The state and federal Environmental Protection Agency investigated and, in October, 1978, ordered the Air Force to take several corrective measures including cleanup.

In August, 1979, Attorney General Frank Kelly filed suit claiming that the Air Force ignored the order and only tried to cover up the pollution by using an additive to mask the odor of TCE. In November, 1980, the Air Force presented a cleanup plan and paid the state $100,000.

6 AIR POLLUTORS

Six Michigan utilities who, as of August, 1980, had not yet met a mid-1975 federal deadline for reducing air pollution.
1. CONSUMERS POWER
2. DETROIT EDISON
3. HOLLAND BOARD OF PUBLIC WORKS
4. LANSING BOARD OF WATER AND LIGHT
5. NORTHERN MICHIGAN ELECTRIC COOPERATIVE
6. UPPER PENINSULA POWER COMPANY

7 WATER POLLUTORS

On August 1, 1977, seven companies, identified by the State Attorney

General's office, Department of Natural Resources, and Water Resources Commision as the state's worst water pollutors at that time, agreed to pay the state almost $3.5 million in fines and install $150 million worth of pollution-control devices.

State officials at the time felt that the pollution-control agreement was the biggest and best ever in the nation and that Michigan's major water-pollution problems would be cured in one stroke. The companies that settled with the state were:

1. FORD MOTOR COMPANY

Ford paid $1.6 million in fines and agreed to install $38 million in equipment at its Rouge, Monroe and Wixom plants, which had dumped wastes into the Detroit, Raisin and Huron rivers.

2. GREAT LAKES STEEL

The company paid a $1.25-million fine and were scheduled to install $45.4 million in equipment, mostly at its Zug Island blast furnace which had discharged oils and iron into the Detroit and Rouge rivers.

3. THE ABITIBI CORPORATION

The Alpena-based corporation paid $200,000 to the state and said they would spend $2.5 million to clean organic discharges described as the worst odor problem in the state.

4. THE PENNWALT CHEMICAL COMPANY

Pennwalt paid a $150,000 fine and agreed to spend $3 million to reduce chemical discharges into the Detroit River from its Wyandotte plant.

5. DETROIT EDISON

The utility received a $120,000 fine and planned to spend $55 million to eliminate the discharge of too-much-heated water and solid wastes at twelve power plants.

6. THE HARBISON-WALKER REFRACTORY COMPANY

The Ludington company agreed to spend $600,000 to reduce waste discharges into Lake Michigan.

7. THE HOOKER CHEMICAL COMPANY

The Montague company paid a $75,000 fine and was scheduled to spend $2 million to correct discharges from a plant producing chlorine and caustic soda.

7 POLLUTED RIVERS

In a 1980 report the Michigan Department of Natural Resources advised that fish caught in the following streams should not be eaten:

1. SHIAWASSEE RIVER (M-59 to Owosso)
   Contaminated with PCB.

2. PORTAGE CREEK (Kalamazoo County from Milhan Park to river's mouth)
   Contaminated with PCB.

3. KALAMAZOO RIVER (Kalamazoo to Saugatuck)
   Contaminated with PCB.

4. CHIPPEWA RIVER (Isabella County)
   Contaminated with PBB.

5. PINE RIVER (Downstream from St. Louis)
   Contaminated with PBB.

6. TITTABAWASEE RIVER (Downstream from Midland)
   Contaminated with PBB and Dioxin.

7. SAGINAW RIVER
   Contaminated with PBB and Dioxin.

Litter - ally Speaking
2 CASES OF TRASH

State roadside surveys made before and after Michigan's beverage container deposit law took effect December, 1976, showed the following comparisons:

	Total Accumulated Litter	Pieces of Trash Per Roadside Mile
1. BEFORE THE LAW	1.7 billion items	6,222
2. AFTER THE LAW	170 million items	652

MICHIGAN'S 4 BEST CITIES

In 1975 the Midwest Research Institute of Kansas City, Missouri, studied and rated the quality of life in 243 small, medium and major metropolitan areas of the United States. Researchers based the rankings on economic, environmental, political, social, educational and health factors.

The four Michigan cities that ranked highest in this federally funded study were:

1. LANSING
   Rated seventh of the eighty-three mid-size metropolitan areas studied.

2. KALAMAZOO
   Rated eighth of the eighty-three mid-size metropolitan areas studied.

3. ANN ARBOR
   Rated tenth of the eighty-three mid-size metropolitan areas studied.

4. GRAND RAPIDS
   Rated eleventh of the sixty-five major metropolitan areas studied.

11 RANKING CITIES

In their book, *Places Rated Almanac* (Rand McNally, 1981), authors Richard Boyer and David Savageau rated 277 American metropolitan areas on climate, housing, health care, crime, transportation, education, recreation, arts and economics. Eleven Michigan cities that were surveyed and how they ranked overall:

1. DETROIT - 43rd
2. LANSING - 58th
3. GRAND RAPIDS - 71st
4. ANN ARBOR - 88th
5. BATTLE CREEK - 154th
6. KALAMAZOO - 155th
7. BAY CITY - 165th
8. FLINT - 180th
9. MUSKEGON - 187th
10. SAGINAW - 230th
11. JACKSON - 242d

4 MOST SCHOLARLY COUNTIES

The four counties with the highest percentage of population attending public or private schools in 1978-79.

1. MONTCALM	31.1%
2. OSCEOLA	31.0%
3. OTSEGO	30.7%
4. TUSCOLA	30.2%

4 MOST UNINSTRUCTED COUNTIES

The four counties with the lowest percentage of population attending public or private schools in 1978-79.

1.	KEEWEENAW	1.5%
2.	LAKE	13.4%
3.	ISABELLA	14.3%
4.	ALCONA	15.3%

3 MOST LEARNED YEARS

The three years with the most pupils enrolled in the public school system.

1.	1967	3,448,802
2.	1968	3,434,754
3.	1966	2,620,663

5 SCHOOL DISTRICTS WITH THE MOST STUDENTS

Based on 1977-78 enrollment.

1. DETROIT CITY SCHOOL DISTRICT	233,049
2. FLINT CITY SCHOOL DISTRICT	38,086
3. GRAND RAPIDS CITY SCHOOL DISTRICT	37,407
4. WARREN CONSOLIDATED SCHOOLS	31,155
5. LANSING PUBLIC SCHOOL DISTRICT	30,675

5 SCHOOL DISTRICTS WITH THE FEWEST STUDENTS

Based on 1977-78 enrollment for kindergarten through twelfth grade (K-12) schools.*

1. BEAVER ISLAND COMMUNITY SCHOOLS	54
2. WHITEFISH SCHOOLS	113
3. MACKINAC ISLAND PUBLIC SCHOOL DISTRICT	136
4. BURT TOWNSHIP SCHOOLS	141
5. MARENISCO SCHOOL DISTRICT	148

*Bois Blanc Island's Pine School District has only four pupils but is not classified as a K-12 school.

3 COUNTIES WITH THE MOST MINORITY STUDENTS

As a percentage of the 1978-79 public school enrollment.

1. WAYNE	47.4%
2. LAKE	42.6%
3. LEELANAU	39.3%

5 COUNTIES WITH THE FEWEST MINORITY STUDENTS

As a percentage of the 1978-79 public school enrollment.

1. KEEWEENAW	0.0%
2. DICKINSON	0.2%
3. MISSAUKEE	0.3%
4. PRESQUE ISLE	0.3%
5. ROSCOMMON	0.3%

3 COUNTIES WITH THE HIGHEST PRIVATE SCHOOL ATTENDANCE

Based on non-public school attendance as a percentage of total 1978-79 enrollment.

1. BAY	20.6%
2. OTTAWA	19.0%
3. LEELANAU	17.2%

8 COUNTIES WHERE NO ONE ATTENDS PRIVATE SCHOOLS

Based on 1978-79 enrollment.

1. ALCONA	5. KEEWEENAW
2. ARENAC	6. LAKE
3. BENZIE	7. MACKINAC
4. IRON	8. ONTONAGON

3 MOST INSTRUCTIVE YEARS

The three years with the most teachers in the Michigan public school system.

1. 1974	94,221
2. 1973	93,852
3. 1975	93,580

6 LARGEST COLLEGES

Based on 1978 enrollment.

1. MICHIGAN STATE UNIVERSITY (East Lansing)	46,567
2. UNIVERSITY OF MICHIGAN (Ann Arbor)	36,577
3. WAYNE STATE UNIVERSITY (Detroit)	33,423
4. WESTERN MICHIGAN UNIVERSITY (Kalamazoo)	22,447
5. EASTERN MICHIGAN UNIVERSITY (Ypsilanti)	18,655
6. CENTRAL MICHIGAN UNIVERSITY (Mt. Pleasant)	17,802

7 NOTABLE CHURCHES

1. MACKINAW CITY
The Church of the Straits conducts half-hour, non-denominational services on a ferry boat that carries tourists under the Mackinac Bridge.

2. DETROIT
The nation's first trailer church, St. Paul's Wayside Cathedral, began operation October 1, 1937.

3. DETROIT
Central United Methodist Church is Michigan's oldest Protestant church with congregations dating from 1822.

4. HIGHLAND PARK
The nation's first Mosque was built in 1901.

5. HOLIDAY INN MOTEL ROOMS
In June, 1968, Holiday Inn motels throughout Michigan began conducting non-denominational services in motel rooms furnished with altars, chord organs and other religious items. Guest pastors perform half-hour Sunday services for travelers and employees.

6. TRAVERSE CITY
Temple Beth-El, founded in 1885, is the oldest synagogue building in continuous use in Michigan.

7. BLOOMFIELD HILLS
The world's second-largest carillon, seventy-seven bells weighing sixty-six tons, peals from the Kirk-in-the-Hills Presbyterian church.

Central United Methodist Church

Kirk-In-The-Hills Presbyterian Church

Temple Beth-El

169

3 CONSPICUOUS CROSSES

1. INDIAN RIVER
The largest crucifix in the world, a seven-ton bronze figure of Christ hanging on a 55-foot-high redwood cross, overlooks the waters of Burt Lake. The Indian River Shrine, as it is known, is dedicated to Kateri Tekakwitha who, her supporters hope, will become the first American Indian saint.

The sculptor, Marshal M. Fredericks, who also did *The Spirit of Detroit*, cast the crucifix in Norway and shipped it to Michigan in 1959. Masses are said at the shrine each Sunday and are held outdoors in front of the crucifix during the summer months.

2. REED CITY
A large cross identifies the home of Methodist minister Rev. George Bennard who composed the famous hymn, *The Old Rugged Cross*.

3. POKAGON
A wooden cross and granite boulder mark the spot where *The Old Rugged Cross* was first sung.

2 RELIGIOUS GROUPS WITH NATIONAL HEADQUARTERS IN MICHIGAN

1. CHRISTIAN REFORMED CHURCH (Grand Rapids)
2. ROMAN ORTHODOX EPISCOPATE OF AMERICA (Jackson)

8 MOST POPULAR DENOMINATIONS

Eight most common denominations as a percentage of the 1970 population.

1. ROMAN CATHOLIC	25.4%
2. LUTHERAN	5.3%
3. METHODIST	3.9%
4. PRESBYTERIAN	2.1%
5. BAPTIST	1.2%
6. JEWISH	1.0%
7. 7TH DAY ADVENTIST	0.3%
8. MORMON	0.2%

Indian River Shrine

Marker at the home of composer Rev. George Bennard.

Original Pokagon Methodist church where the hymn, *The Old Rugged Cross,* was first sung in 1913.

3 UNUSUAL RITUALS

1. GRAND RAPIDS - July, 1981
A Baptist minister, using a homemade electric chair—a stool equipped with wire screens connected to a six-volt battery—jolted Bible School youngsters to show them what could happen if they failed to heed God's word.

2. ANN ARBOR - June, 1975
A 29-year-old yoga instructor mysteriously died while experimenting in a rare form of Hindu meditation. The completely healthy man, with no history or evidence of medical problems, was discovered dead in a classic yoga position. Doctors at first speculated that he had died while in a deep self-induced trance that somehow had slowed his heart to the point his brain received too little blood. Yoga practitioners felt he had projected his soul through "astral projection" to a different time and place. An autopsy ultimately revealed that he had died from an overdose of cocaine.

3. SAGINAW COUNTY - October, 1979
Reports of bizarre forest rituals and tales of satanism terrified residents in southwestern Saginaw County for several weeks.

In what appeared to be the aftermath of a worship ritual, many residents reported seeing a dead dog staked between four posts about five feet off the ground in a remote wooded area. Several people also said that unknown telephone callers had told them their children would be the next to be sacrificed. Though law-enforcement officers investigated, no charges were filed and no official complaints were received in the future.

It's My Body And I'll Do What I Want To
2 UNIQUE EXAMPLES OF MEDICAL RESEARCH

1. HERE'S JOHNNY - March, 1979
Volunteers in the Detroit area stopped at a portable toilet company in suburban Utica and used their privys so that medical researchers could test the feasibility of large-scale urine collection. The researchers installed small boxes in the portable units to collect urokinase, an enzyme extracted from urine that can break up blood clots. Developers of the box were searching for a method of urine collection that would lower the $240 per dose price of producing the beneficial enzyme.

2. SKINNED ALIVE
College students routinely participate in psychological and some medical experiments to help finance their education. Generally, such par-

ticipation pays $3 to $10 per experiment so consider the industry of a University of Michigan medical student from Saginaw who, as of January, 1979, had earned over $700 by selling swatches of his skin to psoriasis and hypertension researchers.

5 NOTABLE WEIGHT WATCHERS

1. BILL EVERTON (Port Huron) - 1974
   The six-foot, three-inch, 640-pound man became the biggest weight-loser ever checked by Weight Watchers, U.S.A., when he lost 417 pounds in thirty-one months.

2. MICHAEL BURNS (Pontiac) - 1979
   A judge ordered the five-foot, ten-inch, 400-pound parole violator to lose weight or be put on a forced diet in the county jail. Twenty-six-year-old Burns was a qualified television repairman but couldn't get a job because of his weight.

3. PATRICK GAYNOR (Novi) - 1977
   The 37-year-old man was one of fifty-three Americans who died while on the controversial liquid protein diet which became popular after publication of *The Last Chance Diet.*

4. SHERRY and MARY ARNDT (Troy) - 1975
   The 186-pound mother and her seventeen-year-old, 248-pound daughter had their mouths wired shut to lose weight, the first mother-daughter combination to do so.

5. REV. WILLIAM A. RAYMOND (Flint) - 1976
   The 298-pound preacher, inspired by *I Corinthians 9:25,* lost 125 pounds in one year.

8 MOMENTOUS ORGAN TRANSPLANTS

1. FIRST MICHIGAN KIDNEY TRANSPLANT (University of Michigan) - March 30, 1964
   The operation involved identical twins, Janice (the recipient) and Joan (the donor) Ottenbacher (Richmond). Both women, now nurses, are married with children and lead normal lives.

2. FIRST MICHIGAN HEART TRANSPLANT (University of Michigan) -September 19, 1968

Philip T. Barnum (Kalamazoo) received the heart of a Southern Michigan prison inmate who had died during an operation to remove a brain tumor. The five-and-a-half-hour transplant was the first in Michigan and the 51st in the world. The 38-year-old inmate, who was serving time for robbery, told relatives he would donate his heart because he wanted to do some good. Barnum died a little more than a year later of infection and rejection of the transplanted heart.

3. LONGEST-LIVING MICHIGAN HEART TRANSPLANT (University of Michigan) - December 2, 1968

On the eve of the first anniversary of the world's first heart transplant, Donald Kaminski (Alpena) received the heart of a 22-year-old Fenton man killed in an auto accident. Kaminski lived an active life hunting, fishing and boating until his death May 15, 1973, making him the world's longest-living heart transplant at that time.

4. FIRST MICHIGAN LUNG TRANSPLANT (University of Michigan) -September 1, 1969

Albert Lee Carnick (Bloomfield Hills) received the lung of a seventeen-year-old Jackson High School traffic accident victim in Michigan's first lung transplant. He died four days later.

5. FIRST DOUBLE HEART TRANSPLANT (University of Michigan) -January 16, 1970

When doctors could not halt rejection of his first transplanted heart, Gerald Kenneth Rector (Livonia and Shelbyville) received a second ten months later. At the time it was only the third double transplant operation in medical history. Rector died less than two weeks later of lung, kidney and liver infection.

6. THYMUS GLAND TRANSPLANT (Michigan State University) -January 24, 1977

Michigan State University physicians successfully performed a rare thymus gland transplant, the first in Michigan, on 1½-year-old Eric Metzger (Marshall) to strengthen his immunity against infection and disease.

7. MICHIGAN'S ONLY LIVER RECIPIENT (Denver, Colorado) - March 10, 1979

Ron Smolinski (Bay City), suffering from a rare primary cancer of the liver, received the liver of a seventeen-year-old boy. The eight-hour operation, only the 24th in the country, cost $250,000.

8. YOUNGEST MICHIGAN KIDNEY RECIPIENT (University of Michigan) - December 4, 1980

During a rare, eight-hour operation, 36-year-old Mary Brookout (South Lyon) donated a kidney to her sixteen-month-old daughter Angela.

7 SUCCESSFUL LIMB RE-ATTACHMENTS

1. TODD TUYLS (Battle Creek) - August 29, 1980

Unaware that he had severed four fingers and a thumb, the ten-year-old ran into his home after flipping his off-road vehicle during a nighttime ride. As his mother comforted him, Todd's father returned to the accident scene, searched with a flashlight and found the missing digits in the dirt.

With his fingers packed in ice, Todd flew in an air ambulance to Jewish Hospital (Louisville, Kentucky) where doctors spent twenty hours pinning together broken bones, restoring veins and arteries and reconnecting nerves.

2. MARCIA GRIMM (Manistique) - January 3, 1971

The six-year-old slid on a saucer into the path of a running snowblower and plunged her arm into the rotating blades. An air ambulance rushed Marcia, her arm dangling by only two stretched nerves, to Detroit's Henry Ford Hospital where doctors, in three separate operations, pinned her bone together, restored circulation and spliced nerves together.

3. LLOYD HOEPPNER (Merrill) - November 20, 1964

The twelve-year-old caught his sleeve in a tractor power take-off which jerked him past the moving gears and severed his right ear. When doctors at St. Luke Hospital (Saginaw) found that they could not immediately re-attach the ear to the boy's head, they temporarily grafted it to his left arm to sustain it.

4. ROBERT BERRY (St. Louis) - November 21, 1979

Using microscopes attached to television cameras, two surgeons at Lansing's Sparrow Hospital re-attached both hands of the 48-year-old tool and die maker who had nearly severed them while changing a machine die.

5. LAURA RICHARDS (Mikado) - October 23, 1979

In a delicate, extensive, fourteen-hour operation, six surgeons at Detroit's Harper Hospital successfully re-attached Mrs. Richard's left arm which had been severed between the wrist and elbow by a power auger. During the 170-mile trip to the hospital, the severed hand and forearm were sealed in a plastic bag and coverd by ice.

6. EDWARD SIMLAR (Livonia) - September 19, 1980

Six months after he had sawed off two fingers and a thumb with a power saw, Detroit Harper Grace Hospital doctors used Simlar's second toe to replace his thumb. The physicians had successfully re-attached his index and middle fingers shortly after the accident.

7. TODD NADEAU (Northville) - September 26, 1979

The high-school basketball star cut off his hand with a power saw while cutting aluminum. Doctors at Detroit's Harper Hospital successfully re-attached it in a thirteen-hour operation and, after several more operations, the physicians felt that the young athlete would be able to compete without much handicap.

8

MAKING CENTS

5 UNIQUE BUDGET PROBLEMS

1. IT ALL CAME OUT IN THE WASH (Detroit) - 1977
   A man who had hidden over $200,000 in cash in the basement of his mother's house lost nearly $75,000 after the basement flooded and the $100 bills swelled, rotted, mildewed and became compressed into a solid mass. After drying the money on heat registers and with hair dryers, the construction business owner and his fiance were able to reconstruct almost $74,000, but the Department of the Treasury concluded that the remaining mess of currency was worth only $54,750.

2. BARELY ESSENTIAL (East Lanisng) - October, 1979
   In a budget-cutting move at Michigan State University's College of Arts and Letters, the Board of Trustees eliminated payment for nude models. But after loud protests from students and professors who called the models "an essential element in the education of artists," the models were reinstated.

3. SCHOOL'S OUT (Alpena) - October, 1981
   After three back-to-back millage defeats, the county-wide school system ran out of cash, declared itself broke and closed. The first and only school district closing in the history of Michigan closed fourteen schools and sent 6,800 students home for two weeks when a renewal millage finally passed.

4. TAKE YOUR MONEY AND SHOVE IT (Willow Run) - 1965
   The University of Michigan received a $188,252 Federal Office of Economic Opportunity grant to administer a self-help program to Willow Run's 4,500 "impoverished" residents. The village demanded that the Feds take their money back saying that they were not impoverished and didn't want that stigma to lower property values and deter business development.

5. TABLECLOTH CRISIS (Muskegon) - 1981

A fund-raising drive sponsored by a Muskegon newspaper to help avert what was termed "a terrible tablecloth crisis" by a Reagan White House Social Secretary netted sixteen cents, a piece of thread, two safety pins, a Band-Aid, two paper clips, a Christmas seal, a peso, a broken comb, a turkey wishbone and an empty book of food stamps.

2 CITIES THAT WERE BOUGHT AND SOLD

1. NAHMA (Population 450) - 1953

The American Playground Device Company (Anderson, Indiana) purchased the entire Upper Peninsula town including 4,300 acres of land, a community center, several miles of railway, 102 dwellings, docks to accommodate ships, a seventeen-room hotel, a golf course, an eight-bed hospital, an airfield, a one-chair barbershop, an eighty-bed boarding house and extensive Lake Michigan beach frontage.

The town's sole industry, the Bay de Noquet Lumber Company, which owned nearly all of the physical assets of the town, had ceased operation so the entire town was offered for sale at an asking price of $250,000. American Playground, the nation's largest manufacturer of playground equipment, needed more space for its operations and planned to develop Nahma as a model industrial-recreation community.

2. HAMTRAMCK POLETOWN (Population 3,400) - 1981

The City of Detroit purchased more than five hundred homes and businesses in the Hamtramck neighborhood so that they could then raze the buildings to make way for a new $500-million General Motors assembly plant.

GENERAL MOTORS' 4 LARGEST QUARTERLY LOSSES

General Motors has only experienced twelve quarterly losses in the company's history. The four largest:

1. THIRD QUARTER, 1980	$567	million
2. THIRD QUARTER, 1981	$468	million
3. SECOND QUARTR, 1980	$412	million
4. FOURTH QUARTER, 1970	$134.8	million

4 INCREDIBLY LARGE LOSSES

1. The Chrysler Corporation lost 1.17 billion dollars in 1980, the largest annual loss ever for any U.S. company.

2. Ford Motor Company reported a $1.54 billion loss for 1980, the largest annual loss in their history.

3. General Motors reported an annual loss for 1980 of $763 million, its worst in history and its first annual loss since 1921.

4. American Motors lost $198 million in 1980, the largest annual loss in the company's history.

2 RECENT BANK FAILURES

1. In 1966 the Public Bank of Detroit, with $117 million in deposits, was declared insolvent in the biggest U.S. Bank failure since the 1930's.

2. In 1971 the Bloomfield Bank of Michigan, with $57.5 million in deposits, failed.

3 MAJOR CITIES THAT HAVE DEFAULTED

1. DETROIT - 1933
   Detroit defaulted after a number of cost-cutting measures failed to close the widening gap between receipts and expenses.

2. GRAND RAPIDS - 1933
   Grand Rapids failed to make payments on its debts because of mounting tax delinquencies, increasing debt service costs, and bank closings.

3. JACKSON - 1933
   Jackson defaulted when cash reserves ran out and credit was impossible to obtain.

4 MOST NEEDY COUNTIES

Three counties with the largest percentage of population receiving general assistance or aid to dependent children in 1979.

1. WAYNE	13.0%
2. LAKE	12.0%
3. VAN BUREN	11.3%
4. SAGINAW	10.1%

4 MOST FINANCIALLY INDEPENDENT COUNTIES

Three counties with the lowest percentage of population receiving general assistance or aid to dependent children in 1979.

1. MACOMB	0.3%
2. LENAWEE	2.0%
3. OTTAWA	2.1%
4. LIVINGSTON	2.7%

3 MOST SOCIALLY SECURE COUNTIES

Three counties with the highest percentage of their residents' 1977 incomes comprised of Social Security benefits.

1. LAKE	18.4%
2. ROSCOMMON	18.3%
3. KEEWEENAW	17.5%

3 MOST SOCIALLY INSECURE COUNTIES

Three counties with the lowest percentage of their residents' 1977 incomes comprised of social security benefits.

1. WASHTENAW	3.2%
2. OAKLAND	3.6%
3. MIDLAND	3.6%

7 POOREST COUNTIES

Based on 1978 per capita personal income.

1. OSCODA	$4,383
2. MECOSTA	$4,551
3. OGEMAW	$4,754
4. ALGER	$4,779
5. LAKE	$4,812
6. MISSAUKEE	$4,879
7. KALKASKA	$4,921

5 RICHEST COUNTIES

Based on 1978 per capita personal income.

1. OAKLAND	$10,877
2. MACOMB	$9,385
3. WAYNE	$9,238
4. WASHTENAW	$9,160
5. GENESEE	$9,016

5 LARGEST BANKS

As ranked according to 1981 assets by the *Michigan Investor*.
1. NATIONAL BANK OF DETROIT
2. DETROIT BANK AND TRUST
3. MANUFACTURERS NATIONAL BANK OF DETROIT
4. MICHIGAN NATIONAL (Detroit)
5. MICHIGAN NATIONAL (Lansing)

6 SMALLEST BANKS

As ranked according to 1981 assets by the *Michigan Investor*.
1. MORLEY STATE BANK
2. FIDELITY BANK OF TROY
3. OLD KENT BANK OF GRANDVILLE
4. NORTHERN MICHIGAN BANK OF KINGSFORD
5. FIDELITY BANK OF BINGHAM FARMS
6. MANUFACTURER'S BANK OF NOVI

6 RICHEST CITIES

Based on 1977 per capita income in incorporated cities of population 2,500 or more. Bloomfield Hills holds the distinction of being the wealthiest community in the entire United States. Grosse Pointe Shores is seventh in the nation.

1. BLOOMFIELD HILLS	$38,371
2. GROSSE POINTE SHORES	$22,304
3. BIRMINGHAM FARMS	$20,279
4. BARTON HILLS	$16,273
5. GROSSE POINTE FARMS	$15,790
6. FRANKLIN	$15,238

Michigan's smallest bank

8 POOREST CITIES

Based on 1977 per capita income of incorporated cities.

1. COPPER CITY		$2,752
2. MARRIETTA		$2,856
3. LUTHER		$3,213
4. PELLSTON		$3,242
5. LAKE LINDEN		$3,266
6. HILLMAN		$3,415
7. COPEMISH		$3,470
8. WALDRON		$3,472

8 MOST DISTRESSED PLACES

Eight places in Michigan listed as most distressed in a 1981 survey by the Michigan Department of Commerce. Several factors including unemployment, income, taxes, percentage of population living below poverty level and property values were statistically combined to determine the distressed rankings. Those rankings in order:

1. BENTON HARBOR
2. CROSS VILLAGE TOWNSHIP (Emmet County)
3. CHIPPEWA COUNTY
4. MONTMORENCY COUNTY
5. ONAWAY
6. HOUGHTON COUNTY
7. HIGHLAND PARK
8. MANTON

6 COUNTIES WITH THE SMALLEST PAYCHECKS

Six counties with the lowest average weekly earnings as reported by establishments covered under the state Unemployment Insurance Program in 1978.

1. LAKE		$134.00
2. MONTMORENCY		$142.01
3. LEELANAU		$142.04
4. KEEWEENAW		$143.97
5. ALCONA		$144.60
6. ROSCOMMON		$146.81

5 INCOMING YEARS

Per capita income in Michigan for five selected years since 1942.

1.	1942	$1,047
2.	1950	$1,701
3.	1960	$2,324
4.	1970	$4,058
5.	1978	$8,442

6 COUNTIES WITH THE LARGEST PAYCHECKS

Six counties with the highest average weekly earnings as reported by establishments covered under the state Unemployment Insurance Program in 1978.

1.	GENESEE	$344.59
2.	MIDLAND	$334.78
3.	WAYNE	$322.89
4.	MACOMB	$312.93
5.	SAGINAW	$309.24
6.	WASHTENAW	$307.59

2 ANCHORMEN'S SALARIES

As published in *Forbes Magazine* December 7, 1981.

1. BILL BONDS (WXYZ Channel 7 - Detroit)
$300,000 per year.

2. MORT CRIM (WDIV Channel 4 - Detroit)
$250,000 per year.

5 DETROIT TIGER ARBITRATION CASES

	PLAYER WANTED	TIGERS OFFERED	ARBITRATOR AWARDED
1. STEVE KEMP - 1980	$210,000	$150,000	$210,000
2. ALAN TRAMMELL -1980	$130,000	$105,000	$130,000
3. LOU WHITAKER - 1980	$130,000	$105,000	$130,000
4. STEVE KEMP - 1981	$600,000	$360,000	$600,000
5. JACK MORRIS - 1982	$650,000	$450,000	$450,000

5 RECORD PROFITS

1. GM'S RECORD YEARLY PROFIT
   $3.5 billion - 1978.

2. GM'S RECORD QUARTERLY PROFIT
   $1 billion - fourth quarter, 1978.

3. FORD'S RECORD YEARLY PROFIT
   $1.7 billion - 1977

4. FORD'S RECORD QUARTERLY PROFIT
   $540 million - second quarter, 1978.

5. AMERICAN MOTORS RECORD QUARTERLY PROFIT
   $32 million - first quarter, 1979.

MICHIGAN'S 8 RICHEST MEN

From *The Very Rich Book*, by Jacqueline Thompson (Morrow Publishing)

1. HENRY FORD II (Grosse Pointe)
   Estimated worth is $600 million to $1 billion. His family controls the Ford Motor Company through stock ownership.

2. ALEX MANOOGIAN (Detroit)
   Estimated personal worth is $100 to $200 million. He is the founder of Masco Corporation, manufacturers of faucets and metal products.

3. RICHARD DEVOS (Grand Rapids)
   Estimated personal worth is $100 to $200 million. Co-founder of Amway, makers of household products sold door-to-door.

4. JAY VAN ANDEL (Grand Rapids)
   Estimated personal worth $100 to $200 million. Co-founder of Amway.

5. WILLIAM B. DAVIDSON (Bloomfield Hills)
   Estimated personal worth $50 to $100 million. President of Guardian Industries and principal owner of the Detroit Pistons.

6. MAX FISHER (Franklin)
   Estimated personal worth $50 to $100 million. Retired director of

Marathon Oil Company.

7. EDWARD J. FREY (Grand Rapids)
Estimated personal worth $50 to $100 million. President of Great Lakes Financial Corporation.

8. RICHARD E. RIEBEL (Grand Rapids)
Estimated personal worth $50 to $100 million. President of Foremost Insurance Company.

4 STATE OFFICIALS' SALARIES

1982 salaries.

1. GOVERNOR	$70,000 plus $20,000 expenses
2. LT. GOVERNOR	$50,000 plus $ 7,000 expenses
3. SUPREME COURT JUSTICES	$69,000 plus $ 5,000 expenses
4. LEGISLATORS	$31,000 plus $ 6,200 expenses

5 LARGE STATE GOVERNMENT EXPENSES

State government expenditures in 1978.

1. SOCIAL SERVICES	$2,247,372,000
2. SCHOOL AID	$1,654,028,000
3. OTHER EDUCATION	$1,108,872,000
4. COLLEGES AND UNIVERSITIES	$ 646,232,000
5. HIGHWAY FUND	$ 629,116,000

5 COUNTIES THAT GET
THE MOST DEFENSE DOLLARS

Based on federal defense spending in 1979.

1. MACOMB	$1,064,334,00
2. WAYNE	$ 195,913,000
3. MUSKEGON	$ 133,938,000
4. OAKLAND	$ 108,464,000
5. MARQUETTE	$ 76,666,000

4 LARGEST FEDERAL GOVERNMENT DISPERSALS

Federal government disbursements in Michigan for fiscal year 1979.

1. GENERAL RETIREMENT AND
   DISABILITY INSURANCE $4,397,492,000
2. DEFENSE/MILITARY $2,102,899,000
3. HEALTH CARE SERVICES $1,948,872,000
4. PUBLIC ASSISTANCE $ 987,583,000

5 TAXING YEARS

Per capita state and local taxes for five selected years.
1. 1957 $186
2. 1965 $288
3. 1970 $457
4. 1975 $685
5. 1977 $878

7 LEAST TAXING CITIES

Seven cities with the lowest millage rates based on 1978 tax rate per $1,000 evaluation.
1. BRIDGMAN   32.96
2. STEPHENSON   34.49
3. HARRISVILLE   34.65
4. BAD AXE   37.08
5. MACKINAC ISLAND   37.50
6. ESSEXVILLE   37.64
7. WHITTEMORE   38.23

6 MOST TAXING CITIES

Six cities with the highest millage rates based on 1978 tax rate per $1,000 evaluation.
1. HIGHLAND PARK   80.16
2. DETROIT   75.16
3. OAK PARK   74.38
4. EAST LANSING   74.34
5. HAZEL PARK   74.12
6. YPSILANTI   74.06

5 MOST GENEROUS SCHOOL DISTRICTS

Five school districts that spent the most per pupil in 1977-78.
1. OAK PARK CITY $2,662.16
2. NORTHVILLE $2,551.06
3. DEARBORN CITY $2,435.72
4. SOUTHFIELD $2,323.04
5. SOUTH REDFORD $2,319.70

5 MOST FRUGAL SCHOOL DISTRICTS

Five school districts that spent the least per pupil in operating expenses for 1977-78.
1. CASS CITY $1,048.66
2. ULBY $1,058.06
3. LAKE CITY $1,070.95
4. MATTAWAN $1,073.89
5. VASSAR $1,083.56

5 SCHOOL DISTRICTS
THAT PAY THEIR TEACHERS THE MOST

Based on average teacher salaries for 1977-78.
1. DEARBORN CITY $22,461
2. RIVER ROUGE CITY $21,515
3. GROSSE POINTE $21,292
4. SOUTH REDFORD $21,073
5. ALLEN PARK $20,892

4 SCHOOL DISTRICTS
THAT PAY THEIR TEACHERS THE LEAST

Based on average teacher salaries for 1977-78.
1. MACKINAC ISLAND $10,113
2. ELLSWORTH $10,135
3. ALBA $10,608
4. MACKINAW CITY $10,656

5 MOST INEXPENSIVE COLLEGES

Five four-year colleges with the lowest annual resident tuition and fees for 1979-80.

1. WESTERN MICHIGAN UNIVERSITY (Kalamazoo)		$820
2. SAGINAW VALLEY STATE COLLEGE (University Center)		$846
3. EASTERN MICHIGAN UNIVERSITY (Ypsilanti)		$849
4. FERRIS STATE (Big Rapids)		$850
5. LAKE SUPERIOR STATE (Sault Ste. Marie)		$852

5 MOST EXPENSIVE COLLEGES

Five four-year colleges with the highest annual resident tuition and fees for 1979-80.

1. SUOMI COLLEGE (Hancock)		$4,400
2. KALAMAZOO COLLEGE (Kalamazoo)		$4,191
3. ALBION COLLEGE (Albion)		$4,017
4. HILLSDALE COLLEGE (Hillsdale)		$3,840
5. ALMA COLLEGE (Alma)		$3,781

3 LARGEST FOUNDATIONS

Michigan is the home of 774 private and community foundations, each awarding grants to $1,000 or more annually. The three largest, based on 1978-79 assets:

1. KELLOGG FOUNDATION (Battle Creek)		$792.2 million
2. KRESGE FOUNDATION (Troy)		$486.9 million
3. MOTT FOUNDATION (Flint)		$396.8 million

12 TOP POLITICAL CAMPAIGN CONTRIBUTORS

Twelve special interest groups that raised the most money for 1980 political campaigns in Michigan through mid-August, 1980, as compiled by the Secretary of State's office.

1. UNITED AUTO WORKERS		$1,011,310
2. MICHIGAN EDUCATION ASSOCIATION		$ 343.247
3. AFL-CIO		$ 310,822
4. MICHIGAN REALTORS		$ 224,327
5. DETROIT AUTO DEALERS		$ 131,790
6. G.M. CIVIC		$ 64,948
7. SAVINGS AND LOANS		$ 59,934

8.	MICHIGAN BANKERS	$	56,774
9.	MICHIGAN CONTRACTORS	$	49,013
10.	MICHIGAN PHARMACISTS	$	45,924
11.	CONSUMERS POWER EMPLOYEES	$	44,341
12.	MICHIGAN AUTO DEALERS	$	41,830

7 LOBBYISTS' UNUSUAL GIFTS

Michigan congressmen have received many gifts from lobbyists. Eight of the most unusual.

1. TUNA CAN WITH A HIPPOPOTAMUS ON TOP
2. PEAT MOSS
3. A DART BOARD ENTITLED *INSTANT LEGISLATIVE ASSISTANT*
4. GREEN BAGELS
5. PEN FILLED WITH OIL
6. CERAMIC ROBIN
7. MUSHROOMS

3 HOUSE WINNERS

1. JIM and BETH VANDERBY (Midland) - 1981
When the Midland Jaycees raffled off a house as a fund-raiser, Mrs. Vanderby's parents bought a $100 ticket and presented it to the couple as a sixth wedding anniversary gift. The gift turned out to be the winning ticket for the $130,000 house.

2. ARLYN and KRISTINA ALDERINK (Jenison) - December, 1981
The couple won a $60,000 house and furnishings in a contest sponsored by a local radio station and contracting company. But, faced with a $35,000 tax bill on the value of the winnings, they decided to sell the "dream" home.

3. RANDY ARMSTRONG (Windsor) - January, 1982
The high-school student won a $235,000 Oakland County house raffled off by the East Detroit Goodfellows.

5 LARGE LOTTERY PAYOUTS

1. On January 17, 1977, as a result of a special bicentennial lottery promotion, David Shepherd (Onsted) won $1,893,742 in the biggest lottery prize in U.S. history to that time. The 23-year-old carpenter received $1 for every

Michigan vote cast for the presidential election candidate (Gerald Ford) who carried the state.

2. On January 29, 1971, nearly a year before Michigan began its lottery, Charles Klotz (Detroit) won $1 million in the New York State lottery.

3. Payoff for the "Daily" lottery game broke all weekly records for the week ending December 21, 1981, when $8 million was paid to 51,076 players.

4. The largest pay-out for the legal "numbers" game occurred on Saturday, March 24, 1980, when number 222 paid $3,026,750 to 8,478 winners.

5. A record $251 million was paid into the state's treasury as a result of record lottery ticket sales for fiscal year 1980-81.

FIRST 3 LOTTERY MILLIONAIRES

1. HERMUS MILLSAPS (Taylor) - February 22, 1973
    The man's former wife, whom he divorced in 1969, filed suit the next day asking for a share of the prize. The judge denied her request.

2. CHRISTINE FERRIZIS (Detroit) - April 5, 1973
    The 46-year-old woman, who had emigrated from Greece eight years before, was accompanied on stage for the millionaire drawing by a friend who acted as interpreter.

3. MARY ODELL (Sterling Heights) - May 10, 1973

3 RECORD LOTTERY SALES

1. A record $501.3 million worth of lottery tickets were sold for fiscal year 1980-81.

2. The "Daily" game saw its highest sales in one week, $8.4 million, for the week ending December 7, 1981.

3. The highest single day of wagering in Michigan lottery history occurred on December 21, 1981, when $1.6 million was spent on tickets.

5 UNIQUE LOTTERY NUMBERS

1. 444
    The number of days the Iranian hostages (see page 80) were held cap-

tive was the highest bet number in lottery history. On January 20, the day the hostages were released, 50,000 people bet on number 444.

2. & 3. 130 and 544

These numbers were drawn on November 23, 1972, in the state's first lottery drawing.

4. & 5. 937 and 385

The only two numbers ever to be drawn two days in a row. 385 was drawn on successive days in December, 1978, and 937 was drawn on two successive days in November, 1981.

9

GETTING DOWN TO BUSINESS

7 MEMORABLE PROMOTIONAL CAMPAIGNS

1. YES TO MICHIGAN - NO TO MICHIGAN ADVERTISERS - 1981
    The first contract for *Say Yes To Michigan*, a taxpayer-funded, na-
tional campaign designed to promote the state as a good place to live, do
business and travel, was awarded to an out-of-state advertising firm.

2. GETTING TO THE KORR OF THE MATTER - 1976
    When the Geyer Brewing Company (Frankenmuth) marketed a beer
called "Korr's," the makers of Coors, a nationally popular western-brewed
beer, promptly filed suit claiming Korr's too closely resembled their
product. The Korr's logo, printed in a similar type style and color as Coors,
displayed the slogan, *America's Finest and Lightest Beer*. Coors slogan
reads, *America's Fine Light Beer*. A court injunction ordered Korr's off
store shelves and Geyer halted production rather than appeal.

3. FREAK OF THE WEEK - 1979
    In an effort to drum up new business, win back old customers and
counteract the effect of numerous police raids, Detroit dope dealers conducted a *Freak of the Week* campaign in which they handed out cards, good
for one free pack of dope, to selected customers.

4. OUR LEGS FIT YOUR LEGS
    Mrs. Alta Becker (Livonia) wrote a letter to a panty hose manufacturer
in praise of their product. The company liked her spontaneous endorsement
so much they asked her to read it for a radio commercial which was then
broadcast hundreds of times daily in forty-nine cities.

5. BUY A HOUSE - GET A CAR - September, 1981
    In an all-out effort to sell homes General Motors had purchased from
transferred employees, the corporation offered a new car with each house.
During the month-long campaign GM sold forty-six homes, but rather than
accept the car, all buyers opted to deduct the car's sticker price from the

home's sale price.

6. DON'T CHEW ADVERTISE ON BARNS
In November, 1974, barn advertising in Michigan became illegal and forty-seven barns, which displayed advertisements, mostly for chewing tobacco, were painted over at a cost to the taxpayers of $7,534.

7. COMMERCIAL VEHICLES - 1975
When the Chrysler Corporation found itself with a surplus of 269,000 cars and a shortage of cash, they bartered their autos for television advertising time with one $5,000 car traded for $10,000 in air time.

5 TOP ADVERTISERS

Five Michigan companies that spent the most for national advertising in 1979.

1. GENERAL MOTORS CORPORATION	$323.4 million
2. K MART	$287.1 million
3. FORD MOTOR COMPANY	$215.0 million
4. CHRYSLER CORPORATION	$118.0 million
5. KELLOGG COMPANY	$ 91.6 million

6 UNIQUE PRODUCTS

1. In June, 1980, a Birmingham stamp and coin dealer offered a $2,700-year-old Egyptian mummy for sale. He had purchased the unusual piece of merchandise from a salesman who had bought it from a museum. The same dealer once sold a pair of missionaries' shrunken heads as bookends.

2. A U.S. biological supply firm pays Joe Thomas (Detroit) $1,500 for each quart of his blood. According to the *1981 Guinness Book of World Records*, Thomas' blood contains the highest known count of Anti-Lewis B, a rare blood antibody.

3. Since 1975 the Decatur Shop (North Adams) has manufactured and sold more than five thousand neckties embroidered with tiny gold Adam Smith portraits. Customers have included White House Counselor Ed Meese, former President Gerald Ford, columnist William F. Buckley, economist Milton Friedman and Reagan budget director David Stockman. Adam Smith was an 18th-century economist who said that government should not interfere with private entrepreneurs.

4. Through a chemical-mechanical process, Will Leese (Jonesville) turns ordinary household garbage into concrete-like fence posts, patio blocks and

Once popular, now illegal, very few barn ads remain along Michigan's highways.

other building materials.

5. Sarns, Incorporated (Ann Arbor), supplies about half the U.S. market for electro-mechanical hearts used as stand-ins during an estimated 160,000 open-heart surgeries performed each year. The console model heart, about the size of a picnic cooler, comes equipped with up to five pumps and sells for approximately $45,000.

6. A Traverse City woman makes clothes out of fluff from her poodle and fuzz balls from her collie.

11 MICHIGAN INVENTORS

1. LEWIS BULLARD (Kalamazoo) invented the first folding daybed and one of the first successful slot machines in the early 1900's.

2. JACK RABINOVITCH (Saginaw) invented the no-nail picture hanger in 1949. The familiar hanger consists of an adhesive-backed, rectangular piece of cloth with a metal hook inserted in the cloth.

3. HANS RUPP (Saginaw) invented the "tip-up," an ice-fishing device that notifies a fisherman when a fish has taken bait and when to set the hook. Rupp worked on the device from 1940 until he patented his "Trip-A-Matic" in 1953.

4. MELVILLE REUBEN BISSELL (Grand Rapids) invented the carpet sweeper in 1876.

5. GEORGE F. GREEN (Kalamazoo) invented the electric dental drill which he patented in 1875.

6. JOSEPH GIBBONS (Adrian) invented the seeding machine in 1840.

7. W. A. BURT (Mt. Vernon), in 1829, patented the first typewriter called a "typographer."

8. CHARLES BRADY KING invented the pneumatic hammer in 1890.

9. DR. ALFRED B. SWANSON (Grand Rapids), in 1969, designed and perfected a silicone rubber joint implant to replace human joints misshapened because of disease or accident.

10. STEPHEN PLATT (Grand Haven), in 1969, invented a two-pound, indestructible, hand-operated record player.

11. WILLIAM DAVIS (Detroit), a fish-market owner, patented the first refrigerator car in 1868.

4 MICHIGAN PRODUCTION FIRSTS

1. The Detroit Aircraft Corporation constructed the world's first dirigible made completely of metal in 1929.

2. In the 1920's William B. Stout produced America's first all-metal airplane. Working with Henry Ford, he later developed the plane into the famous Ford Trimotor.

3. Industrial Browhoist Corporation (Bay City) built the world's first wrecking crane in 1883.

4. J. W. Page (Adrian) opened America's first woven wire fence factory in 1883.

4 WARTIME AUTO INDUSTRY PRODUCTS

In February, 1942, the last civilian cars of the World War II era rolled off Detroit's assembly lines as they geared up for defense jobs.

1. Packard built torpedo boat engines.
2. Ford built B-24 Liberator bombers.
3. Chrysler built Sherman tanks.
4. Willys-Overland built the most famous vehicle to come out of the war, the jeep.

22 PRODUCTS OF THE YEAR

Each year since 1959 the Great Michigan Foundation has designated one Michigan-made product as their "Product of the Year." The winners:

1. *MICHIGAN FISHERMAN* MAGAZINE (Lansing) - 1980

2. CARRY-CABIN (Muskegon) - 1979
   An insulated cabin for camping or temporary shelter.

3. EFFIKAL AUTOMATIC FLUE DAMPER (Troy) - 1978
   Automatically closes flue pipe conserving heat.

4. IT'S A BUMMER (New Hudson) - 1977
   A new concept in bicycle seating.

5. THERMAL-PROCESSED POTATO (Edmore) - 1976
   A vacuum-packed, ready-to-eat potato product.

6. PLASTIC SHOWER HEAD (Grand Rapids) - 1975
   Conserves energy by allowing only three gallons of water per minute to flow.

7. MASTER TEE (Grand Rapids) - 1974
   A golf tee with protruding lip in which the tee edge is the target.

8. CYCLE BURRO (Hazel Park) - 1973
   An aerodynamically designed, one-wheeled motorcycle trailer.

9. COMFORT-AIRE TWIN PAC REMOTE AIR CONDITIONING SYSTEMS (Jackson) - 1972

10. CARTRETTE (Tecumseh) - 1971
    A tiny tape cartridge.

11. MODULAR HOUSING UNITS (Charlotte) - 1970

12. READY-TO-FEED MODILAC (Fremont) - 1969
    A liquid infant formula.

13. ANTI-THEFT STEERING COLUMN LOCK (Saginaw) - 1968

14. ADD-A-CLASS (Marlette) - 1967

15. THE PETTIBONE CARRY-LIFT (Baraga) - 1966

16. F-28 (Menominee) - 1965
    A three-place helicopter.

17. E 2100 (Plymouth) - 1964
    Electronic direct accounting computer.

18. PARADOME PORTABLE BUILDING (Chelsea) - 1963

19. APACHE CAMPING TRAILER (Lapeer) - 1962

20. METRECAL (Zeeland) - 1961
    A liquid diet food.

21. HUSH PUPPY SHOE (Rockford) - 1960

22. *ANATOMY OF A MURDER* MOVIE (Ishpeming) - 1959.

3 MOST EXTRAVAGANT COUNTIES

Three counties whose residents spend the most money based on per-capita retail sales by retail trade establishments for 1977.

COUNTY	EACH RESIDENT SPENT AN AVERAGE OF
1. EMMET	$5,599
2. GRAND TRAVERSE	$4,963
3. WEXFORD	$4,868

4 MOST FRUGAL COUNTIES

Four counties whose residents spend the least money based on per-capita sales by retail trade establishments for 1977.

COUNTY	EACH RESIDENT SPENT AN AVERAGE OF
1. KEEWEENAW	$1,537
2. BARRY	$1,678
3. LAKE	$1,802
4. CASS	$1,868

6 RARE BUSINESSES

1. MERCENARY OPERATIONS UNLIMITED (Muskegon)

David T. McGrady is a professional mercenary soldier who has acted as the bodyguard for Rhodesia's Ministry of Health, guarded a Rhodesian cattle ranch, hunted terrorists for bounty, fought Cuban and East German-supported forces in Southwest Africa and fought PLO terrorists in southern Lebanon.

The 31-year-old family man, who founded Mercenary Operations Unlimited in 1977, keeps a file of some two hundred fifty people including ex-Green Berets, Legionnaires, Rangers, helicopter pilots, armor crews and CIA agents.

2. WASP COLLECTING (Ypsilanti)

Gary Rodabaugh collects live hornets and wasps, freezes them and sends them to Vespa Laboratories. Vespa then extracts and uses the venom to manufacture serum for people allergic to stings. The Eastern Michigan University student is one of a very few select individuals under contract to Vespa.

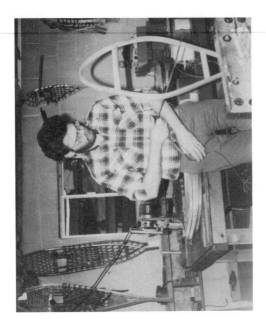

Clockwise from top left: Adeline Polom, long-time employee of Michigan's only remaining cigar maker, rolls cigars with a hand-powered "bunching" device; John Clark of Iverson's Snowshoes weaves reinforced neoprene lace through a white ash "bear paw" frame; Tundra Kennels and Outfitters sends dogsleds like this one to customers throughout the world; Charles Bengelsdorf prepares tobacco used to wrap his *Berndt's Specials* and *Flor de Berthold's*.

3. PILLOW TALK and FANTASY PHONE (Detroit)

During late 1981 Michigan's first two sexually explicit telephone services began operation. In return for a fee paid by credit card, operators at the two businesses provide up to a half-hour of conversation on any subject the caller desires.

4. SNOWSHOE MANUFACTURER (Shingleton)

Clarence Iverson operates Michigan's only snowshoe business. With the help of local residents, who bind the ash frames with plastic lacings, Iverson ships more than four thousand pairs each year to the U.S. Forest Service, Michigan Department of Natural Resources and backpackers throughout the country.

5. SAN TELMO CIGAR COMPANY (Bay City)

Charles Bengelsdorf, 86, operates the only surviving cigar company in Michigan. By hand he and 77-year-old Adeline Polom wrap, roll, trim, press and box more than 100,000 *Flor de Berthold* and *Berndt's Specials* each year.

6. DOGSLED MAKER (Nunica)

Tun-Dra-Kennels and Outfitters is the world's top producer of dogsleds. The mail-order business also sells other Arctic gear including headbands and socks knitted from Siberian husky hair.

FOREIGN INVESTMENTS
IN 32 MICHIGAN COMMUNITIES

Foreign-owned business operating in thirty-two Michigan communities as of 1975.

CITY	BUSINESS	C O U N T R Y
1. ADRIAN	Animal food	United Kingdom
2. ALMA	Oil refining	France
3. ALPENA	Truck attachments	Canada
4. ANN ARBOR	Bearings Photo equipment	Japan Liechtenstein
5. BENTON HARBOR	Electronics Steel Strip	Netherland Antilles Sweden
6. BIG RAPIDS	Machine tool accessories	Japan

7. BIRMINGHAM	Paperboard	Canada
8. BRIDGMAN	Steel wire	France
9. COLDWATER	Polyfoam	Japan
10. DETROIT	Bank	Saudi Arabia
	Machine tools	Belgium
	Tractors	Canada
	Metal stamps	Germany
	Pneumatic tools	United Kingdom
11. DUNDEE	Cement	Switzerland
12. EDMORE	Magnetics	Japan
13. EDWARDSBURG	Steel Springs	Germany
14. FERNDALE	Warehouse	Japan
15. GRAND RAPIDS	Cookies	United Kingdom
16. HOLLY	Foundry Machinery	Switzerland
17. JACKSON	Sheet Aluminum	Switzerland
	Electric Gears	United Kingdom
18. KENTWOOD	Musical instruments	Japan
19. LANSING	Epoxy resins	Switzerland
20. LOWELL	Seed-sorting machinery	United Kingdom
21. MOUNT CLEMENS	Pottery	Japan
22. MUSKEGON	Casings	France
23. MUSKEGON HEIGHTS	Gasoline pumps	Canada
24. PLYMOUTH	Chemicals	United Kingdom
25. PORT HURON	Strapping	Canada
	Phone equipment	Canada
26. SAGINAW	Food machinery	United Kingdom

27. SAULT STE. MARIE	Steel tubing	Canada
28. SOUTHFIELD	Metal presses	Germany
29. SOUTH HAVEN	Pianos	Japan
30. SPRINGFIELD	Cookies	Canada
31. TROY	Chemical Machine tools	Canada Germany
32. WYANDOTTE	Chemicals	Germany

3 MICHIGAN BUSINESSES OWNED BY TED NUGENT

Rock star and Michigan native, Ted Nugent, has produced two gold and five platinum albums. The money from those sales has been invested in many diversified businesses including these three in Michigan
1. TROUT FARM (East Lansing)
2. HYATT REGENCY HOTEL (Flint) - Limited partner.
3. KING MINK RANCH - Mink and Clydesdale horses.

22 FORTUNE-500 COMPANIES

Twenty-two Michigan companies that made *Fortune* magazine's list of the five hundred largest American corporations in 1980 as measured by sales.

COMPANY	RANK
1. GENERAL MOTORS	3
2. FORD MOTOR COMPANY	6
3. DOW CHEMICAL	25
4. CHRYSLER	32
5. BENDIX	87
6. BURROUGHS	137
7. AMERICAN MOTORS	155
8. WHIRLPOOL	170
9. KELLOGG COMPANY	176
10. FRUEHAUF	180
11. UPJOHN	206
12. CLARK EQUIPMENT	226
13. EX-CELL-O	297
14. WHITE MOTOR	350
15. MAACO	359

16. TECUMSEH PRODUCTS	368
17. FEDERAL-MOGUL	377
18. DOW CORNING	396
19. MCLOUTH STEEL	427
20. GERBER PRODUCTS	434
21. HOOVER UNIVERSAL	439
22. FREDERICK & HERRUD	480

4 NATIONAL FRANCHISES HEADQUARTERED IN MICHIGAN

1. AMWAY (Grand Rapids)
   The home products, direct sales operation employs 1,835 workers.

2. LITTLE PROFESSOR BOOK CENTERS (Livonia)

3. CIRCUS WORLD TOY STORES (Taylor)
   The largest privately owned toy specialty chain in the country with 135 stores in twenty-two states.

4. SUSAN'S PETS (Oak Park)
   One hundred thirty-one representatives sell sexual aids at Tupperware-style house parties.

5 LARGEST MOTEL CHAINS

Numbers of establishments operated by major lodging chains or franchisors in Michigan in 1979.

1. HOLIDAY INN	49
2. BEST WESTERN	33
3. RAMADA INN	16
4. HOWARD JOHNSON'S	14
5. RED ROOF INNS	13

5 LARGEST DEPARTMENT STORE EMPLOYERS

Based on the number of employees in 1978.

1. K MART	37,600
2. J. C. PENNEY	16,577
3. DAYTON-HUDSON	16,297

National franchises headquartered in Michigan

Amway headquarters

| 4. SEARS ROEBUCK | 15,500 |
| 5. MEIJER | 12,000 |

6 INTERESTING OCCUPATIONS LICENSED BY THE STATE

1. DEAD STOCK HAULER
2. BUTTER GRADER
3. DEAD ANIMAL DISPOSAL PLANT OPERATOR
4. GARBAGE FEEDER
5. MINNOW DEALER
6. HOT WALKER

A Family Affair

3 RELATIVE PROFESSIONS

1. The Michigan Department of Natural Resources' Corp of Conservation officers includes a father-daughter-son. John Bezolte has worked in the Upper Peninsula for thirty-three years, his daughter Kathy (Pontiac) became the first woman DNR officer in 1978 and son John is a conservation officer in Sandusky.

2. In 1981 Francine Goodrich coached the Michigan State University women's cross-country team while husband John coached the women's cross-country team at arch rival University of Michigan.

3. Robert Breakey (Ann Arbor) graduated from the University of Michigan Medical School in 1980, the fifth-generation graduate of the same family from the same school.

Professionally Speaking

11 LICENSED PROFESSIONS

Numbers of people licensed for selected professions in Michigan in 1979.

1. LICENSED PRACTICAL NURSE	72,221
2. REGISTERED NURSE	33,507
3. PHARMACISTS	7,518
4. DENTISTS	6,317
5. HYGIENISTS	4,030
6. BARBERS	3,294
7. ARCHITECTS	3,152

8. PHYSICIANS	2,985
9. VETERINARIANS	2,019
10. CHIROPRACTOR	1,112
11. PODIATRISTS	431

3 MOST DANGEROUS JOBS

According to the Michigan Department of Labor in December, 1975, the chances of getting killed on the job are highest for the following three categories:
1. RETAIL CLERK
2. CAB DRIVER
3. GAS STATION ATTENDANT

4 MOST WORKING YEARS

Four years since 1947 with the fewest people collecting unemployment in Michigan.

1.	1965	38,200
2.	1948	40,300
3.	1966	40,500
4.	1953	40,800

6 MOST JOBLESS YEARS

Six years from 1947 through 1979 with the most people collecting unemployment in Michigan.

1.	1975	255,300
2.	1958	199,800
3.	1974	163,400
4.	1976	161,400
5.	1961	131,900
6.	1971	125,600

8 MOST UNEMPLOYED CITIES

Based on the 1980 unemployment rates as measured by the Michigan Department of Commerce.

1.	ONAWAY	34.9%
2.	BENTON HARBOR	25.1%

3. CROSWELL	23.9%
4. PONTIAC	23.4%
5. PERRY	22.0%
6. CHEBOYGAN	21.7%
7. HARRISVILLE	21.4%
8. MANTON	21.1%

2 CONSPICUOUS RESIGNATIONS

1. MARY CUNNINGHAM (Detroit) - October, 1980

The 1979 graduate of Harvard jumped from a relatively minor post with the Bendix Corporation to vice president in a little over a year. National headlines displayed the rumor that Cunningham had received the promotion because of a romantic involvement with William Agee, Bendix chairman. Both Agee and Cunningham denied the rumors but she resigned and was immediately hired as a vice president at Joseph E. Seagram and Sons, Incorporated (New York City).

2. BOB BRAUN (Pontiac) - November, 1981

The Internal Revenue (IRS) employee alleged to *60 Minutes* television reporter Morley Safer that the IRS engages in unfair collection practices against small businesses. Though the IRS denied that he was heavily pressured to do so, Braun resigned two days before the broadcast.

3 MOST STRIKING YEARS

Three years since 1941 with the most work stoppages in Michigan.

1. 1944	562
2. 1945	478
3. 1943	145

3 LEAST STRIKING YEARS

Three years since 1941 with the fewest work stoppages in Michigan.

1. 1963	135
2. 1949	139
3. 1960	145

4 NOTABLE STRIKES

1. FIRST BASEBALL STRIKE

The Detroit Tigers staged baseball's first strike on May 18, 1912, to protest the suspension of their star player, Ty Cobb, who had slugged a critical fan. Faced with a $100-per-day fine, the Tigers ended their strike after missing one game and forcing the re-scheduling of another.

2. CRESTWOOD STRIKE

On December 30, 1974, the Crestwood School District Board of Education (Dearborn Heights) fired 184 striking teachers after ordering them to either report to work or resign. The union appealed the action all the way to the U.S. Supreme Court which upheld the firings.

3. ATHEISTS STRUCK

A dispute with Easter-celebrating kitchen workers left an American Atheists convention foraging for food at a Southfield hotel, April, 1980. The catering employees walked off the job because they were upset with anti-religious jokes.

4. MICHIGAN'S FIRST STRIKE

In 1837 Detroit journeymen carpenters carrying signs saying, "Ten hours a day and two dollars for pay" walked off their jobs in Michigan's first organized protest against lower wages and increased hours.

3 YEARS WITH THE MOST STRIKERS

Three years since 1941 with the most Michigan workers involved in work stoppages.

1. 1944	568,700
2. 1945	521,000
3. 1941	333,600

4 YEARS WITH THE FEWEST STRIKERS

Four years since 1941 with the fewest Michigan workers involved in work stoppages.

1. 1975	35,000
2. 1963	36,800
3. 1972	54,200
4. 1960	65,300

5 SIGNIFICANT AUTO STRIKES

1. DECEMBER 30, 1936
Workers at Flint Fisher Body plants began a sit-down strike that eventually lasted forty-four days, affected 150,000 workers and closed more than sixty plants in fourteen states. The strike resulted in a one-page, nine-paragraph document in which General Motors guaranteed, for the first time, that it would recognize the United Auto Workers as its employees' bargaining agent. Strikes in 1937 at Chrysler and 1941 at Ford gained UAW recognition at those companies.

2. 1945-1946
The UAW struck General Motors for a record 119 days and won an 18.5-cent hourly wage increase.

3. 1949
Following a 24-day strike at two Ford plants, the UAW won the automobile industry's first non-contributory pension plan.

4. 1967
Strikes at all "Big Three" automakers gained nearly a dollar-an-hour-wage-and-benefits increases, a guaranteed annual income and pension increases.

5. 1970
A 67-day strike at GM succeeded in taking the ceiling off cost-of-living increases and obtaining retirement for workers over age 55 who had thirty years service.

2 LARGEST AUTOMOBILE RECALLS

1. LARGEST RECALL BY A SINGLE MANUFACTURER
In 1971 General Motors recalled 6.7 million cars to fix engine mounts.

2. LARGEST YEARLY TOTAL RECALLS
In 1977 U.S. auto manufacturers and importers recalled 12.6 million motor vehicles.

23 MODELS MADE IN MICHIGAN

Automobile models manufactured and produced in Michigan in 1980.
1. ASPEN (Hamtramck) - Dodge

2. CAPRI (Dearborn) - Ford
3. CENTURY (Flint) - Buick
4. CHECKER (Kalamazoo) - Checker Motor
5. CUTLASS (Lansing) - Oldsmobile
6. ELECTRA (Flint) - Buick
7. GRANADA (Wayne) - Ford
8. GRAND PRIX (Pontiac) - Pontiac
9. LeMANS (Pontiac) - Pontiac
10. LeSABRE (Flint) - Buick
11. MARK V (Wixom) - Lincoln
12. MONARCH (Wayne) - Mercury
13. MUSTANG (Dearborn) - Ford
14. NEWPORT (Detroit) - Chrysler
15. NEW YORKER (Detroit) - Chrysler
16. NOVA (Willow Run) - Chevrolet
17. OMEGA (Willow Run) - Oldsmobile
18. PHOENIX (Willow Run) - Pontiac
19. REGAL (Flint) - Buick
20. SEVILLE (Detroit) - Cadillac
21. SKYLARK (Willow Run) - Buick
22. VERSAILLES (Wayne) - Lincoln
23. VOLARE (Hamtramck) - Plymouth

Going In Style
6 COUNTIES WITH THE MOST NEW CARS

Based on the total new-car registrations per 100,000 people in 1979.

1. OAKLAND	9,567
2. MACOMB	8,801
3. WAYNE	7,930
4. SAGINAW	7,899
5. INGHAM	7,357
6. GENESEE	7,301

Clunking Around
5 COUNTIES WITH THE FEWEST NEW CARS

Based on total new-car registrations per 100,000 people in 1979.

1. HOUGHTON	2,753
2. OSCODA	2,861
3. MENOMINEE	2,897
4. LAKE	3,056
5. LEELANAU	3,057

2 SHORTEST HIGHWAYS

1. M-209
This half-mile highway runs from M-109 to Glen Haven near Sleeping Bear Dunes.

2. The highway that runs from M-106 north of Jackson to the gates of Southern Michigan Prison.

3 UNUSUAL HIGHWAY MATERIALS

1. USED TIRES
More than 10,000 old automobile tires, pulverized into tiny grains, were used in a 1978 paving of M-60 in Branch and St. Joseph counties.

2. STYROFOAM
Styrofoam sheets, bundled together five feet thick, were used as a base for a 1972 bridge approach northeast of Pickford in Chippewa County.

3. COPPER
To stabilize an area of shifting clay, a million tons of waste rock containing one pound of copper per ton was placed on an eight-mile section of U.S. 45 in Ontonagon County in 1959. Prior to the creation of that unusual base, it had been impossible to lay a durable concrete surface and the stretch was the last remaining gravel portion on the Gulf of Mexico to Lake Superior route.

7 INCOMPLETE HIGHWAYS

The last major freeway work scheduled to be competed in Michigan.

1. U.S. 131
Howard City to north of Reed City - 50 miles.

2. M-21
Lapeer to Port Huron - 45 miles.

3. U.S. 27
Lansing to Ithaca - 30 miles.

4. U.S. 31
From U.S. 12 (Niles) to I-94 (Scottdale) - 25 miles.

212

5. I-69
   Charlotte to Lansing - 20 miles.

6. U.S. 131
   Cadillac to Manton - 15 miles.

7. U.S. 31
   Ludington to Pentwater - 11 miles.

6 BRICK HIGHWAYS

As of 1977 only 3.3 miles of brick state highway remained in Michigan. The six largest remaining brick highways:

1. 1.4 miles on U.S. 12 (Wayne)
2. .4 mile on M-54 business route (Flint)
3. .3 mile on I-94 business loop (St. Joseph)
4. .3 mile on M-99 (Albion)
5. .2 mile on M-46 (Muskegon)
6. .1 mile on M-43 (Kalamazoo)

5 MACKINAC CROSSINGS

Total number of vehicles that have crossed the Mackinac Bridge during five selected years.

1. 1958	1,390,390
2. 1965	1,328,641
3. 1970	1,947,862
4. 1975	2,285,784
5. 1979	2,539,620

4 LEAST TRUCKING COUNTIES

The four counties with the fewest new-truck registrations per 100,000 people in 1979.

1. HOUGHTON	1,111
2. LEELANAU	1,113
3. KEEWEENAW	1,174
4. WAYNE	1,175

Brick highway, M-54, Flint

Brick highway, M-99, Albion

214

5 MOST TRUCKING COUNTIES

Five counties with the most total new-truck registrations per 100,000 people in 1979.

1. OTSEGO		2,874
2. OSCEOLA		2,657
3. MONTMORENCY		2,571
4. SCHOOLCRAFT		2,448
5. OCEANA		2,417

7 FUELISH YEARS

Gasoline consumed for highway use for seven selected years.

1. 1947	1,345 million gallons
2. 1955	2,238 million gallons
3. 1960	2,564 million gallons
4. 1965	3,241 million gallons
5. 1970	4,097 million gallons
6. 1975	4,650 million gallons
7. 1978	5,220 million gallons

6 OIL REFINERIES

There are nearly four thousand producing gas and oil wells in Michigan and six refineries.

1. BAY REFINING (Bay City)
2. CRYSTAL REFINING COMPANY (Carson City)
3. LAKESIDE REFINING COMPANY (Kalamazoo)
4. TOTAL LEONARD, INCORPORATED (Alma)
5. MARATHON OIL (Detroit)
6. OSCEOLA REFINING COMPANY (West Branch)

4 LARGEST OIL PRODUCING COUNTIES

Based on 1978 production figures.

1. OTSEGO	2.5 million barrels
2. KALKASKA	1.6 million barrels
3. HILLSDALE	1.6 million barrels
4. INGHAM	1.4 million barrels

3 NUCLEAR POWER PLANTS

1. PALISADES (South Haven)
   Consumers Power - 805,000 Kw capacity.

2. BIG ROCK POINT (Charlevoix)
   Consumers Power - 72,000 Kw capacity.

3. DONALD C. COOK (Bridgman)
   Indiana and Michigan Electric Company.
   Reactor #1 - 1,054,000 Kw capacity.
   Reactor #2 - 1,100,000 Kw capacity.

4 LARGEST PORTS

Michigan's four largest ports based on 1979 tonnage handled.
1. DETROIT   24,996,000 tons
2. ESCANABA   13,453,000 tons
3. CALCITE (Rogers City)   10,320,000 tons
4. STONEPORT   9,358,000 tons

Mining Their Own Business
3 MINEFUL COUNTIES

Three counties that extracted the most minerals in 1977 expressed in dollar value of the mined minerals.
1. MARQUETTE $303,429,000
2. MANISTEE $163,705,000
3. GRAND TRAVERSE $ 97,816,000

5 YEARS OF IRON MINES

Number of actively worked iron mines in Michigan for five selected years.
1. 1947   36
2. 1953   40
3. 1960   27
4. 1965   16
5. 1978   6

Donald C. Cook nuclear power plant

Big Rock Point nuclear power plant

5 LEAST MINEFUL COUNTIES

Five counties that extracted the fewest minerals in 1977 expressed in dollar value of the mined minerals.

1. ALGER		$44,000
2. ALCONA		$46,000
3. KEEWEENAW		$47,000
4. OSCODA		$50,000
5. MONTMORENCY		$83,000

5 MOST AGRARIAN COUNTIES

Based on cash receipts from total fruit and vegetable crop marketings in 1977.

1. HURON	$98 million
2. SANILAC	$79 million
3. ALLEGAN	$72 million
4. LENAWEE	$71 million
5. TUSCOLA	$71 million

5 YEARS OF FARMS

Number of farms in Michigan for five selected years.

1. 1920	196,447
2. 1950	155,589
3. 1960	111,817
4. 1970	77,946
5. 1979	64,094

5 LARGEST CASH CROPS

Based on cash receipts from total 1978 marketings.

1. CORN	$244,032,000
2. SOYBEANS	$159,139,000
3. DRY EDIBLE BEANS	$95,891,000
4. APPLES	$68,463,000
5. POTATOES	$67,048,000

4 BREWERIES

1. CARLING (Frankenmuth) - owned by G. Heileman Brewing Co.
2. STROH (Detroit)
3. GOEBEL (Detroit) - owned by the Stroh Brewing Co.
4. GEYER (Frankenmuth)

13 WINERIES

Michigan is the third largest wine-producing region in the nation following California and New York. For a wine to be labeled a Michigan product it must contain 75% state-grown grape juice. Thirteen wineries in Michigan:
1. BOSKYDEL (Lake Leelanau)
2. BRONTE (Keeler)
3. CHATEAU GRAND TRAVERSE (Traverse City)
4. FENN (Fennville)
5. FRONTENAC (Paw Paw)
6. LAKESIDE (Harbert)
7. LEELANAU (Omena)
8. MILAN (Detroit)
9. MOLLY PITCHER (Harbert)
10. ST. JULIAN (Paw Paw and Frankenmuth)
11. TABOR HILL (Bridgman)
12. VENRAMINO (Paw Paw)
13. WARNER (Paw Paw)

5 LARGEST WINERIES

Based on gallons shipped in 1979.

1. WARNER	300,474
2. ST. JULIAN	161,572
3. MILAN	127,517
4. LAKESIDE	99,706
5. BRONTE	98,690

5 MOST COMMON ETHNIC PERIODICALS

Based on the total number of weekly or monthly periodicals published in Michigan for specific ethnic groups in 1979.

1. GERMAN	127

Michigan breweries and beer brewed
and bottled in Michigan.

2. AFRO AMERICAN   92
3. DUTCH   73
4. POLISH   64
5. FINNISH   62

4 SMALLEST NEWSPAPERS

Based on paid circulation for 1981.
1. *ELK RAPIDS PROGRESS*   520
   (ceased publication January 1, 1982.)
2. *CLIMAX CRESCENT*   700
3. *FREEPORT NEWS*   700
4. *GALESBURG ARGUS*   700

10

ATHLETE FEATS

6 REMARKABLE FEATS

1. OVER NIAGARA FALLS IN A BARREL - October 24, 1901
   Annie Edson Taylor, a Bay City schoolteacher, became the first person to survive a barrel ride over Niagara Falls. She took the plunge in a self-designed, wooden barrel made by a Bay City cooperage.

2. 2,200 MILES BY ROWBOAT - 1964
   "Seaway" Tony Calery, a 45-year-old, 200-pound, bachelor lumberjack rowed a fifteen-foot boat from his hometown Sault Ste. Marie to the 1964 World's Fair in New York. The 2,200-mile journey took seventy-five days.

3. MACKINAC STRAITS SWIM - September 4, 1979
   While 23,000 people joined Governor Milliken in the 1979 Labor Day Mackinac Bridge walk, Jack Laporte (Flint) swam in the water underneath. The forty-year-old swam the 4½ miles from the Lower to Upper Peninsula in three hours. During the 1981 Bridge Walk Cathy Daoust, a 22-year-old Northern Michigan University student, repeated the wet, cold journey in just over seven hours.

4. CROSS-COUNTRY BIKE RIDE - 1976
   Mark Johnson (Royal Oak), Scott Ray (Grand Rapids), and Doug Miner (Canton, Ohio) rode their bikes 3,500 miles cross-country. The three Michigan State University roommates put their back tires in the Pacific Ocean at Astoria, Oregon, on June 14 and, forty-two days later, put their front tires in the Atlantic Ocean at Virginia Beach, Virginia.

5. PERIMETER RIDE - 1974
   John King (Jackson) and Michael Ritter (Reading) pedaled bicycles around the perimeter of the United States. The Western Michigan University students completed the 10,000-mile trek in nine months.

. PACIFIC CREST TRAIL
During the summer of 1970 eighteen-year-old Eric Ryback (Belleville) iked 2,313 miles of the Pacific Crest trail from the Canadian-American order, through Washington, Oregon and California to Mexico. In 1972)ean Johnson (Flint) reversed the trip, hiking from Mexico to Canada in 27 days.

9 OLYMPIC GOLD MEDALISTS

. KEN MORROW (Davison) - 1980
The stellar defenseman on the gold-medal-winning ice hockey team ecame the only player in hockey history to win both a gold medal and, as a nember of the National Hockey League's New York Islanders, professional ockey's Stanley Cup in the same season.

. MARK WELLS (St. Clair Shores) - 1980
The forward played regularly on the ice hockey team that stunned the oviets 4-3 and went on to win the gold medal.

. SHEILA YOUNG (Detroit) - 1976
The speed skater broke an Olympic record and won a gold medal by kating 500 meters in 42.76 seconds. She also became the first American to vin three medals at a Winter Olympics by capturing a silver medal in the 500-meter and bronze in the 1000-meter events.

. MICKI KING (Pontiac) - 1972
The diver won a gold medal in the 3-meter springboard competition.

. TERRY McDERMOTT (Essexville) - 1964
The barber won a gold medal by skating 500 meters in a record 40.1 econds.

. ROD PAAVOLA (Hancock) - 1960
The hockey player was a member of the gold-medal-winning squad.

. WELDON OLSEN (Marquette) - 1960
The hockey player was a member of the gold-medal-winning squad.

. EDDIE TOLAN (Detroit) - 1932
Won the 100-meter and 200-meter dashes.

. JACKSON SCHOLZ (Buchanan) - 1924
Won a gold medal in the 200-meter dash.

1. GREG BARTON (Homer)
   Kayak - Men's 500, 1,000 and 10,000-meter flatwater.

2. JIM BELL (Ypsilanti)
   Badminton - Masters mixed doubles (with Ethel Marshall, Williamsville, New York).

3. PAM BRADY (Flint)
   Badminton - Women's doubles (with Judianne Kelly, Costa Mesa, California).

4. MAX CALHOUN (Flint)
   Paddleball - Men's senior doubles (with Joe Roberson, Flint).

5. TAMMY DEWULF (Brighton)
   Roller skating - Junior women's figures.

6. SUE DOOLEY (Farmington Hills)
   Roller skating - 4-woman relay (with Kathy Katovich, Tammy Griffith, and Denise McLeod, all from Farmington Hills).

7. ROB DUNN (Farmington Hills)
   Roller skating - Speed, two-man relay (with Chuck Jackson, Farmington Hills), mixed-couple relay (with Denise McLeod, Farmington Hills), and mixed-4 relay (with Chuck Jackson, Denise McLeod, and Kathy Katovich, all from Farmington Hills).

8. MIKE EATON (Grand Rapids)
   Bowling - ABC men's singles.

9. STEVE GALETTI (Ann Arbor)
   Paddleball - Men's masters doubles (with Rod Grambeau, Kalamazoo).

10. MEADE GEOUGON (Bay City)
    Iceboating - U.S. DN class.

11. GREG GRAMBEAU (Ann Arbor)
    Paddleball - Men's doubles (with Bob Sterken, Ann Arbor).

12. ROD GRAMBEAU (Ann Arbor)
    Paddleball - Men's masters doubles (with Steve Galetti, Ann Arbor).

13. GALE GREENLAND (Kalamazoo)
   Paddleball - Men's golden masters doubles (with Dick Tanner, Kalamazoo).

14. TAMMY GRIFFITH (Farmington Hills)
   Roller skating - 4-woman relay (with Kathy Katovich, Denise McLeod, and Sue Dooley, all from Farmington Hills).

15. YVONNE HACKENBERG (Kalamazoo)
   Platform tennis - Women's doubles (with Hilary Hilton, Glen Ellyn, Illinois).

16. JERRY HARDY (Detroit)
   Tumbling - Men.

17. CHUCK JACKSON (Farmington Hills)
   Roller skating - 2-man relay (with Rob Dunn, Farmington Hills) and mixed-4 relay (with Rob Dunn, Denise McLeod, and Kathy Katovich, all from Farmington Hills).

18. DICK JURY (Williamston)
   Paddleball - Men's open and men's seniors.

19. KATHY KATOVICH (Farmington Hills)
   Roller skating - 4-woman relay (with Denise McLeod, Tammy Griffith, and Sue Dooley, all from Farmington Hills) and mixed-4 relay (with Rob Dunn, Chuck Jackson, and Denise McLeod, all from Farmington Hills).

20. BRUCE KIMBALL (Ann Arbor)
   Diving - A.A.U. indoor platform.

21. TINA KNEISLEY (Brighton)
   Roller skating - Pairs (with Paul Price, Brighton).

22. GRACE LOUWSMA (Ann Arbor)
   Paddleball - Women's doubles (with Judy Shirley, Ann Arbor).

23. LYNETTE LOVE (Detroit)
   Tae Kwon Do - Women's heavyweight division.

24. SUSIE MASCARIN (Grosse Pointe Shores)
   Tennis - U.S. Open juniors.

25. STEVEN McCRORY (Detroit)
   Boxing - Golden Gloves 106-pound division.

26. DENISE McLEOD (Farmington Hills)

Roller skating - 4-woman relay (with Kathy Katovich, Tammy Griffith, and Sue Dooley, all from Farmington Hills) and mixed-4 relay (with Rob Dunn, Chuck Jackson, and Kathy Katovich, all from Farmington Hills).

27. PAM MERCER (Wyandotte)
Speed skating - Indoor.

28. DEBRA OCHS (Howell)
Archery - Junior girls.

29. DALLAS OSKEY (Flint)
Roller skating - Junior men's figures.

30. MARTIN PIERCE (Flint)
Boxing - A.A.U. 165-pound division.

31. PAUL PRICE (Brighton)
Roller skating - Pairs (with Tina Kneisley, Brighton).

32. SUE NOVARA REBER (Flint)
Bicycle track racing - Women's sprint.

33. JOE ROBERSON (Flint)
Paddleball - Men's senior doubles (with Max Calhoun, Flint).

34. SUE SCHAUGG (St. Clair Shores)
Bicycle track racing - Intermediate girl's.

35. CHRIS SEUFERT (Ann Arbor)
Diving - Outdoor women's 3-meter.

36. JUDY SHIRLEY (Ann Arbor)
Paddleball - Women's doubles (with Grace Louwsma, Ann Arbor).

37. BOB STERKEN (Ann Arbor)
Paddleball - Men's doubles (with Greg Grambeau, Ann Arbor).

38. DICK TANNER (Kalamazoo)
Paddleball - Men's golden masters doubles (with Gale Greenland, Kalamazoo).

39. DON TAYLOR (Allen Park)
Paddleball - Men's masters.

40. MICHAEL VASQUEZ (Port Huron)
Tae Kwon Do - Men's flyweight division.

41. BRET WILLIAMS (Northern Michigan University)
   Skiing - NCAA slalom.

42. KENNETH WORDEN (Coldwater)
   Shuffleboard - Men's doubles (with Virgil Pfiser, Canton, Ohio).

43. VIRGINIA WORDEN (Coldwater)
   Shuffleboard - Women's doubles (with Mildred Davis, New Castle, Indiana.

44. JAN ZAKARZECKI
   Judo - A.A.U. women, 106-pound division.

5 1980 WORLD CHAMPIONS

1. SHERI CONFER (Warren)
   Skeet shooting - Champion of champions.

2. ILA HILL (Birmingham)
   Skeet shooting - 28-gauge individual gun.

3. AL MAGYAR, JR. (Taylor)
   Skeet Shooting - Men's overall high.

4. SUE NOVARA REBER (Flint)
   Women's bicycle sprint.

5. SUE WILLIAMS (Dimondale)
   Girl's horseshoe pitching.

2 NATIONAL HALLS OF FAME LOCATED IN MICHIGAN

1. AMERICAN ASSOCIATION OF COLLEGE BASEBALL COACHES HALL OF FAME (Kalamazoo)
   Founded in 1963.

2. NATIONAL SKI HALL OF FAME (Ishpeming)

2 NATIONAL SPORTS ORGANIZATIONS BASED IN MICHIGAN

1. AMERICAN AMATEUR BASEBALL CONGRESS (Battle Creek)

2. AMERICAN POWER BOAT ASSOCIATION (Detroit)

3 ATHLETES OF THE YEAR

Three Michigan athletes selected by the Associated Press as America's Athlete of the Year.
1. JOE LOUIS - 1935
2. TOM HARMON - 1940
3. DENNY McLAIN - 1968

3 RETIRED NUMBERS

Three Michigan professional athletes whose numbers have been retired.
1. LARRY AURIE - #6, Detroit Red Wings.
2. GORDIE HOWE - #9, Detroit Red Wings.
3. AL KALINE - #6, Detroit Tigers.

23 SPORTS ILLUSTRATED COVER ATHLETES

Twenty-three Michigan athletes who have appeared on the cover of *Sports Illustrated* magazine from its inception in 1953 through 1978.
1. EARVIN "MAGIC" JOHNSON — Michigan State basketball player (November 26, 1978)
2. MARK FIDRYCH - Detroit Tigers (April 24, 1978, and June 6, 1977)
3. RICKY GREEN - University of Michigan basketball player (November 29, 1976)
4. RICK LEACH - University of Michigan quarterback (September, 1976)
5. UNIVERSITY OF MICHIGAN BASKETBALL (March 29, 1976)
6. CAMPY RUSSELL - University of Michigan basketball player (December 11, 1972)
7. ALEX KARRAS - Detroit Lions (October 12, 1970, and November 24, 1964)
8. DENNY McLAIN - Detroit Tigers (February 22, 1970, September 23, 1968, and July 29, 1968)

9. BILL FREEHAN - Detroit Tigers (April 14, 1969)
10. AL KALINE - Detroit Tigers (June 5, 1967, May 15, 1964, and May 14, 1956)
11. MICHIGAN STATE FOOTBALL (November 28, 1966)
12. DETROIT RED WINGS (April 26, 1966)
13. GORDIE HOWE - Detroit Red Wings (March 18, 1964, and March 18, 1957)
14. HOWIE YOUNG - Detroit Red Wings (January 28, 1963)
15. NICK PIETROSANTE - Detroit Lions (December 15, 1962)
16. FRANK LARY - Detroit Tigers (April 9, 1962)
17. OAKLAND HILLS - U.S. Open golf (June 13, 1961)
18. TED LINDSAY - Detroit Red Wings (March 18, 1957)
19. TOM MAENTZ - University of Michigan football (November 12, 1956)
20. RON KRAEMER - University of Michigan football (November 12, 1956)

Top bowler Steve Nagy

The Detroit Lions' Doak Walker

Al Kaline and Harvey Kuenn of the Detroit Tigers

Tom Maentz and Ron Kramer: Michigan's great ends

Ted Lindsay and Gordie Howe of the Detroit Red Wings

Detroit Tiger pitcher Frank Lary

Fullback Nick Pietrosante of the Detroit Lions

Detroit Red Wing Howie Young

Al Kaline of Detroit

Detroit's red-hot Red Wing Gordie Howe

Defensive lineman Alex Karras of the Detroit Lions

Chicago vs. Detroit in the Stanley Cup playoffs

Al Kaline and Tigers stalk pennant

Detroit Tigers' pitcher Denny McLain

Detroit's Denny McLain wins his 30th game

Bill Freehan of the champion Detroit Tigers

Pitcher Denny McLain of the Detroit Tigers

Alex Karras, pride of the Detroit Lions

College court star Campy Russell of Michigan's Wolverines

Quarterback Rick Leach of No. 1-rated Michigan

All-America Rickey Green of Michigan

Detroit's Mark Fidrych and friend

"Big Bird" Mark Fidrych whoops it up in Detroit

"Super Soph" Earvin Johnson of Michigan State

21. HARVEY KUEHN - Detroit Tigers (May 14, 1956)
22. DOAK WALKER - Detroit Lions (October 3, 1955)
23. STEVE NAGY - Professional bowler (March 28, 1955)

3 RECORD HOME ATTENDANCES

1. DETROIT RED WINGS - January 17, 1982
20,682 watched Wayne Gretzky and the Edmonton Oilers tie the Wings, 4-4. The Joe Louis Arena crowd was the largest to watch a regular season National Hockey League game anywhere.

2. DETROIT PISTONS - January 11, 1980
28,146 watched "Magic" Johnson and the Los Angeles Lakers beat Detroit, 123-100, at the Pontiac Silverdome.

3. DETROIT TIGERS - July 20, 1947
58,369 jammed into Briggs Stadium to watch a doubleheader between Detroit and the New York Yankees.

19 TIGERS IN THE
NATIONAL BASEBALL HALL OF FAME

	Year Inducted
1. TY COBB	1936
2. DAN BROUTHERS	1945
3. HUGHIE JENNINGS	1945
4. MICKEY COCHRANE	1947
5. HARRY HEILMANN	1952
6. CHARLIE GEHRINGER	1949
7. EDWARD B. BARROW	1953
8. AL SIMMONS	1953
9. HANK GREENBERG	1956
10. SAM CRAWFORD	1957
11. HEINIE MANUSH	1964
12. GOOSE GOSLIN	1968
13. WAITE HOYT	1969
14. BILLY EVANS	1973
15. SAM THOMPSON	1974
16. EARL AVERILL	1975
17. BUCKY HARRIS	1975
18. EDDIE MATHEWS	1978
19. AL KALINE	1980

2 HALL OF FAMERS
WHO SPENT THEIR ENTIRE CAREER IN DETROIT

1. CHARLIE GEHRINGER - Infielder from 1924 to 1942.

2. AL KALINE - Outfielder from 1953 to 1974.

DETROIT TIGERS' FIRST 3 YEARS

Detroit joined the National League and played from 1881 through 1888. Their record for the first three years:

	W	L	PCT	Place
1. 1881	41	43	.488	4th out of 8 teams
2. 1882	42	41	.506	6th out of 8 teams
3. 1883	40	58	.408	7th out of 8 teams

Detroit joined the American League in 1901. The record for their first three American League seasons:

	W	L	PCT	Place
1. 1901	74	61	.548	3rd out of 8 teams
2. 1902	52	83	.385	7th out of 8 teams
3. 1903	65	71	.478	5th out of 8 teams

7 PENNANT-WINNING YEARS

Seven years the Detroit Tigers have won the American League regular season championship.

1. 1907	5. 1940
2. 1908	6. 1945
3. 1934	7. 1968
4. 1935	

2 LONGEST TIGER GAMES

1. 24 INNINGS - July 21, 1945
Detroit and the Philadelphia Athletics were tied, 1-1, when, after four hours and forty-eight minutes, the game was called because of darkness.

2. 22 INNINGS - June 24, 1962

The New York Yankees beat Detroit, 9-7, in a game which took seven hours to play.

3 TIGER ROOKIES OF THE YEAR

Three American League "rookie of the year" awards as selected by the Baseball Writer's Association.
1. HARVEY KUEHN - 1953
2. MARK FIDRYCH - 1976
3. LOU WHITAKER - 1978

6 DETROIT TIGER MOST VALUABLE PLAYERS

Six American League "most valuable players" selected by the Baseball Writer's Association.
1. MICKEY COCHRANE - 1934
2. HANK GREENBERG - 1935
3. CHARLIE GEHRINGER - 1937
4. HANK GREENBERG - 1940
5. HAL NEWHOUSER - 1944 and 1945
6. DENNY McLAIN - 1968

4 AMERICAN LEAGUE HOME RUN CHAMPIONS

	Year	#Hit
1. SAM CRAWFORD	1908	7
	1914	14
2. TY COBB	1909	9
3. HANK GREENBERG	1935	36
	1938	58
	1940	41
	1946	44
4. RUDY YORK	1943	34

8 AMERICAN LEAGUE BATTING CHAMPIONS

1. TY COBB - 1907, 1908, 1909, 1911, 1913, 1914, 1915, 1917, 1918 and 1919.
2. HARRY HEILMANN - 1921, 1923, 1925 and 1927.
3. HEINIE MANUSH - 1926
4. CHARLIE GEHRINGER - 1937
5. GEORGE KELL - 1949
6. AL KALINE - 1955
7. HARVEY KUEHN - 1959
8. NORM CASH - 1961

3 TIGERS WHO HOLD
ALL-TIME MAJOR LEAGUE RECORDS

1. TY COBB
    Highest lifetime batting average (.361), most runs (2,244), and most base hits (4,191).

2. CESAR GUTIERREZ
    Most consecutive base hits in a single game (7).

3. JIM NORTHRUP
    Most grand slams in a single game (2).

7 TIGERS WHO HAVE HIT FOR THE CYCLE

Seven Tigers who have hit a single, double, triple and home run in the same game.
1. BOBBY VEACH - September 17, 1920
2. BOB FOTHERGILL - September 26, 1926
3. GEE WALKER - April 20, 1937
4. CHARLIE GEHRINGER - May 27, 1939
5. VIC WERTZ - September 14, 1947
6. GEORGE KELL - June 2, 1950
7. HOOT EVERS - September 7, 1950

2 TIGERS SIGNED OUT OF PRISON

1. GATES BROWN (Ohio State Reformatory) - 1960
2. RON LEFLORE (Jackson Prison) - 1973

2 WHO MISSED A CHANCE TO MANAGE THE TIGERS BECAUSE THEY WERE ON VACATION

1. BABE RUTH - 1934
   Tiger owner Frank Navin asked Ruth to manage the club but, when Ruth left for Honolulu without giving an answer, Navin hired Mickey Cochrane.

2. "SCHOOL BOY" ROWE - 1955
   When Spike Briggs, Tiger president, decided to change managers, he tried to call his first choice, Rowe. But the former Tiger pitcher had gone fishing and couldn't be reached so Briggs called Fred Hutchinson and gave him the job.

10 ANIMAL NICKNAMES

Ten former Tigers with animal-sounding nicknames.
1. LEON "GOOSE" GOSLIN
2. JOHN "RATSO" HILLER
3. JIM "FOX" NORTHRUP
4. FRANK "PIG" HOUSE
5. HARRY "HORSE" HEILMAN
6. MARK "BIRD" FIDRYCH
7. CHARLEY "SEA LION" HALL
8. DON "COYOTE" WERT
9. WILLIAM "MUTT" WILSON
10. CLYDE "RABBIT" JOHNSON

3 WEIGHTY TIGER NICKNAMES

1. ELMER "SLIM" LOVE
2. BOB "FATTY" FOTHERGILL
3. CHARLES "PIANO LEGS" HICKMAN

AN ALL-TIME, ALL-MICHIGAN-BORN
PROFESSIONAL BASEBALL TEAM

	STARTER	BACK UP
CATCHER	Bill Freehan (Detroit)	Ted Simmons (Highland Park)
FIRST BASE	John Mayberry (Detroit)	Rick Leach (Flint)
SECOND BASE	Charlie Gehringer (Fowlerville)	Bobby Grich (Muskegon)
THIRD BASE	Bill Stein (Battle Creek)	Tom Paciorek (Detroit)
SHORTSTOP	Tom Tresh (Detroit)	Cass Michaels (Detroit)
RIGHT FIELD	Mickey Stanley (Grand Rapids)	Bernie Carbo (Detroit)
CENTER FIELD	Kirk Gibson (Pontiac)	Bill Virdon (Hazel Park)
LEFT FIELD	Ron Leflore (Detroit)	Merv Rettenmund (Flint)
PITCHERS	Hal Newhouser (Detroit)	Dick Raditz (Detroit)
	Frank Tanana (Detroit)	Mike Marshall (Adrian)
	Dave Rozema (Grand Rapids)	Milt Pappas (Detroit
	Larry Sorenson (Detroit)	Vern Ruhle (Coleman)

3 MAJOR LEAGUE UMPS FROM MICHIGAN

1. MIKE REILLY (Battle Creek)
   The five-year American League umpiring veteran had the distinction of being attacked on the field by a fan during the 1981 Milwaukee-New York playoff series. It was the first physical assault by a fan against a major-league umpire in more than forty years.

2. ROCKY ROE (Southfield)
   Became an American League umpire in 1980.

3. LEE WEYER (Imlay City)
   Has umpired in the National League since 1965.

3 NATIONAL AMATEUR SOFTBALL CHAMPIONS

1. BURCH GAUGE & TOOL (Detroit) - 1964
2. MIDLAND - 1979
3. McCARDLE PONTIAC-CADILLAC (Midland) - 1980

236

5 NATIONAL COLLEGE FOOTBALL CHAMPION YEARS

1. 1932 - University of Michigan
2. 1933 - University of Michigan
3. 1948 - University of Michigan
4. 1952 - Michigan State University
5. 1965 - University of Michigan (tie with Alabama)

9 COLLEGE FOOTBALL HALL OF FAMERS

Nine Michigan college players selected to the College Football Hall of Fame. The date is the last year of play.
1. WILLIE HESTON (University of Michigan) - 1904
2. A. BENBROOK (University of Michigan) - 1914
3. JOHN MAULBETSCH (University of Michigan) - 1914
4. HARRY KIPKE (University of Michigan) - 1923
5. BENNY FRIEDMAN (University of Michigan) - 1926
6. HARRY NEWMAN (University of Michigan) - 1932
7. TOM HARMON (University of Michigan) - 1940
8. ELROY HIRSCH (University of Michigan) - 1943
9. DON COLEMAN (Michigan State University) - 1951

3 HEISMAN TROPHY WINNERS
DRAFTED BY THE DETROIT LIONS

The Heisman Trophy is presented annually by the Downtown Athletic Club of New York City to the nation's outstanding college football player as determined by a poll of sportswriters and sportscasters.
Three winners who were drafted by the Lions:
1. HOWARD "HOPALONG" CASSADY (Ohio State) - 1955
2. STEVE OWENS (Oklahoma) - 1969
3. BILLY SIMS (Oklahoma) - 1978

5 HALL OF FAME LIONS

Five Detroit Lions who have been inducted into the Pro Football Hall of Fame.

1. BILL DUDLEY
   Running back, 1942-1953

2. RICHARD "NIGHT TRAIN" LANE
   Defensive back, 1948-1962

3. BOBBY LAYNE
   Quarterback, 1948-1962

4. JACK CHRISTIANSEN
   Defensive back, 1951-1958

5. JOE SCHMIDT
   Linebacker, 1953-1965

6 NFL ROOKIES OF THE YEAR

Six Detroit Lions voted the National Football League's Rookie of the Year as selected by United Press International (UPI).
1. NICK PIETROSANTE - 1959
2. GAIL COGDILL - 1960
3. MEL FARR - 1967
4. EARL McCULLOUGH - 1968
5. AL "BUBBA" BAKER - 1978
6. BILLY SIMS - 1980

4 LION ALL-TIME PRO RECORDS

Four professional football records held by the Detroit Lions.

1. MOST CONSECUTIVE SHUTOUT WINS - 7 (1934)

2. FEWEST PENALTIES IN A SEASON - 19 for 139 yards (1937)

3. MOST SEASONS LEADING THE LEAGUE IN PUNT RETURNS - 8

4. MOST TOUCHDOWNS RETURNING PUNTS - 8 (Jack Christiansen, 1951-1958)

2 WHO DIED WHILE PLAYING FOR THE LIONS

1. CHUCK HUGHES - October 25, 1971
   With a minute left in a game against the Chicago Bears, the 28-year-old wide receiver collapsed on the field and died less than an hour later of a

238

heart attack brought on by hardening of the arteries.

2. LUCIAN REEBERG - February 1, 1964
    After completing his rookie season with the Lions, the six-foot, three-inch, 290-pound tackle checked into a hospital in late January and died ten days later of cardiac failure brought on by uremic poisoning.

4 NFL CHAMPIONSHIPS

Four years the Lions won the National Football League playoff championship.
1. 1935
2. 1952
3. 1953
4. 1957

9 COLLEGE HOCKEY CHAMPIONSHIPS

Nine years in which a Michigan college team has won the NCAA Hockey Championship.
1. 1951 - University of Michigan
2. 1952 - University of Michigan
3. 1955 - University of Michigan
4. 1956 - University of Michigan
5. 1962 - Michigan Technological University
6. 1964 - University of Michigan
7. 1965 - Michigan Technological University
8. 1966 - Michigan State University
9. 1975 - Michigan Technological University

2 FORMER NAMES OF THE RED WINGS

They became the Red Wings in 1932-33. Before that they were called:
1. DETROIT FALCONS
2. DETROIT COUGARS

11 NHL LEAGUE CHAMPIONSHIP YEARS

Eleven years in which the Detroit Red Wings won the National Hockey League's regular season championship.

1. 1943	7. 1953
2. 1948	8. 1954
3. 1949	9. 1955
4. 1950	10. 1957
5. 1951	11. 1965
6. 1952	

7 STANLEY CUP CHAMPIONSHIPS

Seven years in which the Red Wings won the National Hockey League's Stanley Cup playoffs.

1. 1936	5. 1952
2. 1937	6. 1954
3. 1943	7. 1955
4. 1950	

3 RED WING WINNERS OF THE HART TROPHY

Awarded each year to the National Hockey League's most valuable player.
1. EBBIE GOODFELLOW - 1940
2. SID ABEL - 1949
3. GORDIE HOWE - 1952, 1953, 1957, 1958, and 1963

6 RED WING LADY BYNG WINNERS

Awarded to the NHL player who combines excellent play with sportsmanship.
1. MARTY BARRY - 1937
2. BILL QUACKENBUSH - 1949
3. RED KELLEY - 1951, 1943 and 1954
4. EARL REIBEL - 1956
5. ALEX DELVECCHIO - 1959, 1966, and 1969
6. MARCEL DIONNE - 1975

3 NBA RECORDS HELD BY
DETROIT PISTON KEVIN PORTER

1. MOST ASSISTS IN A SEASON - 1,099 (1979)
2. MOST ASSISTS IN A GAME - 29 (1979)
3. HIGHEST ASSIST AVERAGE PER GAME - 13.4 (1979)

2 NBA RECORDS SET BY THE DETROIT PISTONS

1. HIGHEST FIELD GOAL PERCENTAGE
   On January 29, 1979, the Pistons hit 56 of 81 shots (69.1%) from the field in a 128-118 victory over San Diego.

2. LONGEST LOSING STREAK
   The Pistons lost a record twenty-one games in a row (the last fourteen games of the 1979-80 season and the first seven of the 1980-81 season) before they beat Houston, 112-109.

7 PROFESSIONAL BOXING CHAMPIONS

1. GEORGE "KID" LAVIGNE (Bay City)
   World lightweight champion, 1896-1899.

2. STANLEY KETCHEL (Grand Rapids)
   World middleweight champion, 1908-1910.

3. AD WOLGAST (Cadillac)
   World lightweight champion, 1910-1912.

4. SUGAR RAY ROBINSON (Detroit)
   Welterweight champion, 1946, and middleweight champion, 1951.

5. JOE LOUIS (Detroit)
   Heavyweight champion, 1937-1949.

6. THOMAS HEARNS (Detroit)
   WBA welterweight champion, 1980.

7. HILMER KINTY (Detroit)
   WBA lightweight champion, 1980.

8 A.B.C. HALL OF FAMERS

Eight Michigan bowlers selected to the American Bowling Congress Hall of Fame.
   1. JOHN CRIMMINS (Detroit)
   2. BASIL FAZIO (Detroit)
   3. THERMAN GIBSON (Detroit)
   4. JOE JOSEPH (Lansing)

5. ED LUBANSKI (Detroit)
6. STEVE NAGY (Detroit)
7. LOUIS SIELAFF (Detroit)
8. GEORGE YOUNG (Detroit)

4 BOWLERS WITH SIX OR MORE SANCTIONED 300 GAMES

1. ED LUBANSKI (Detroit) - 11
2. WALTER KING (Detroit) - 8
3. JOE JOSEPH (Lansing) - 6
4. BOB STRAMPE (Detroit) - 6

2 HIGHEST SANCTIONED SERIES

The two highest sanctioned three-game series bowled in Michigan.

1. 877
   During three qualifying games for the Bonanza Michigan Majors Tour circuit, Chris Wu (Ann Arbor) bowled 278 - 299 - 300 on October 23, 1981.

2. 867
   Gostan Marois (Detroit) got thirty-three out of a possible thirty-six strikes while bowling 300 - 278 - 289 on March 3, 1970.

6 BOWLERS OF THE YEAR

Six Michigan bowlers who have been selected by the Bowling Writer's Association of America as their annual national Bowler of the Year.

1. JOHNNY CRIMMINS (Detroit) - 1942

2. VAL MIKIEL (Detroit) - 1948 and 1949

3. LEE JOUGLARD (Detroit) - 1951

4. MARION LADEWIG (Grand Rapids) - 1951, 1952, 1953, 1954, 1957 and 1958.

5. ANITA CANTALINE (Detroit) - 1956

6. ED LUBANSKI (Detroit) - 1959

242

5 NATIONAL COACHES OF THE YEAR

Only five Michigan high-school coaches have ever been selected as national coaches of the year in the history of the National High School Athletic Coaches Association. They are:

1. BOB WOOD (Grosse Pointe University Liggett)
   Tennis - 1981

2. JO LAKE (Flint Kearsley)
   Volleyball - 1978

3. HARLEY PIERCE (Sturgis High)
   Tennis - 1978

4. LOFTON GREEN (River Rouge)
   Basketball - 1971

5. MIKE RODRIQUEZ (Detroit Catholic Central)
   Wrestling - 1971

INDEX

A

Accidents 12, 15, 63, 68, 93, 94, 119, 161, 175
    airplane 2, 6, 7, 12
    boating 13, 14, 32, 42
    deadly 3, 4, 5, 6, 13, 62
    drowning 13
    falls 7, 8, 10, 13, 24
    hunting 14
    nuclear 2, 3
    odd 1, 2, 10, 11, 12, 23, 92, 93
    skydiving 7, 23
    traffic 2, 4, 10, 13, 14, 15, 20, 33, 42, 59, 74, 91, 92, 174, 175
    train 3, 4
Ada 58, 106
Adrian 45, 47, 98, 106, 113, 120, 128, 162, 196, 197, 201, 236
Advertising 74, 193, 194, 195
Aetna Township 109
Africa 197
Agate 133
Airplanes 2, 6, 7, 12, 23, 40, 41, 62, 79, 80, 111, 120, 148, 175, 197
Airports,
    Bishop 148
    Detroit City 7
    Detroit Metro 12, 40, 79, 120
    Ionia 7
    Nahma 178
    Pontiac Municipal 113
    Tecumseh 147
    Tri-City 6
Alabaster 48
Alaska 40, 69
Alba 188
Albion 68, 189, 213
Alcona County 154, 166, 167, 183, 218
Alger County 17, 180, 218
Allegan 87, 126, 127
Allegan County 87, 110, 142, 218
Allen Park 188, 226
Allendale 106
Alma 32, 144, 189, 201, 215
Alma County 16
Almira Township 107
Alpena 6, 26, 45, 48, 106, 163, 174, 177, 201
Alpena County 136
Amway 185, 204
Anchorage, Alaska 91
Anderson, Indiana 178
Animals 4, 32, 34, 69, 89, 90, 107, 141, 142, 143, 144, 145, 146, 201, 203, 235
    albino 144
    endangered 143
Ann Arbor 6, 26, 30, 45, 54, 60, 61, 62, 68, 78, 82, 98, 101, 104, 105, 106, 111, 118, 122, 147, 154, 165, 168, 172, 196, 201, 206, 224, 225, 226, 242
Ann Landers 58
Antrim County 16, 107, 132, 160
Appliances, common 159
Arcadia, California 40
Archery 226
Arenac County 26, 167
Arenas (see *Stadiums*)

Argentine Township 7
Arizona 53
Armada 21, 138
Asia 28
Astoria, Oregon 222
Astronauts 62, 138
Athletes of the year 229
Atlanta, Georgia 9
Atlanta, Michigan 136
Attendances,
    athletic 68, 69, 231
    legislative 53
    rock concert 52, 148
    school 57, 167
Au Gres 157
Augusta 45
Automobile,
    models 91, 92, 113, 114, 116, 210, 211
    new 211
    patents 114
    recalls 210
    salespeople 52, 114, 116, 123
    strikes 210
Automobile companies 52, 59, 113, 114, 116, 119, 197
    American Motors 179, 185, 203
    awards levied against 91, 92
    Chrysler Corporation 178, 194, 203, 210
    Ford Motor Company 91, 110, 159, 163, 179, 185, 194, 203, 210
    General Motors 91, 116, 178, 179, 185, 193, 194, 203, 210
Automobiles, assembled 68
Autopsies 16, 17, 172

B

Bad Axe 187
Badminton 224
Baltrusol, New Jersey 24
Banks 72, 85, 119, 179, 181
Baraga 198
Baraga County 26, 110, 154, 199
Barryton 32
Barton Hills 181
Baseball 25, 115, 126, 184, 209, 227, 229, 231, 232, 233, 234, 235, 236
Basketball 11, 24, 120, 175, 240, 241, 243
Bath 81, 82
Battle Creek 23, 46, 106, 122, 128, 147, 165, 175, 189, 229, 236
Bay City 11, 58, 71, 72, 85, 90, 94, 98, 137, 144, 165, 174, 197, 201, 215, 222, 224, 241
Bay County 136, 167
Beauty pageants 53, 54
Bedford Township 158
Beer and breweries 29, 193, 219, 220
Belgium 202
Bellaire 47
Belleville 46, 223
Bellevue 55, 111
Benton Harbor 21, 41, 48, 58, 70, 74, 101, 151, 183, 201, 207
Benzie County 34, 107, 133, 136, 167
Benzonia 34
Berrien County 137

Berrien Springs 83, 101
Bessemer 72, 135
Beverly Hills 70
Bicycling 197, 222, 226, 227
Big Bay 28
Big Rapids 106, 189, 201
Bigfoot 33, 34
Billiards 115, 116
Bingham Farms 181
Birmingham, Alabama 79
Birmingham Farms 181
Birmingham, Michigan 53, 54, 194, 202, 227
Births 93, 150, 151, 152, 153
    multiple 152
    surrogate 151, 152
    unique 151
    young 152
Black Legion 85, 86
Bloomer Township 109
Bloomfield Hills 28, 35, 52, 76, 92, 168, 174, 181, 185
Bloomingdale 127
Blizzards and snowstorms 6, 7, 11, 36, 128, 131
Boats and boating 13, 14, 34, 40, 107, 108, 109, 168, 174,
    222, 224, 229
Books 26, 27, 28, 32, 50, 60, 96, 97, 101, 119, 165, 173,
    185, 204
Bowlers of the year 242
Bowling 69, 224, 241, 242
Boxing 50, 225, 226, 229, 241
Boyne City 46
Branch County 126, 142, 212
Breweries (see Beer)
Bridges 4, 43, 86, 119, 212
    Ambassador 42
    Bluewater 42
    Houghton-Hancock 42
    International 44
    Mackinac 6, 8, 41, 42, 44, 50, 122, 147, 168, 213, 222
    Manistee River 15
    Manistique 44
    Zilwaukee, new 42
    Zilwaukee, old 42
Bridgman 2, 187, 202, 216, 219
Briggs Stadium 231
Brighton 18, 224, 225, 226
Bronson 47
Brownstone Township 50
Buchanan 23
Budget problems 177, 178
Buel Township 107
Buildings,
    old 98, 101
    tallest 44
Burt Township 166
Burton 47
Businesses,
    foreign-owned 201, 202, 203
    Fortune-500 203, 204
    rare 199, 200, 201
Byron 145

                        C

Cadillac 15, 26, 136, 213, 241
Cairo, Egypt, 80
Calhoun County 161
California 11, 33, 126, 145, 149, 156, 157, 223
Calumet 3, 36, 126, 128, 131
Canada 17, 30, 44, 76,97, 109, 157, 201, 202, 203
Cannonsburg 36
Canton, Ohio 222, 227
Canton Township 55

Caro 33
Carson City 215
Caseville 138
Cass City 188
Cass County 83, 98, 137, 142, 199
Castles 101, 102, 159
Cedar 36
Cemeteries 19, 20, 22, 73, 74
Centenarians 62, 63
Centerline 71
Centreville 98
Cesspools 160
Champions,
    national 137, 138, 224, 225, 226, 227, 236, 237, 239
    olympic 223
    professional 50, 223, 232, 233, 234, 239, 240, 241
    world 57, 227
Charlevoix 2, 47, 48, 49, 101, 216
Charlevoix County 133, 136
Charlotte 4, 198, 213
Chassell 46
Cheboygan 87, 208
Cheboygan County 35, 87, 132, 133
Chelsea 37, 87, 198
Chesaning 40
Chicago, Illinois 17, 77, 85, 93, 103, 113, 132
Chippewa County 35, 132, 136, 155, 183, 212
Churches 89, 98, 169
Circus 4, 21, 24, 148
Cities,
    all-American 68
    best 164, 165
    criminous 70
    defaulted 179
    ghost 110
    growing 157
    largest 154
    oldest 98
    poorest 183
    purchased 178
    ranking 165
    richest 181
    safest 70
    shrinking 156
Clark Lake 45
Clawson 70
Cleveland, Ohio 79
Climax 161, 221
Clinton 93
Clinton County 81, 158
Clio 55, 151
Coaches of the year 243
Cobo Hall 53
Coincidences, unusual 10, 151, 152
Coldwater 45, 126, 202, 227
Coleman 236
Colleges and universities 105, 156, 168, 186, 189
    Albion 105, 189
    Alma 31, 32, 189
    Central Michigan 168
    Cooley Law School 151
    Detroit Medical 73
    Eastern Michigan 82, 105, 168, 189, 199
    Ferris State 83, 189
    Harvard 208
    Hillsdale 63, 105, 189
    Hope 63
    Kalamazoo 105, 189
    Lake Superior State 189
    Michigan State 19, 54, 57, 81, 105, 106, 115, 128, 137,
        145, 168, 174, 177, 206, 222, 237, 239
    Michigan Technological 36, 105, 239
    Northern Michigan 222, 226

246

Ohio State 68, 237
Olivet 81, 105, 18
Oxford 57
Saginaw Valley State 189
Smith 123
Suomi 189
University of Alabama 237
University of Oklahoma 237
University of Michigan 2, 6, 53, 54, 56, 65, 68, 73, 82, 105, 115, 118, 119, 122, 159, 168, 173, 174, 177, 206, 237, 239
Wayne County Community 34
Wayne State 16, 17, 19, 63, 81, 168
Western Michigan 168, 189, 222
Colon 109
Colorado 41
Concord 103
Congressional Medal of Honor 59
Constantine 59, 98
Consumers Power 2, 3, 131, 144, 162, 216
Cooper 106
Copemish 183
Copper City 156, 183
Copper Harbor 103
Cornerstone 103, 104
Costa Mesa, California 224
Counties,
  animal populations 142
  elderly 154
  defense spending 186
  fastest growing 157
  financially independent 180
  largest 136
  largest families 158
  largest paychecks 184
  least populous 154
  minority students 167
  most mobile homes 159
  most populous 154
  most septic tanks 160
  needy 179
  no hospitals 16
  no veterinarians 143
  oldest 98
  one mortuary 17
  poorest 180
  population density 155
  private school attendance 167
  richest 180
  scholarly 165
  shrinking 155
  smallest 136
  smallest paychecks 183
  socially insecure 180
  socially secure 180
  uninstructed 166
  water facts 132
  youthful 154
Covington, Kentucky 110
Covington Township 110
Crawford County 18, 135, 140
Cross Village Township 183
Crosses 170, 171
Croswell 208
Cuba 79, 80, 120, 124, 199
Curene 162
Curling 115
Czechoslovakia 17

D

Daggett 106
Dansville 1

Darts 116, 190
Davison 65, 223
Davison Township 148
Day Township 109
Dearborn 8, 29, 45, 46, 53, 58, 60, 94, 152, 188, 211
Dearborn Heights 152, 209
Deaths 2, 3, 4, 5, 6, 7, 8, 9, 11, 13, 14, 15, 16, 20, 23, 24, 32, 42, 58, 62, 63, 68, 72, 73, 79, 80, 81, 82, 83, 84, 85, 86, 87, 89, 90, 91, 93, 94, 95, 124, 125, 128, 131, 132, 140, 142, 172, 173, 174, 207, 238, 239
  odds against 12
Deerfield 21
Delta County 110
Denver, Colorado 174
Detroit 2, 3, 9. 10, 15, 17, 18, 19, 20, 21, 23, 24, 25, 26, 28, 40, 42, 44, 45, 46, 47, 52, 53, 54, 55, 57, 59, 60, 61, 62, 68, 76, 77, 79, 80, 81, 83, 84, 85, 86, 90, 91, 92, 93, 94, 97, 98, 103, 104, 105, 106, 107, 111, 113, 114, 115, 116, 118, 119, 120, 122, 123, 124, 126, 131, 132, 145, 147, 149, 151, 152, 154, 165, 166, 168, 172, 177, 178, 179, 181, 184, 185, 187, 191, 193, 194, 197, 201, 202, 208, 211, 215, 216, 219, 223, 225, 229, 236, 241, 242, 243
Detroit Edison 12, 131, 162, 163
Detroit Lions 24, 229, 237, 238, 239
Detroit Pistons 185, 231, 240, 241
Detroit Red Wings 229, 231, 239, 240
Detroit State Fairgrounds Coliseum 24
Detroit Tigers 184, 209, 229, 231, 232, 233, 234, 235
Dexter 30
Dickinson County 88, 167
Dimondale 56, 227
Dioxin 164
Disabled winners 54, 55
Diseases 9, 12, 15, 17, 68, 73, 124, 125, 174
Diving 223, 225, 226
Divorces 58, 59, 149, 150, 191
Dogs 1, 32, 33, 48, 69, 145, 172, 196, 201
Domestic winners 55
Drinking and driving,
  penalties 78
  rights 77
Drowning 8, 14
Duluth, Minnesota 30
Dundee 202
Durand 4, 123

E

Eagle River, Wisconsin 35
Earthquakes 126, 127
East Detroit 40, 190
East Germany 199
East Lansing 19, 40, 60, 70, 146, 168, 177, 187, 203
East Tawas 13
Eaton County 155
Eau Claire 52
Ecorse 156
Edmore 198, 202
Education (see also *Students* and *Teachers*) 69, 88, 105, 118, 119, 165, 166, 167, 168, 177, 186
  finances 172, 173, 188, 189
  strikes 209
Edwardsburg 202
Egypt 17, 194
Elections 61, 65, 82, 120, 122, 123, 191
  contributors 189, 190
Elk Rapids 221
Ellsworth 188
Elmira 106
Emmet County 160, 183, 199
Empire 22, 23, 109

Employment (see also *Unemployment*) 204, 206, 207, 208
England 97
Entertainers 21, 22, 23, 24, 25, 45, 56, 71
Escanaba 216
Essexville 187, 223
Executions 81, 83, 84, 85, 118
Expenditures 199
  federal government 186, 187
  state government 186
Explosions 5, 6, 13, 59, 82, 93, 126, 145

F

Falls Church, Virginia 81
Falmouth 56
Farmington 46, 57
Farmington Hills 7, 46, 131, 224, 225, 226
Farms and farming 4, 41, 50, 56, 72, 94, 101, 127, 131, 161, 218
Farwell 37, 46
Fayette 110
Fennville 219
Fenton 31, 32, 109, 174
Ferndale 65, 202
Festivals,
  ethnic 47
  food 46
  historic 46, 47
  music 45, 46
Fine arts centers 44
Fires 4, 13, 62, 82, 84, 85, 86, 91, 110
  forest 4, 5
Firsts,
  national 4, 29, 37, 54, 61, 62, 68, 85, 104, 105, 111, 113, 114, 115, 116, 118, 119, 122, 123, 124, 137, 147, 152, 168, 170, 173, 181, 196, 197, 209, 210, 222, 223
  state 8, 9, 41, 62, 76, 84, 96, 104, 113, 119, 120, 122, 123, 138, 147, 173, 174, 177, 191, 192, 201, 206, 209, 232
  women 122, 123, 124, 206
  world 41, 62, 96, 116, 119, 133, 170
Fish and fishing 4, 34, 35, 36, 69, 115, 137, 143, 164, 174, 196, 203, 235
Flint 7, 9, 12, 18, 19, 25, 40, 45, 47, 53, 54, 56, 57, 59, 60, 68, 70, 71, 90, 92, 93, 95, 104, 111, 126, 128, 144, 145, 148, 152, 154, 165, 166, 173, 189, 203, 210, 211, 213, 222, 223, 224, 226, 227, 236, 243
Flint Township 34, 151
Floods 131, 132, 177
Florida 4, 16, 149, 156
Football 24, 68, 69, 95, 115, 145, 229, 237, 238, 239
Foundations 189
Fourths, national 69
Fowlerville 236
France 97, 201, 202
Franchises, national 204, 205
Frankenmuth 47, 193, 219
Franklin 181, 185
Freeland 6
Freeport 221
Fremont 198
Fruit 48, 52, 68, 69, 141, 218
Fruitport Township 93
Fulton 34
Funerals 17, 18, 19, 73, 88, 89, 95

G

Gaines Township 74
Galesburg 92, 221
Gangs 85, 86
Garden City 65
Gasoline consumption 215

Gaylord 61
Genesee County 71, 76, 88, 109, 148, 154, 155, 159, 160, 181, 184, 211
Geographic points 136
Germany 157, 202, 203
Ghost towns 110
Glen Ellyn, Illinois 225
Glen Haven 10, 135, 212
Gogebic 72
Gogebic County 35, 106, 133, 154, 156
Golf 3, 11, 24, 178, 198
Grand Haven 35, 63, 196
Grand Junction 56
Grand Ledge 7, 45
Grand Rapids 10, 11, 21, 26, 44, 45, 48, 60, 62, 68, 72, 73, 83, 98, 105, 111, 115, 119, 123, 127, 128, 131, 152, 154, 165, 166, 170, 172, 179, 185, 186, 196, 198, 202, 204, 222, 224, 236, 241, 242
Grand Traverse County 199, 216
Grandville 181
Gratiot County 88, 132, 160
Grave robbing 73, 74
Grayling 33, 50, 103
Greece 191
Greenland 36
Greenville 47, 111
Grosse Pointe 32, 94, 184, 188, 243
Grosse Pointe Farms 181
Grosse Pointe Park 23
Grosse Pointe Shores 181, 225
Grosse Pointe Woods 70
Guinness world record holders 48, 50, 52, 53, 194
Gulf of Mexico 212

H

Halls of fame 227, 228
  members 231, 232, 237, 238, 241, 242
Hamilton 63
Hamtramck 57, 178, 210, 211
Hancock 36, 189, 223
Harbert 219
Harbor Springs 36, 68
Harper Woods 156
Harrison 37
Harrisville 187, 208
Hartford 93
Hartwick Pines 135, 140
Hastings 45, 126
Hazel Park 65, 187, 198, 236
Haunted houses 30, 31, 32
Heisman Trophy winners 237
Helena Township 107
Hell 149
Heroes 59, 80, 106
Hetherton 136
Highests, world 52
Highland Park 24, 70, 152, 156, 168, 183, 187, 236
Highways and roads 2, 7, 37, 74, 111, 113, 119, 124, 128, 131, 132, 142, 159, 164, 186, 212, 213
  brick 213, 214
  dangerous 15
  dullest 38, 39, 40
Hillman 183
Hillsdale 113, 189
Hillsdale County 215
Hockey 223, 229, 231, 239, 240
Holland 37, 45, 47, 87
Holly 46, 144, 202
Hollywood 56
Homer 224
Honolulu, Hawaii 235
Horseshoes 227

Hospitals 3, 11, 16, 23, 72, 78, 79, 91, 92, 93, 94, 118, 151, 175, 178, 239
Hostages 87, 156, 191, 192
  Iranian 80, 81
Hotels (see also *Motels*) 7, 8, 44, 50, 51, 52, 53, 77, 92, 107, 178, 203, 209
Houghton 30, 36, 37
Houghton County 133, 135, 183, 211, 213
Houghton Lake 7
Houses 98, 101, 103, 158, 193
  haunted 30, 31, 32
  mobile 159
  old 99, 100
  unique 158, 159
  winners of 190
Houston 241
Howard City 15, 212
Howell 46, 56, 73, 226
Hunters and hunting 14, 32, 33, 34, 69, 89, 174
  monster 33, 34
  old-fashioned 34
Huron County 4, 142, 218
Hypnosis 89

I

Ice storms 130, 131
Iceboating 224
Illinois 16, 128, 149, 156, 157
Imlay City 37, 236
Immigrants 62, 92, 156, 157, 191
Income and salaries 69, 75, 180, 181, 183, 184, 185, 186, 188, 218
Indian River 63, 170
Indiana 16, 80, 128, 149, 156, 157
Ingham County 84, 211, 215
Insects 2, 199
Interlochen 44
Inventors 196
Ionia 3, 7, 87
Ionia County 120, 142
Ira Township 2
Iran 156
Ireland 10, 40
Iron County 88, 132, 156, 167
Iron River 127
Ironwood 37, 47, 113
Isabella County 155, 164, 166
Ishpeming 3, 50, 61, 110, 128, 198, 227
Islands,
  Beaver 101, 166
  Belle Isle 86
  Bois Blanc 166
  Gull 33
  Mackinac 12, 29, 44, 50, 53, 98, 122, 135, 166, 187, 188
  Zug 163
Israel 101
Italy 109, 157
Ithaca 212

J

Jackson 9, 20, 30, 35, 37, 60, 61, 62, 63, 79, 86, 87, 122, 137, 142, 148, 165, 170, 174, 179, 198, 202, 212, 222
Jackson County 36
Jacksonville, Florida 40
Jails (see also *Prisons*) 87, 173
  county 71, 88
Japan 201, 202, 203
Jenison 190
Jobs (see *Occupations*)
Joe Louis Arena 231
Jonesville 194

Judo 227

K

Kalamazoo 17, 44, 50, 68, 70, 103, 105, 113, 116, 117, 122, 164, 165, 168, 174, 189, 196, 211, 213, 215, 224, 225, 226, 227
Kalamazoo County 98, 106, 160, 161, 164
Kalkaska 84, 127
Kalkaska County 18, 88, 157, 180, 215
Kansas City, Missouri 164
Kayak 224
Keeler 219
Keeweenaw 46, 154
Keeweenaw Bay 131
Keeweenaw County 16, 18, 26, 88, 135, 143, 155, 156, 166, 167, 180, 183, 199, 213, 218
Kent City 35
Kent County 35, 106, 154, 155, 160, 161
Kentucky 126
Kentwood 72, 202
Kings 101
Kingsford 181
Kinross 87
Kirtland Warbler 5, 143
Korea 124

L

Labor,
  strikes 3, 208, 209, 210
  unions 69, 122, 189
    teamsters 81
    UAW 62, 189, 210
Lady Byng winners 240
Lake City 188
Lake County 16, 143, 154, 156, 166, 167, 179, 180, 183, 199, 211
Lake Leelanau 219
Lake Linden 126, 183
Lakes 132
  Big Wolf 36
  Black 133
  Burt 132, 170
  Charlevoix 133
  Crooked 35
  Crystal 133
  Dodge 35
  Erie 136
  Gogebic 133
  Grand Mere 137
  Higgins 133, 147
  Houghton 132
  Huron 5, 13
  Indian 103
  Kent 35
  Lake of the Clouds 135
  Lime 35
  Loch Ness 34
  Long 35
  Manistique 133
  McKeever 13
  Michigan 2, 23, 40, 101, 110, 163, 178
  Mullett 35, 133
  Portage 133
  Silver 35
  Superior 30, 96, 135, 212
  Thousand Island 35
  Torch 132
  White 161

L'Anse 131, 133

Lansing 25, 33, 54, 60, 70, 71, 94, 95, 103, 131, 132, 138, 145, 148, 151, 154, 165, 166, 181, 197, 202, 211, 212, 213, 241, 242
Lapeer 4, 15, 90, 101, 198, 212
Lapeer County 155, 158
Largest,
    national 91, 135, 163, 173, 178, 190, 204, 231
    state 34, 35, 36, 72, 132, 136, 138, 141, 144, 154, 158, 168, 181, 184, 187, 189, 191, 204, 215, 216, 218, 219
    world 42, 48, 49, 50, 170
Las Vegas, Nevada 56
Lasts, state 72, 85
Lawsuits 9, 17, 18, 90, 91, 92, 93, 94, 162, 191, 193
Lebanon 199
Leelanau County 18, 87, 109, 136, 143, 167, 183, 211, 213
Leland 87
Lenawee County 98, 103, 142, 180, 218
Leslie 79
Liechtenstein 201
Life expectancies 13
Lincoln Park 47
Litter, roadside 164
Littlefield Township 160
Livingston County 35, 107, 155, 157, 158, 180
Livonia 19, 50, 154, 174, 175, 193, 204
Lobbyists 190
London, England 40, 115
Longests,
    state 62, 133
    world 42, 50, 174
Losses, corporate 52, 178, 179
Lottery 120, 190, 191, 192
Lowell 147, 202
Lower Peninsula 131, 133, 136, 140, 147, 222
Luce County 18, 87, 88, 132, 133, 155
Ludington 35, 37, 163, 213
Lumbering 4, 63, 77, 103, 107, 110, 222
Luther 183
Luxembourg 62

M

Mackinac County 18, 97, 132, 133, 167
Mackinac Straits 97, 222
Mackinaw City 6, 36, 42, 46, 168, 188
Macomb County 73, 92, 98, 132, 154, 155, 158, 159, 160, 161, 180, 181, 184, 186, 211
Madison Heights 65
Magazines 15, 26, 54, 181, 184, 197, 229
Maine 33, 41
Male pinups 54
Manchester, England 116
Manchester, Michigan 45
Manistee 80
Manistee County 35, 216
Manistique 103, 175
Manton 40, 183, 208, 213
Maps 66, 67
    additions 65, 68
    omissions 65
Marenisco 106, 166
Marine City 98
Marion Township 107
Marlette 198
Marquette 26, 28, 87, 115, 137, 144, 223
Marquette County 28, 88, 132, 135, 136, 186, 216
Marriage (see also Weddings) 88, 92, 147, 148, 149, 150
Marrietta 183
Marshall 174
Mason 12
Mattawan 188
Mayville 138
Mecosta County 109, 180

Medical research 16, 17, 19, 73, 172, 173, 199
Melstrand 133
Mendon 98
Menominee 10, 198
Menominee County 17, 106, 211
Merrill 175
Meteorites 127
Mexico 223
Michigan Center 36
Michigan state government,
    attorney general 162, 163
        opinions 88, 89
    board of cosmetology 89
    court of appeals 77
    crime victims compensation board 94
    department of agriculture 72, 160
    department of commerce 65, 183, 207
    department of corrections 88
    department of labor 207
    department of natural resources 13, 71, 141, 160, 16 163, 201, 206
    department of public health 160
    department of transportation 37
    department of treasury 76
    employment security commission 183, 184
    expenditures 186
    governor 41, 57, 63, 75, 94, 138, 186, 222
    highway commission 65
    legislature 145, 186
        House of Representatives 53, 71, 76, 89
        Senate 76, 80, 89, 123
    lieutenant governor 123, 186
    secretary of state 38, 189
    state police 69, 119
    supreme court 28, 74, 75, 186
    water resources commission 163
Midland 7, 44, 164, 190, 236
Midland County 155, 180, 184
Mikado 175
Milan 85
Milford 36
Millington 48
Mills, water-powered 111, 112
Milwaukee, Wisconsin 77, 92, 144, 236
Mines and mining 3, 30, 96, 110, 126, 216, 218
Minnesota 5, 149
Mio 5, 127
Miss America winners 53
Missaukee County 16, 137, 143, 167, 180
Missing persons 81
Money winners 55, 56
Monroe 1, 2, 4, 33, 61, 98, 104, 113, 152, 163
Monroe County 88, 98, 158, 160
Monsters 32, 33
    Loch Ness 34
Montague 53, 163
Montana 61
Montcalm County 109, 165
Montmorency County 16, 88, 154, 183, 215, 218
Montreal, Canada 23
Montrose 46, 52
Morley 181
Mortuaries 17, 18, 72
Most valuable players 233, 240
Motels (see also Hotels) 168, 204
Mount Clemens 45, 48, 90, 111, 202
Mount Morris Township 74
Mount Pleasant 56, 126, 168
Mount Vernon 196
Mountain ranges 135
Movie theatres 29, 120
Movies 27, 28, 29, 90, 198
Mummies 17, 194

Munger 46
Munising 13, 133, 135
Munith 79
Murder 12, 15, 17, 28, 57, 70, 72, 74, 75, 79, 81, 82, 83, 84, 85, 86, 95, 101
Museum 45, 56, 87, 101, 103, 194
Music (see *Rock Music*)
Muskegon 20, 40, 53, 56, 70, 77, 87, 93, 159, 165, 178, 197, 199, 202, 213, 236
Muskegon County 160, 186
Muskegon Heights 202

N

Nahma 80, 178
Names 152
   assumed 71, 76
   changes 88, 148, 239
   cities after women 106
   cities, former 106
   colleges original 105
   nicknames 12, 235
   places unusually named 109
   ships named Michigan 107
   townships after stoves 110
   townships after women 107
Nashville, Tennessee 55
Natural landmarks 137
Nebraska 149
Netherlands 201
New Castle, Indiana 227
New Greenleaf 101
New Haven 90
New Hudson 197
New Jersey 7
New Troy 111
New York 114, 149, 157, 191, 222, 236
New York City 56, 58, 114, 116, 208, 237
New Zealand 62
Newago 46
Newberry 72, 87, 147
Newspapers 38, 41, 60, 104, 118, 120, 144, 178
   ethnic 219, 221
   smallest 221
Niles 46, 97, 212
Nobel Prize 61
Normandy 111.
North Adams 94
North Branch Township 20
North Dakota 30
Northville 175, 188
Norway 170
Nova Scotia 40
Novels (see *Books*)
Novesta Township 110
Novi 173, 181
Nuclear power plants 79, 216, 217
Nudity 53, 54, 70, 71, 177
Numbers, retired 229
Nunica 201

O

Oak Park 187, 188, 204
Oak Ridge, Tennessee 79
Oakland County 83, 98, 128, 137, 140, 154, 155, 159, 160, 180, 181, 186, 190, 211
Occupations and professions 206, 207
   dangerous 207
Oceana County 215
Oceans,
   Atlantic 40, 41, 61, 222
   Arctic 124

Pacific 222
Offenses, non-criminal 75
Ogden, Utah 36
Ogemaw County 180
Ohio 16, 63, 65, 113, 128, 149, 156, 157
Oil,
   production 2, 56, 215
   refining 201, 215
Okemos 78
Oldest, state 20, 62, 63, 88, 97, 98, 104, 105, 111, 145, 168
Olympia Stadium 53
Olympics 61, 223
Omena 219
Onaway 133, 183, 207
Onsted 190
Ontario 73
Ontonagon 37
Ontonagon County 133, 135, 136, 143, 155, 167, 212
Orchard Lake 115, 123, 126
Oregon 223
Organ transplants 173, 174
Orlando, Florida 79, 138
Osceola County 165, 215
Oscoda 144, 162
Oscoda County 16, 18, 143, 154, 155, 180, 211, 218
Otsego County 84, 106, 136, 165, 215
Ottawa County 106, 142, 158, 161, 167, 180
Owosso 61, 101, 138, 164

P

Paddleball 224, 225, 226
Pageants 54, 71
Paradise 135, 138
Paris, France 96
Parks,
   roadside 37, 120
   state 37, 68, 110, 122, 135
Paulding 135
Paw Paw 46, 219
Paychecks (see *Income*)
PBB 56, 94, 161, 164
PCB 164
Pellston 183
Pentwater 213
Pequaming 110
Perry 208
Pet rocks 19
Petoskey 32, 60, 72
Philadelphia, Pennsylvania 25
Pickford 212
Pictured Rocks National Lakeshore 135
Pinconning 35, 146
Plymouth 3, 11, 28, 87, 198, 202
Plymouth Township 7
Poison and poisoning 8, 9, 13, 78, 79, 94, 160, 161, 162, 239
   botulism 8
   salmonella 9
   toxic shock syndrome 9
Poisonous plants 140, 141
Pokagon 170
Poland 157
Pollution 160, 161, 162, 163, 164
Pontiac 8, 28, 56, 68, 74, 79, 91, 104, 113, 173, 206, 208, 211, 223, 236
Pontiac Silverdome 24, 44, 48, 52, 231
Pool (see *Billiards*)
Population 153, 154, 155, 156, 157, 158
Port Huron 5, 15, 42, 68, 74, 84, 97, 106, 113, 118, 120, 173, 202, 212, 226
Portland, Oregon 114
Ports 216

Powers 17
Presque Isle 120
Presque Isle County 133, 167
Prison (see also *Jails*) 59, 73, 74, 75, 87, 90, 121, 122
  inmates 57, 61, 69, 71, 79, 82, 86, 87, 90, 173, 174, 235
  Michigan State 30
  Ohio State Reformatory 235
  riots 86, 87
  Southern Michigan 79, 82, 86, 87, 174, 212, 235
  Tennessee State 90
Products,
  firsts 197
  product of the year 197, 198
  unique 194, 196
  wartime 197
Professions (see *Occupations*)
Profits, corporate 52, 116, 185
Promotions (see *Advertising*)
Prostitution 76, 77
Public officials, convicted 61, 75, 76
Pulitzer Prize 60
Purple Gang 85

Q

Quadruplets 152

R

Radio 25, 26, 104, 105, 115, 119, 123, 190, 193
Railroads 3, 113, 118, 120
Rape 70, 75, 79, 82, 90
Reading 222
Redford 188
Redford Township 80, 122
Reed City 127, 170, 212
Religion 209
  denominations 170

Reno, Nevada 83
Resignations 208
Rhodesia 199
Richmond 173
Richville 37
Riots,
  interracial 86, 120
  prison 86, 87
Rituals, unusual 172
Rivers 131, 132
  Au Sable 133
  Cass 101
  Chippewa 164
  Detroit 42, 133, 163
  Doan Creek 10
  Grand 133, 144
  Huron 159, 163
  Kalamazoo 164
  Little Big Horn 61
  Manistee 133
  Manistique 44
  Menominee 133
  Mississippi 144
  Pine 35, 164
  polluted 163, 164
  Portage Creek 164
  Raisin 163
  Red Cedar 131
  Rouge 156, 163, 188, 243
  Saginaw 42, 133, 164
  St. Clair 42
  St. Joseph 109
  St. Lawrence 96
  St. Mary's 44
  Shiawassee 164

Tittabawassee 164
Riverview 37
Roads (see *Highways*)
Rochester 123
Rock music and musicians 21, 23, 25, 52, 148, 203
Rockford 25, 58, 198
Rockwood 126
Rogers City 48, 216
Roller skating 147, 224, 225, 226
Romeo 46
Rookies of the year 233, 238
Roscommon 7
Roscommon County 16, 132, 133, 137, 154, 156, 157, 167,
  180, 183
Rose City 127
Rose Township 160
Roseville 72
Royal Oak 8, 9, 21, 28, 58, 68, 105, 131, 222
Russia 59

S

Sacramento, California 91
Saginaw 21, 42, 47, 50, 68, 113, 123, 165, 173, 196, 198,
  202
Saginaw County 172, 179, 184, 211
Saigon 80
St. Clair County 2, 98
St. Clair Shores 72, 223, 226
St. Ignace 42, 97, 103
St. Joseph 41, 54, 97, 106, 213
St. Joseph County 98, 109, 142, 212
St. Louis, Michigan 164, 175
St. Louis, Missouri 80
Salaries (see *Income*)
Salem 3
Saline 40
San Diego, California 241
Sandusky 85, 206
Sanilac County 4, 107, 132, 142, 218
Santa Ana, California 91
Saranac 120
Sarnia, Ontario 42, 113
Saudi Arabia 202
Saugatuck 45, 46, 63, 164
Sault Ste. Marie 42, 44, 76, 96, 97, 98, 109, 189, 203, 222
Sawyer 37, 145
Schoolcraft County 35, 136, 137, 154, 155, 215
Scientists 60, 61
Scotland 34
Scottdale 212
Seconds,
  national 5, 26, 69, 159
  world 168
Seneca 127
Seney 40
Seney Wildlife Refuge 5
Septic tanks 160
Sequoia National Park, California 11
Sex change 74, 89
Shelby 46
Shelbyville 174
Shiawassee County 109, 132, 158
Shingleton 40, 201
Ships (see *Boats*)
Shootings 1, 8, 12, 14, 74, 79, 81, 82, 83, 84, 86, 90, 94,
  227
Shuffleboard 227
Siberia 59
Sicily 92, 109
Silver Buffalo award 60
Singapore 110
Sister Lakes 33
Skandia 13

252

Skeet shooting 227
Skiing 36, 37, 115, 227
Skydiving 7, 147
Skyjackings 79, 80, 120
Sleeping Bear Dunes 10, 135, 212
Smallest, state 88, 136, 156, 181, 182, 183, 221
Smokers and smoking 3, 52, 53, 56, 57, 201
Snowmen 36
Snowmobile,
    fatalities 68
    races 36
    trips 40, 41
Snowstorms (see *Blizzards*)
Social security 180
Softball 236
Sound winners 55
South Haven 2, 46, 203, 216
South Lyon 157, 174
Southfield 24, 54, 59, 159, 188, 203, 209, 236
Spain 97
Speed skating 223, 226
Speeding excuses 78
Spratt 136
Springfield 203
Springfield Township 160
Stadiums and arenas 24, 44, 48, 52, 53, 126, 231
Standale 128
Stanwood 46
State symbols 137
Stephenson 187
Sterling Heights 150, 191
Stockholm, Sweden 147
Stoneport 216
Students (see also *Education*) 10, 23, 32, 36, 54, 57, 73, 74,
    78, 80, 82, 83, 84, 90, 122, 165, 166, 167, 172, 173,
    177, 190, 199, 206, 222
Sturgis 62, 243
Suicide 8, 12, 15, 74, 84
Surgery 1, 11, 12, 89, 94, 173, 174, 196
    limb re-attachments 175
    sex change 74, 89
Swartz Creek 46, 53, 57
Sweden 201
Switzerland 202

T

Tae Kwon Do 225, 226
Tampa Bay, Florida 42
Taxes 69, 76, 118, 120, 158, 183, 187, 190, 208
Taylor 6, 150, 191, 204, 227
Teachers (see also *Education*) 40, 81, 82, 83, 84, 88, 105,
    167, 168, 188, 209, 222
Tecumseh 144, 198
Teheran, Iran 80, 81
Telephone and telephone calls 10, 34, 116, 147, 159, 160,
    201
Television 24, 26, 28, 36, 55, 56, 58, 59, 61, 71, 84, 88, 90,
    115, 119, 123, 145, 159, 173, 175, 184, 194, 208
Tennis 225, 243
    platform 225
Texas 81, 149, 156
Theatres 53
    movie 29, 120
    summer 45
Thefts 70, 71, 72, 73, 75, 77, 85
    unusual 25
Thirds,
    national 69, 97, 128, 219
    world 174
Thompsonville 36
Three Oaks 138

Tidal wave 131
Tiger Stadium 24, 53, 126
Toledo, Ohio 24, 73, 113, 120, 158
Tornadoes 59, 128, 129
Toronto, Ontario 79
Townships named after women 107
Toxic shock syndrome 9
Track 206, 223
Trash and litter (see also *Waste Dumps*) 194
Traverse City 1, 10, 23, 36, 45, 46, 168, 196, 219
Trees 68, 71, 72, 137, 138, 139, 140, 141
Trenton 70, 126
Triplets 10, 152
Trips and voyages, unusual 40, 41, 50, 55, 61, 114, 115,
    222, 223, 235
Troy 40, 53, 55, 59, 92, 93, 98, 122, 173, 181, 189, 197, 203
Trucks, new 213, 215
Tumbling 225
Tunnels 5, 30, 44, 81, 113, 126, 159
Turtles 10, 127
Tuscola County 4, 110, 158, 165, 218
Tustin 157
Twins 10, 151, 152, 173

U

UFO's 30
Ulby 188
Umpires 25, 236
Unemployment (see also *Employment*) 80, 89, 183, 207,
    208
United Kingdom 157, 201, 202
United States government,
    ambassador 62
    attorney general 61, 64
    budget director 194
    bureau of alcohol, tobacco and firearms 18
    cabinet members 64
    congress 190
        House of Representatives 75
    department of commerce and labor 64, 113
    department of defense 64
    department of health, education and welfare 64
    department of housing and urban development 64
    department of the interior 5, 64, 137
    department of the treasury 64, 177
    environmental protection agency 160, 162
    expenditures 186, 187
    federal bureau of investigation 69, 75, 80, 81
    forest service 201
    internal revenue service 208
    office of economic opportunity 177
    president 45, 61, 64, 65, 128, 138, 156, 178, 194
    supreme court 61, 63, 209
    white house counselor 194
Universities (see *Colleges*)
University Center 189
Upper Peninsula 28, 36, 40, 41, 65, 88, 96, 103, 110, 136,
    140, 147, 178, 206, 222
Utica 172

V

Van Buren County 160, 179
Vanderbilt 127
Vanity plates 37, 38
Vassar 37, 188
Vegetables 48, 50, 68, 69, 141, 207, 218
Venice Township 109
Vermontville 46
Veterinarians 63, 143, 145, 207
Vienna Township 8
Vietnam 124

Virginia Beach, Virginia 222
Volleyball 243

W

Waldron 183
Warren 57, 65, 106, 144, 154, 166, 227
Wars,
    Civil 59, 61, 123, 124
    Korean 124, 125
    Revolutionary 97, 106
    Spanish-American 124, 125
    Vietnam 124, 125
    War of 1812 97
    World War I 124, 125
    World War II 124, 125
Washington, 145, 223
Washington, D.C. 91, 159
Washtenaw County 26, 30, 35, 98, 106, 138, 142, 155, 160,
    180, 181, 184
Waste dumps, toxic 160, 161
Waterfalls 133, 134, 135
    Niagara 107, 222
    Tahquamenon 128, 135
Waterford 57
Wayne 213
Wayne County 16, 17, 74, 88, 93, 94, 98, 119, 126, 154,
    155, 157, 167, 179, 181, 184, 186, 211, 213
Weather extremes 127, 128
Weddings (see also *Marriage*) 41, 92, 147, 148, 149
Weight and weight loss 89, 173, 235
Welfare 179, 180
West Bloomfield 28, 59, 123, 215
Westland 29, 35
Wexford 136
Wexford County 15, 199
Whiskey 29
White Lake 54
Whitefish 166
Whitehall 7, 161
Whitmore Lake 28
Whittemore 187
Williamsburg 1, 2
Williamston 10, 225
Williamsville, New York 224
Willow Run 177, 211
Windsor, Ontario 42, 47, 90, 190
Wineries 219
Winners 50, 52, 53, 54, 55, 56, 57, 60, 61, 65, 68, 115, 137,
    138, 190, 191, 197, 198, 223, 224, 225, 226, 227, 229,
    232, 233, 234, 236, 237, 239, 240, 241, 243
Wisconsin 16, 149
Wixom 157, 163, 211
Women,
    cities named after 106
    first 122, 124, 206
Woodhaven 157
Worsts,
    national 8, 161
    state 6, 13, 82, 86, 128, 160, 163
Wrestling 243
Wyandotte 21, 47, 80, 116, 163, 203, 226
Wyoming, Michigan 10

Y

Yorktown, Indiana 35
Ypsilanti 1, 7, 34, 46, 72, 82, 87, 124, 157, 168, 187, 189,
    199, 224

Z

Zanesville, Ohio 115
Zeeland 198
Zilwaukee 5

THE AUTHOR

Gary W. Barfknecht is a free-lance writer and director of amateur hockey programming. He, his wife Ann, and their two daughters, Amy and Heidi, live in Davison, Michigan.

Mr. Barfknecht's previous publishing credits include: *A Father, A Son, And A Three Mile Run* (Zondervan, 1974), *33 Hikes From Flint* (Friede Publications, 1975), and articles in the *Reader's Digest, Science Digest, Lion, Sign, Science & Mechanics, Lutheran Standard, Modern Maturity* and other magazines.

MICHIGAN